S0-BRZ-557

Beyond MaxiMarketing: The New Power of Caring and Daring

Other Books by Stan Rapp and Thomas L. Collins

MaxiMarketing: The New Direction in Advertising, Promotion, and Marketing Strategy

The Great Marketing Turnaround

Beyond MaxiMarketing: The New Power of Caring and Daring

Stan Rapp
Thomas L. Collins

McGraw-Hill, Inc.

New York San Francisco Washington, D.C. Auckland Bogotá
Caracas Lisbon London Madrid Mexico City Milan
Montreal New Delhi San Juan Singapore
Sydney Tokyo Toronto

Library of Congress Cataloging-in-Publication Data

Rapp, Stan.
Beyond MaxiMarketing : the new power of caring and daring / Stan Rapp, Thomas L. Collins.
p. cm.
Includes index.
ISBN 0-07-051343-0 :
1. Marketing—Case studies. 2. Sales promotion—Case studies.
I. Collins, Thomas L. II. Title.
HF5415.R3245 1994
658.8—dc20 93-23545
CIP

1 2 3 4 5 6 7 8 9 0 DOC/DOC 9 9 8 7 6 5 4 3

ISBN 0-07-051343-0

The sponsoring editor for this book was Philip Ruppel, the editing supervisor was Jane Palmieri, and the production supervisor was Pamela Pelton. It was set in Palatino by McGraw-Hill's Professional Book Group composition unit.

Printed and bound by R. R. Donnelley & Sons Company.

INTERNATIONAL EDITION

When ordering this title, use ISBN 0-07-113622-3.

This book is printed on recycled, acid-free paper containing a minimum of 50% recycled de-inked fiber.

This book is dedicated to
the memory of Jerome S. Hardy
—gentleman, visionary, mentor, client, and friend

Contents

Introduction

The swiftness or slowness by which the world around us changes affects our perception of time itself. The more swiftly things change, the faster we appear to be hurtling into the future and the further behind us the events of only yesterday seem to be.

As we write this, it is a little less than a decade since the two of us sat down together to write our first book, *MaxiMarketing*. It seems much longer. Things have been moving very fast indeed.

Do you remember when there were still typewriters in the office—and those little bottles of "white out" used to correct typing errors?

Think of it. In 1985, the personal computer introduced by mighty IBM was only a few years old. Apple's new Macintosh was looked upon by the business world as little more than a quaint toy with funny little icons instead of businesslike commands. There were few fax machines, almost no E-mail, and today's ubiquitous mobile telephone was a new idea on the horizon. In offices all across the land, Wang word processors and typewriters were a familiar presence.

In those days, business managers in the United States were making the most of the ready cash put into consumer pockets by the expanded defense budget and ballooning deficit spending. Rumblings of a coming adjustment to a new information-based economy were shrugged off as irrelevant to the prosperous eighties. What turned out to be a fatal fallacy for many companies was the failure to understand just how fast new consumer attitudes and the new media and telecomputing technologies would unravel the business assumptions of the past.

In the preface to *MaxiMarketing*, we said that the eighties would be remembered as a decade of transition:

From "get a sale *now* at any cost" to managing long-term relationships and maximizing the lifetime value of each customer

From crudely accountable "creativity" in advertising to the scientific accountability of each advertising expenditure

From reliance on a company's familiar single channel of distribution to a multi-channel mode that breaks rules as it breaks down walls

"As the cost of accumulating and accessing the data drops, the ability to talk directly to your prospects and customers—and to build one-to-one relationships with them—will continue to grow," we wrote in 1986. "A rising tide of technological change has brought this golden moment of opportunity."

The marketing transformation predicted in the preface to *MaxiMarketing* is now history, but many marketers still don't get it. By and large, the marketing/advertising establishment seems unwilling to let go of the past. Far too many managers remain ill-prepared philosophically to deal with today's world of constant risk taking, customer empowerment, and the complex process of turning likely prospects into long-term customer relationships.

As auto magnate and onetime presidential candidate George Romney told author David Halberstam, "There is nothing more vulnerable than entrenched success. You become prisoner to what you've done in the past."

This is in marked contrast to the emerging winners of today. James E. Burke, the man who led the search for the new CEO to replace John F. Akers at IBM, had this to say about the entrepreneurial companies that shook IBM: "They move quickly and they love to take risks."

We work in an age when a sweeping revolution brought about by the convergence of telephone and computer technologies is irrevocably changing the commercial landscape. Today, companies in every category are ready to strike out in the new direction we wrote about in *MaxiMarketing* and are eager to know how to succeed. So a new book was needed to help management get moving in the right direction.

At the time we wrote *MaxiMarketing*, we could barely see the outlines of where the future would take us. Now that almost a decade has passed, those outlines have become much clearer. There is a need for a new look at what leads to business success in the current shift from an Industrial-Age economy to an Information-Age economy—from the time when most business was production-based and dealt with the customer at arm's length to a time when what you do to interact with your customers can be critical to your company's future.

The necessity for a new outlook was underscored for us at a meeting with Fabienne Petit, the marketing director of Nestlé Baby Food, at the corporate headquarters outside Paris in May of 1992. Two years had passed since we had written about the early success of Nestlé's relationship-driven strategy in our second book, *The Great Marketing Turnaround*.

Between 1985 and 1989, the Nestlé Baby Food Company made a whopping gain of 10 share points in the French baby food market. They went from No. 3 to No. 2, outdistancing Gerber and closing the gap separating them from the market leader, Bledina. At the time, the managing director gave much of the credit for the outstanding performance to the company's dialogue with parents and their other innovative customer-involvement activities.

"What happened in 1990 and 1991 after your earlier success?" we asked Mme. Petit. "Were you able to withstand the Bledina advertising bombardment, outspending you more than 7 to 1?"

Her reply was an eye-opener: "Our market share continued going up—we went from 26.5 percent in 1989 to 40 percent in 1991."

Since the total category barely grew in those two years, the gain translates into a whopping increase in sales while the competition was going nowhere. When asked what made this further spurt in growth possible in a category where year-to-year advances are measured by a point or two, she confided: "I cannot speak with passion about my advertising, but I am passionate about my links with the consumer—we are totally committed to making an improvement in the life of the parents who purchase our products."

As we looked more closely at the driving force behind her success and at how this remarkable growth could take place without the benefit of an advertising or promotion breakthrough, we saw something quite different from accepted marketing know-how. Something was happening at this Nestlé company that went beyond the common variety of marketing—even beyond what we wrote about in *MaxiMarketing*.

The Nestlé Baby Food Division in France had demonstrated what can happen when a well-run business puts someone in charge of loving the customer and repositions the entire marketing process to put the customer's interests first. (The story of how Nestlé Baby Food management in France put together their 24-share-point rise is told in Chapter 7. And you will also learn in Chapter 8 about a bold experiment by Nestlé corporate management in Switzerland to reposition a global pasta brand on the basis of a one-to-one relationship with the consumer.)

Shortly after the visit to Nestlé, we decided to seek out other companies that were obtaining sensational results by taking the MaxiMarketing approach to new heights. We wanted to know what was behind the business success of these MaxiMarketing winners and to put a spotlight on what they were doing differently and how they were thinking differently. The result is this book, a close-up look at some of the best-performing companies in America, Europe, and around the globe. These are companies that scored extraordinary gains while so many other firms were suffering setbacks in the difficult early years of this decade.

With it, we complete the trilogy begun with the publication of *MaxiMarketing*.

We wrote our first book at a time when the move from mass marketing to a more fragmented marketplace was picking up momentum—and nothing seemed quite what it had been before. A new world was stirring to life: a world in which dealing with a faceless mass market was giving way to direct interaction with known prospects and customers; a new reality in which the discontinuity of each separate step in the selling process was being replaced by an organic continuum.

MaxiMarketing presented a process for dealing with the disintegration of the mass market and offered a new nine-step model (see the boxed summary on the next three pages) that seemed destined to replace it. When we started looking for companies that demonstrated mastery of this process, we found there were almost none to write about at the time. We did, however, find examples of companies beginning to get some of it right, so that the reader could envision the potential in putting the pieces together.

We saw the forerunners of the new world of database-driven marketing creating new opportunities for getting closer to the customer and gaining incremental profits after the sale is made. A new reality was emerging—a reality in which direct interaction with individual prospects and customers was replacing the mass-market mentality of the past.

With the MaxiMarketing model, we saw a way to improve performance along the entire continuum which turns likely prospects into longtime customers. It offers a unified strategic approach in which people who are actually or potentially your best customers are identified, contacted, motivated, activated, and cultivated in order to maximize sales and profits.

Our second book, *The Great Marketing Turnaround*, released in 1990, described and illustrated 10 broad trends away from yesterday's mass marketing and toward the new individualized marketing of the postindustrial era. What had seemed a radical transformation of how goods and services would be sold when *MaxiMarketing* first appeared was by then winning a succession of new adherents.

The turnaround from unknown to identified prospects and customers, from passive consumers to involved participants, from creativity-driven to response-driven advertising, and the other shifts in direction anticipated in our first book had become part of an unstoppable chain of events.

Now, in the mid-nineties, this book puts a spotlight on the keys to business success of the emerging MaxiMarketing winners. What started as a more targeted and customer-focused approach to the marketplace of the 1980s has grown into a new imperative for business management, embracing every aspect of business planning today.

We will show how the smartest companies can gain a compet-

The nine-step model presented in *MaxiMarketing* reduced the traditional ways of doing business to their three common denominators: reaching the prospect, making the sale, and developing the relationship. MaxiMarketing does not mean giving up what your company is already doing. It means examining every step of your selling process, from visualizing your prospect to what you do after the sale is made, and maximizing performance all along the way. It means adding powerful new capabilities to what you are already doing very well.

1. **Maximized Targeting.** The ideal selling process begins with the traditional step of learning as much as possible about your prospect. But it includes, whenever and wherever possible, building a prospect database that allows you to approach your target prospects as individuals. The most cost-efficient object of your advertising and promotion expenditures is the individual who needs or wants your product or service and is ready and able to buy it. With each year of the computer era, singling that ideal prospect out of the mass consumer market at less cost is more easily accomplished.
2. **Maximized Media.** You will want to examine carefully—and to explore as your budget permits—the dazzling, almost bewildering, array of new media options that are available now or soon will be. But you will want to keep this exploration under control. Most media tested should be held directly accountable and made to prove their value—whenever feasible, by tabulated phone, mail, and fax responses to offers made in the advertising.
3. **Maximized Accountability.** With the increased competition for customers, the winners will be those who make their advertising expenditures more accountable. They will evaluate and rank media buys by the proven advertising cost per response or purchase. And they will improve copy by comparing how two different split-test promises or treatments in the real-world advertising environment actually attract prospects or customers.

4. **Maximized Awareness.** A great deal of awareness advertising suffers from a high degree of misguided creativity. MaxiMarketing addresses the need to maximize the impact of awareness advertising by appealing to both the left and right brain (that is, to both the rational and nonrational sides of our nature). The highest creative challenge will be to appeal to the whole brain of the prospect. This becomes even more important in an environment driven by the value of information provided and feedback obtained.
5. **Maximized Activation.** Activation includes, but is broader than, sales promotion. Activation simply means making something happen by means of your advertising. That something might be promoting a purchase, or it might be inviting the prospect to call or write for more information. MaxiMarketing calls for applying the stern yardstick of accountability to promotion activity. It calls for giving your follow-up material just as much careful attention as you give your up-front advertising.
6. **Maximized Synergy.** By making your advertising do two or more jobs at the same time, you can achieve a synergistic explosion of energy and profitability. With the rise in media costs, there is an urgent need to review your advertising plans and ask yourself how the cost might be spread over, and justified by, more than one purpose. By building a direct-response offer into your advertising you can identify the most interested prospects for your product or service. Modern-day advertising is usually most efficient when it does double duty, combining both building awareness and direct response.
7. **Maximized Linkage.** Too often, advertising leaves the prospect dangling, with no idea of what to do next, where to buy, or how to obtain more information. At the very least, the ideal advertising and marketing process should bridge this gap between advertising and sale by offering—and providing—additional information. We call this "linkage"; it involves reaching out in meaningful ways—far more than merely offering where-to-buy information.

8. **Maximized Sales with Customer Database.** All the steps in the MaxiMarketing process outlined so far should, if well planned and effectively executed, result in a significant increase in sales and profits. But MaxiMarketing does not end with making the first sale to a new customer. What happens after that sale has a profound effect on the bottom line. MaxiMarketing adds something new to the picture: a customer database and an after-the-sale interactive customer relationship. Once you start acquiring, storing, and analyzing names and addresses and other relevant information, you possess a powerful new marketing instrument. You have a private advertising medium you can use cost-effectively for repeat sales and for building commitment to your brand. When combined with the many ways to build a brand image, the result is greater than either can achieve alone.
9. **Maximized Distribution.** How can your company continue to grow when your retailers refuse to offer you more shelf space? Or your sales force agents can't find or get appointments with enough new prospects? Or your mail-order catalog is swamped by a horde of competitors in the mail box? Many companies have found the answer in opening up a new channel of distribution. It's like extending your business activities to another continent, but without the complication of foreign language, customs, and currency conversion to worry about.

The common wastefulness of the mass-advertising approach of the Industrial Age is giving way to the newly affordable ability to locate and communicate directly with a company's best prospects and customers. The MaxiMarketing concept outlined in 1986 is still valid today. But in using these principles, the best and boldest MaxiMarketers have taken the basic steps to a higher level, with results often exceeding our wildest expectations when the model was first set down.

itive edge by going beyond the fundamentals of marketing—the manipulation of pricing, distribution, advertising, and promotion—and by rethinking how the business relates to its reason for being, the individual customer. We will show how the arrival of the information superhighway, connecting everything to everybody and everyone to everyone else, opens up a new world of endless opportunity. We will show how to outsmart the competition at a time when the flow and control of information has become more important than the hum of machines turning out products on the factory floor.

In writing this book, we revisited some of the trailblazers cited in our first two books to see how their earlier accomplishments were holding up. But we didn't stop there. We singled out additional companies around the world doing exceedingly well despite the economic slowdown of the early 1990s. These are daring innovators that have overcome seemingly insurmountable obstacles, scored phenomenal gains against the competition, or solidified their dominance of a category they already own. We went inside these companies to interview the key players and ferret out what was behind their surprising results.

We also gained insights from hundreds of business men and women with whom we interacted on our speaking and seminar tours of 28 countries around the world. And, as two of the principals of the CCR Consulting Group, we saw firsthand what is possible when MaxiMarketing strategies are carried out by far-sighted clients.

When we were through, we had singled out 24 of the best-performing MaxiMarketers we could find in the United States and abroad at that time. The process of examining and analyzing the achievements of these companies slowly but surely brought us to a startling conclusion. There was a common philosophy underlying the ingenious actions taken to meet the wide range of challenges they faced: a winning attitude that can best be described as *a passion for Caring and Daring.*

What we saw were companies meeting the essential challenge of business today: the necessity for (and the profitability of) creating a unique, enduring, and caring relationship with the customer.

We are not talking about the superficial "customer satisfaction" programs that are standard business procedure nowadays. As you will see in the pages of this book, we are talking about something quite different: about finding daring new ways to improve the quality of life of those who purchase what your company has to offer; about adding value to the sales transaction by exceeding expectations and developing an ongoing involvement with the customer.

We saw a new breed of "caring" marketer ready to find new ways for the buyer, as well as the seller, to win.

We saw winning managers putting their own imaginative spin on the new directions offered by the MaxiMarketing approach.

We saw a movement away from the "Sell! Sell! Sell!" dictum of the past marketing era to the "Tell! Tell! Tell!" marketing style of a new Information Age.

We saw a new kind of corporate culture that faults managers for not being risk takers—with CEOs in the most successful companies questioning the effectiveness of a manager who didn't fail once in a while.

The spectacular accomplishments chronicled in the pages of this book are a stunning testament to the payoff from adopting a "Caring and Daring" corporate culture.

These innovators are at the cutting edge of a vast change that has gradually taken place over the last decade almost without anyone realizing it. As you watch the evening's television programming or page through your favorite magazine, try picking up a pencil and making a mark on a scratch pad every time you note an ad or a commercial inviting a response. You may be astonished at how many pencil marks you accumulate. The people, services, and equipment required to service the ubiquitous toll-free 800-number connection between the advertiser and the consumer have grown into a $7 billion to $8 billion service industry of its own.

Often the invitation to respond is poorly handled, with an 800 number flashed across the television screen for a second or two, or buried in the body copy of a magazine ad. But every mark on your scratch pad means that somebody, somewhere, is at least taking the first small move toward beginning an interaction with prospective customers. And at least some of these hesitant first steps will evolve into a real dialogue with the marketplace by the time the twenty-first century rolls around.

Just how much has changed since we began writing our first

book in the mid-eighties can be seen in the startling figures compiled by John Cummings & Partners to show the number of packaged-goods companies that are using database marketing. They tracked 525 brands with an end-user database during the second quarter of 1993, up 19 percent over the year before. In less than five years time, what was widely considered irrelevant by most companies—a one-to-one relationship with the consumer—has become a common practice.

But, we have to ask, in how many instances is there actually a real commitment to the new marketing concepts rather than only rudimentary experimentation and mere mimicry of what is rapidly becoming "the thing to do"? Why are a relatively few innovative marketers zooming ahead so dramatically while so many others lag behind?

Indeed, we see many of these winning marketers carrying out the various steps of the MaxiMarketing continuum and taking advantage of the Turnaround Trends we described in our second book. We see them adding the "Double D" of dialogue and database to the classic "four Ps"—product, price, place, promotion—of the marketing mix. But they are also doing something more. They are pushing beyond the marketing wisdom of the late twentieth century into the marketing of the future. They are exhibiting qualities of heart and guts and vision that can't be taught by rules alone and that go beyond the tactical steps of the MaxiMarketing process.

Marketing leadership is shifting to the "Caring and Daring" companies we see racing beyond the rules and ahead of the competition. To businesses large and small, as the case histories in this book will show you, this means:

- Caring enough about your prospects and customers to push beyond the Total Quality Management or TQM of the 1980s to the new mandate for the 1990s—TRC or Total Relationship Commitment.
- Daring enough to seek to hold onto customers for life by pushing beyond customer satisfaction and achieving true customer astonishment—not just once but over and over again.
- Caring enough to put the customer's interests first—even if it means temporarily putting the corporate bottom line second.

- Daring enough to lead the way in exploration of the new media technologies and blast through the cluttered environment of today's fragmented media scene.
- Caring enough to create a feedback loop that empowers customers to play a role in shaping the company's destiny.
- Daring enough to go back to square one and to rethink your entire marketing expenditure from the bottom up, using today's new marketing math.

To fail to understand all this and more—everything you will be reading about in this book—is to risk putting yourself at a tremendous disadvantage in the remaining years of the decade.

We can't tell you the exact rules for how to invent a "Caring and Daring" company, any more than the Cowardly Lion in *The Wizard of Oz* could be taught the rules for having courage. But we believe that the inspiring examples provided by our MaxiMarketing winners, and the keys to business success that they reveal, can breathe new life into your company and your own business career and carry you far beyond where you are now.

The troubled marketplace described in the opening chapter, "The Decade of the Rude Awakening," is not a temporary aberration brought on by a global economic slowdown. It is the fallout from living in a time of discontinuous change, from leaving behind the mass-production orientation of the past while not yet feeling completely comfortable with the computer-driven individualized orientation replacing it.

"The advanced economy could not run for thirty seconds without computers," Alvin Toffler reminds us in his latest work, *Powershift*. "The new complexities of production, the integration of many diverse (and constantly changing) technologies and the de-massification of markets continue to increase, by vast leaps, the amount and quality of information needed to make the system produce wealth. It explains why the battle for control of knowledge and the means of communication is heating up all over the world."

As the battle heats up, the pressure on marketers to forgo past assumptions and adjust to the new "informationalized" economy will continue to grow.

Since our first book, there have been a number of works published on the subjects of customer service, integrated marketing, database marketing, one-to-one marketing, relationship marketing, and other contemporary views of marketing success. Each of these works has something valuable to say about one or another aspect of the business scene. But too often they are limited by being narrowly focused on a single aspect of the solution to the complexities of competing in the current economy.

We believe that a much broader view is needed to be a winner in today's blazing competition for market share. The likelihood of matching the impressive performances illustrated by the case histories on the following pages is dramatically increased whenever there is a willingness to look at how a company measures up at every point of contact with the marketplace.

The keys to business success highlighted in this book cover a wide spectrum of marketing scenarios. Taken together, they demonstrate a new standard of excellence needed to survive and prosper in the Age of the Individual.

As in our previous books, we have sought to be as specific as possible about actions and results. We name names and quantify sales and growth to the extent that the companies involved are willing to make the information known or that can be deduced from public records.

We have directed the primary focus not just on successful companies, but on *impressively* successful companies whose gains (or equally impressive defense of market share) can be attributed in large part to a vision that often goes where no company has gone before. If you believe that good ideas can be contagious, you will enjoy reading about how these excellent companies went beyond the boundaries of commonly accepted business practice to score their singular gains.

Your journey will not be limited to what is happening here in America. In today's globalized economy, what happens in the commercial arena of any single developed or developing country anywhere in the world has relevance everywhere else as well. So, in writing this book, we ranged far and wide to bring you the best examples we could find to illustrate our themes.

Our chosen MaxiMarketing winners cover almost the entire

business spectrum. Yet most, or possibly all, of our examples may not be from your particular category. And many will not be from your geographical part of the world.

It doesn't matter. The business acumen illustrated here has universal application—whether you manufacture a product, deliver a service, ring up sales at retail, or play a vital role in the distribution chain—whether the breakthrough took place in Asia, Europe, or the Americas.

By analyzing and comparing what these MaxiMarketing winners are doing, we were able to identify seven keys to business success in today's economy that you can use in your own company's situation. These are not pat "how-to-do-it" formulas. Rather they are ways of thinking and acting that are characteristic of these leading companies. It is what we found driving their remarkable progress while competitors were slipping backward or spiraling downward.

This book puts in your hands the insights needed to start you on the road to your own success in the mid-nineties. We believe you can become a champion of the new power of "Caring and Daring"—moving your thinking and your company into new MaxiMarketing achievements and beyond, and reaping the rewards of reaching your own ultimate goal.

Acknowledgments

We owe a special debt of gratitude to some very special people who helped make this book possible.

Janet A. Smith and Karen Soule were tireless, inventive, and unfailingly cooperative researchers in helping us dig out the success stories and pin down the facts in them.

Our years of work alongside Richard Cross, our third colleague in the CCR Consulting Group, has laid the groundwork for understanding the different degrees of customer bonding and has made possible a deeper appreciation of what relationship marketing can accomplish.

The convictions about the power of daring reflected in this book are due in good measure to our participation over the years in the idea generation workshops of Liz Forrest Rapp, president of Innovation Labs. She showed us that bold new ideas can be generated by the collective talent of any company open to the creative thinking process, and that these ideas can be developed into profitable new directions and breakthroughs.

We also owe a large debt of thanks to the senior executives and middle management of the MaxiMarketing winners examined in this book for their generosity in sharing with us not only their thoughts but their costs and results as well. Once again, we have found that the best companies are also the most open and most willing to share insights that can benefit the entire business community.

And without the encouragement, understanding, and support of our editor, Philip Ruppel, and editing supervisor, Jane Palmieri, at McGraw-Hill, this book would never have seen the light of day.

We thank you all.

The Authors

PART 1

New Needs, New Answers

1

The Decade of the Rude Awakening: The New Reality of the Nineties

There is a phenomenon in behavioral psychology called the mechanism of denial. That's shorthand for trying to make the storm clouds go away by pretending they don't exist.

In business and marketing, the 1980s was a time of distant thunder and, for many, a time of denial—an unwillingness to face the coming storm and prepare for it. After all, the great brands, retailers, and media company names still shone serenely in the sky like eternal constellations. IBM, AT&T, Philips, Volkswagen, Sears, Macy's, NBC, CBS. It was unthinkable that they would ever be shaken by new upstart competitors, new forms of competition, or a changed business climate.

The great advertising agencies still vied with one another to create advertising that would get a high recall score, win the most awards, and inspire the most chuckles. "If an idea makes me laugh, that's a sure sign it's a good idea," explained one top creative director, living in his own dream world.

Certainly there were early warnings of impending change.

As far back as 1980, a cover story in *Fortune* warned of a coming Knowledge Age that would transform everything. *Business Week* in 1983 proclaimed: "Vast economic and social changes have made better marketing an imperative." But during the rest of the decade, in a period of record profits fueled by tripled U.S. defense budgets and soaring deficit spending, such warnings seemed to many to be merely far-distant thunder on a sunny summer day.

If the 1980s was, in the words of the artful Reagan campaign advertising, "morning in America," it was also a time for oversleeping and ignoring the alarm clock.

Today the alarm can no longer be ignored.

Just as the 1980s was the decade of drifting and dreaming, the 1990s will be remembered as the decade of the rude awakening.

"The Fall of the Dinosaurs"

"The hurricane winds of change have already toppled some corporate giants that seemed as indestructible as California redwoods," we wrote in 1986. "And more are threatened." Seven years later, in March of 1993, *Newsweek* did a grim roundup of what they called "The Fall of the Dinosaurs."

Perhaps "fall" was too strong a word. Nonetheless, some of the most solid companies were experiencing serious difficulty. Here was Sears closing down its 97-year-old big catalog and eliminating 50,000 jobs. General Motors had lost $23.5 billion in its most recent year, a world's record of dubious distinction. IBM had lost over $5 billion and laid off 25,000 workers, with another 40,000 scheduled to be let go in 1993. Later in the year, the new chairman announced that another 35,000 jobs must go. Between February 15, 1991, and December 18, 1992, the value of IBM stock dropped 68 percent.

A few months later, *The Wall Street Journal* reported that RJR

Nabisco had canceled its $1.7 billion stock offering because of the poor market for food stocks: "Standard & Poor Corp.'s food group has dropped more than 8 percent in the past three months as investors have focused on the threat to branded products from private-label offerings." And on Fifth Avenue in New York City, the cavernous block-long B. Altman department store had been sitting empty and sad for years, a mournful reminder of past glory.

The dismal business scene was not only a U.S. happening. By the end of 1992, business failures in England and Wales were up to 76 a day. Figures from the British Chambers of Commerce showed 1 out of every 38 companies failing during the prior year. At the headquarters of Europe's biggest automaker, the $51 billion Volkswagen colossus, new CEO Ferdinand Piech was puzzling over a curious fact: The more cars Volkswagen sold, the more red ink it seemed to face.

Of course, the recession at the time was a factor. But that didn't explain why other, more nimble companies were thriving and the MaxiMarketing winners included in this book were scoring truly astonishing gains.

No. Something else was involved.

The world was changing with incredible rapidity. Competition was getting fiercer everywhere. Technology was racing ahead faster than the thinking of many managers and the capability of outdated bureaucratic structures to keep pace. Most important from our point of view, many of the companies in trouble had lost the ability to listen to and respond to their stakeholders (customers, employees, suppliers, and society). In contrast, there was a very different outcome for those companies that *were* listening and responding. They were acting and reacting in daring new ways and looking at improved results despite the hard times.

Commenting on the deteriorating situation at IBM, John R. Graham, president of Graham Communications, wrote in *Brandweek:* "IBM spent the past 25 years convincing customers they were lucky to do business with Big Blue....Dell Computer made it clear that they are in the customer's corner."

Wake-Up Call: All Business Must *Informationalize*

In *MaxiMarketing,* we wrote: "The time has come for all companies to break out of the box of past assumptions. Time to master the new computer capabilities. Time to take direct control of your future and move in a new strategic direction."

The change, we said, would not be evolutionary. When it happened, it would be a discontinuous change, a mighty leap from one marketing era to another. This break with the past and need to undertake new initiatives was underscored in *2020 Vision,* a book coauthored by Stan Davis, a former professor of the Harvard Business School, and Bill Davidson, an associate professor at the School of Business, University of Southern California.

Their message comes across loud and clear: "All business must informationalize. From small Mom-and-Pop stores to giant global corporations, the point to grasp is not merely that all economic activities will depend upon information to create and control their destinies. We've heard that already. And while it's true, this truth manifests itself so slowly—over decades—that people have tired of it. For many, it is unpoured honey. Instead of focusing on its not-so-newness, we must focus on the growing power and consequences of this truth."

The fact is that the value generated by information gained through direct interaction with the consumer is growing significantly faster than the value of traditional advertising and promotion. Peter Brabeck, worldwide chief marketing strategist at Nestlé, offered this comment in a *Financial Times* interview: "For me it is very clear. Advertising is out. Credible communication with the consumer is in."

The future predicted in *MaxiMarketing* and in Davis and Davidson's *2020 Vision* has arrived. But most marketers are still stumbling around in the industrial Stone Age. As we move beyond mass production toward more customization, beyond mass marketing toward targeting niches and a "segment" of just one person, the old beliefs are no longer a safe harbor.

With so much changing so fast, the traditional manager is left without a lodestar. He or she must learn how to master new navigational strategies just at a time when the marketing horizon itself has been transformed.

There are four "rude awakeners" out there ready to cause trouble for any corporate management that doesn't react soon enough to the changing scene:

1. New media technologies and priorities
2. New consumer attitudes and demands
3. New retail control of the selling process
4. New advertising and marketing realities

Let's take an up-close look at these new realities to see what lies ahead as we move into the middle years of this decade.

1. New Media Technologies and Priorities

Where has everybody gone? By the mid-1980s the average total prime-time network audience for commercials in the United States had sunk to 63 percent of television households. And it was hard to measure how many of this 63 percent were actually watching during the commercial breaks and how many were skipping around to other channels or wandering off to the kitchen. The late Bob Goldstein, president of Procter & Gamble at the time, expressed the opinion that Procter & Gamble was losing as much as 25 percent of its audience for commercials due to zapping alone.

Those were the days when a cable system might offer programming on merely 15 to 30 channels. Today, many systems have doubled that number of viewing options.

But that is just a drop in the bucket compared to what is coming next. *Advertising Age* early in the nineties reported two events that brought the futuristic concept of 500-channel cable systems into the contemporary world.

In December 1992, Tele-Communications Inc., the largest multiple system cable operator, disclosed plans to implement digital compression—and increase the channel capacity of some systems tenfold. The following month, Time Warner said it was installing a demonstration of the "electronic superhighway" serving 4000 subscribers in an Orlando, Florida, suburb that would be fully operational by the second quarter of 1994. TCI then announced implementation of its own version of a 500-channel system in several markets.

The big bucks to be made with mega-channel cable systems brought the Baby Bells into the fray. With the telephone companies' strong finances and experience in interactive services, the future was no longer in doubt—a cable marketplace of staggering dimensions is arriving sooner than expected.

At a meeting with Bruce Judson, general manager of Multi-Media Products and Services at Time Inc., a division of Time Warner Inc., we were told not to confuse the Orlando system with conventional cable channels. "What we will have is information and entertainment on demand, the ability to choose among hundreds of movies, games, a menu of information services, and home shopping," said Judson. "And that's just a small part of it. There will be a wide range of interactive possibilities as well."

Time described the electronic superhighway this way:

> Imagine a medium that combines the switching and routing capabilities of phones with the video and information offerings of the most advanced cable systems and data banks. Instead of settling for whatever happens to be on at a particular time you could select any item you wanted. A movie? Airline listings? Tomorrow's newspaper or yesterday's episode of Northern Exposure? How about a new magazine or book? A stroll through the L.L. Bean catalog? A teleconference with your boss? Just punch up what you want and it appears when you want it.

Geoffrey Holmes, Time Warner's senior vice-president for technology, talked about the advertising implications in a *New York Times* interview: "When you're shopping for a life insurance policy, you can access a detailed explanation. Or think about buying a car. You can bring the showroom to your house and take a 15-minute walk through it."

This new cable technology will also give marketers a chance

to reach the consumer in dramatically new ways. Infomercials could be targeted to households electronically with the same ease as today's selective binding technology targets individual magazine readers with specific interests.

By the summer of 1993, *The New York Times* in a special report on tomorrow's TV was describing the new global computerized information network as "one grand Communicopia." A *New York Times*/CBS News Poll indicated that most Americans are willing to pay for the privilege of controlling what is on their screens.

A preview of the future could be seen in what was happening on the Videoway interactive cable network in Montreal, Canada. Viewers use remote-control pads to play along with *Jeopardy!* and choose which camera angle to watch during baseball games. Watching a Ford commercial, viewers could choose which of four different models they wanted to know more about.

Dr. André H. Caron, director of the University of Montreal's New Technologies Research Laboratory, estimated that subscribers have reduced the amount of "plain old television" they turn on by about six hours a week.

It is true that most of the additional special-interest viewing opportunities will have tiny audiences. But in the aggregate this convergence of telephone, computer, and television technologies will bring about still more leakage out of the great pool of network TV viewers. The number of "plain old television" fans will continue to shrink. The audience for "fancy new telecomputing" will continue to expand.

Based on what is already taking place, some of the audiences for the new cable offerings may not be so small. The TV viewing public will be chopped into both miniscule and maximal niches.

QVC just keeps growing and growing and growing. The business world gasped when the legendary Barry Diller, the onetime head of prime-time television for ABC Entertainment and then of Paramount Pictures, decided, after months of looking around, to invest in and become chairman of—a shopping channel!

But Diller's eyes had been opened to the interactive future of television when he visited the studios of QVC, the premium home shopping channel, with his friend the noted fashion designer Diane Von Furstenberg. There he stood and watched as they introduced a special Diane Von Furstenberg line called Silk Assets, created exclusively for QVC. Thousands of calls poured in, and he was thunderstruck to see the QVC computer system rack up and process $1.2 million in sales in just 100 minutes—$12,000 per minute.

After Diller moved in as chairman of QVC in January of 1993, providing additional credibility to the company, the fashion columnist of *The New York Times* reported that "the center of American fashion seems to be shifting decidedly south of Seventh Avenue. Pilgrimages have begun in force to the West Chester, PA, headquarters of QVC Network."

Saks Fifth Avenue paid a call and then announced that Saks would be the first department store to market its private-label collection, Real Clothes, on the shopping channel. Saks then went on the air twice with the collection and racked up more than $1 million in sales. *Business Week* reported that Saks CEO Philip Miller was "thrilled" by the experience. The chairman of Bloomingdale's was expected to call. And even the legendary Calvin Klein said, "I'm going down to West Chester to look at it."

Then in July of 1993, Diller rocked the world of retailing again when he announced that QVC would merge with its competitor, Home Shopping Network, creating a $2.2 billion home shopping meganetwork available in more than 60 million homes. "RETAILING WILL NEVER BE THE SAME," trumpeted the banner headline on the cover story in *Business Week.*

The millions of home-shopping junkies QVC already has watching may not fit your stereotype of the compulsive TV cubic-zirconia home shopper. Surprisingly, according to a study by Deloitte & Touche, the single largest group of callers is professional people and managers who are too busy to shop and who are fed up with crowds at the department stores.

Innovative programming produced by Diller on the new QVC may draw millions of other men and women who heretofore would have scoffed at the idea of sitting glued to their television sets watching pitches for ceramic figurines and Irish crystal pet bowls. The announcement that Macy's department store is launching its own 24-hour TV home-shopping channel only confirmed that the boom in video shopping by telephone and credit card is picking up speed.

As if network television executives and clients who just love mass-market viewing numbers don't have enough to worry about, consider this. There is a new VCR that can automatically delete commercials when a recorded program is played back. And, on the horizon, there is a remote control that can scan live TV and edit out commercials or switch channels when one comes on.

Marketers still dreaming of the "bigger is better" audience buys of yesterday had better wake up to the priorities of adjusting to and trying out what it means to do business along the digital information highway of the 1990s. The rude awakening to the changing role of the video screen is only one facet of the way that technology is transforming marketing communications in this decade.

Magazine publishers are turning to computer-controlled selective binding to target which reader will get to see which advertisement. With selective ink-jet imaging, the right message for the right reader can be put on each page as well. (See Chapter 6 for the House of Seagram story.)

And with the art and science of predictive computer modeling you can forget about "plain old direct mail," too, and enter the age of mailing less while enjoying greater response than you ever thought possible.

Finding Generation X in the traditional media is also a problem. Throughout the 1980s and into the 1990s, marketers focused intently on understanding and selling to the Baby Boomers. But now the Baby Boomers are aging, and an overlooked, skeptical, hard-to-reach generation is about to follow them as the prime market for many advertisers: the "Busters," or "Generation X."

These roughly 46 million Americans 18 to 29 years old are a $125 billion market. But, according to *Advertising Age,* "marketers seeking to hit this younger target are finding a dearth of outlets through which to communicate their messages. The traditional media preoccupied for years with catering to the needs and tastes of the boomers have virtually ignored the busters, *many of whom have turned away from the big 3 TV networks and mass-market magazines.*" (Italics ours.)

Karen Ritchie, the director of media services for McCann-

Erickson Worldwide in Detroit, warned a gathering of the nation's publishers and editors. "The idea that we can reach this target with boomer media is an idea whose time has come and gone. There is so little on television or in magazines that holds any real meaning for them."

Finding our target market in the old familiar places is a luxury no longer available to the strategic planner of the 1990s. It's time to seek out and find new ways to interact with potential and actual customers, one at a time, in our own private database universe—and in public events that enhance the brand image and customer bonding. (See Chapter 4 for the Harley-Davidson story.)

2. New Consumer Attitudes and Demands

A funny thing happened to consumers in the world's prosperous economies on their way to the mid-1990s. The economic pressure of stagnating wages and the threat of unemployment forced millions to carefully clip coupons, shop for bargains, and throng to discount warehouses.

You may say that there is nothing new about such a development. During hard times, people have always gone bargain-hunting. What is new this time, analysts say, is that people who are *not* necessarily having a hard time are shopping more carefully. It is a change in behavior that has forced marketers in North America and Europe to toss out their timeworn assumptions and to embrace the new verities of Value Marketing.

A national poll conducted for *Adweek's Marketing Week* by Warwick Baker & Fiore found that 9 out of 10 shoppers go shopping for frequently purchased items armed with a specific strategy for saving money. And often they are able to proudly add up how much they have saved over the year.

Brand marketers awakened in the early 1990s to living with a whole new pressure on profit margins. Before long, each in turn would discover that they could no longer automatically produce higher profits by simply raising prices on advertised brands. The consumer just wouldn't stand for it.

Other things being equal, people may still like seeking out a certain brand to get the quality they prefer and can rely upon for satisfaction. But other things are no longer equal. Today, shoppers are demanding both dependable quality *and* the lowest price—even if it means giving up a relationship with a long-famous brand name.

Says Kenneth Stone, economics professor at Iowa State University, "We Americans have gotten into the discount mindset. It's fashionable to be frugal in the 1990s. I don't think a lot of people would have been seen dead in a warehouse store in the 1980s."

According to an article in *The Economist:* "If this trend [toward buying the cheapest brand available] continues, it could spell disaster for America's biggest consumer-goods firms, which live or die on their ability to make their products stand out in the world's most crowded market."

The trend was not restricted to Americans and the way they shop. German discount chains with rock-bottom prices and tough sales tactics were expanding across the European continent and into Great Britain. *The Wall Street Journal* reported that since Aldi GmbH, the pioneer of heavy discounting in Europe, opened its first British store in Birmingham, the spread of deep discounting has been explosive. Analysts expect the number of British grocery food discounters to double in the next few years, moving closer to the German model in which the cheaper stores control 23 percent of the food market. The discounting fever even spread to Japan, where it began to shake up the archaic distribution system.

Private Labels Get Respect. In the late 1970s and early 1980s, low-priced no-name generic products in plain wrappers began appearing on supermarket shelves. But they were not considered a significant threat to advertised brands, and it seemed as if generic products and house brands might eventually fade away. Like the comedian Rodney Dangerfield, they "couldn't get no respect."

Somehow, though, they didn't fade away. They lingered and consumer attitudes gradually changed.

Then the pressure of the economic slump accelerated the trend toward store brands, even in product categories that were considered bastions of brand loyalty in the past.

Retail store managers couldn't be happier. Profit margins are usually 4 percent higher on store brands than name brands.

"The infection is spreading to other parts of the store," observed one consultant in the fall of 1992. "Quality private-label products can now compete in nearly every category in the supermarket."

The share of supermarket shoppers' dollars spent on store brands rose from 12.5 percent in 1989 to 18.3 percent three years later, reaching a total of $35 billion. *Brandweek* reported the predictions of no fewer than three securities analysts that this share would rise to *30 to 45 percent of the market within the next decade.*

"In the past, if I had a national brand I liked, I stuck with it, but I can't afford to do that any more," said a young mother in Alaska. She started out buying house-brand frozen vegetables and fruit juices. She found she liked them just as well, and now she will try the store brand of just about any product.

The trend is also affecting the big brand names in nonprescription drug products. A company called Perrigo took in $410 million in fiscal 1992 supplying "knock-offs" of 857 different name-brand products such as Advil, Pepto-Bismol, and Plax to such chains as Wal-Mart, Kmart, and Rite Aid. The chains then sell the products under their own labels, at 30 to 50 percent less than name-brand prices.

Sales of private-label cold and flu remedies alone hit $105.5 million in the year ending May 1993, up 88 percent over the previous year.

Of course, if you can't lick 'em, join 'em. As a result, big brand companies such as Nestlé, Heinz, Kraft General Foods, Campbell, and Keebler have jumped into contracting to produce the goods for private-label retail marketers. It's still profitable business. But it recasts the role of the once mighty brand marketer from the one who creates consumer demand to *the one who supplies what the retailer demands.*

"We're at the end of an era in terms of national brand loyalty," says Dave Nichol, president of the Canadian supermarket chain, Loblaw's.

He may be overstating the case somewhat. Or, he may not. In either case, the implication is clear. Just spending tens of millions, or even hundreds of millions of dollars, on advertising insisting that you're "the right one" (Coke) or "It's it and that's that" (Miller Lite) is no longer any guarantee of continued growth. (During the Miller campaign, sales declined 5 percent despite an estimated increase in ad expenditure of 33 percent.)

Says high-tech marketing consultant Regis McKenna, "If you want customer loyalty, you must be loyal to the customer."

Increasingly, brand advertisers are going to have to earn their brand loyalty in new ways: by identifying who their loyal customers are and rewarding them for desired behavior, by empowering loyal customers to play a role in creating new products, and by encouraging loyalty with an attractive set of benefits wrapped around the product or service.

The New Consumer Fights Back. As if dealing with a penny-pinching consumer wasn't scary enough, the 1990s marketer also must face the demands of a better educated, street-smart shopper. For example, take the airline industry.

Many passengers, armed with their own on-line information resources and a fierce determination not to be outdone, have found a variety of ways to beat the airlines at their own game. Some of these strategies were highlighted in a *New York Times* article telling how the consumer wages guerrilla war against the marketing strategies of the airlines.

Many passengers look for what are known as "hidden city fares." The industry's hub-and-spoke system makes it possible for a passenger going to New York from Dallas to buy a $346.50 ticket from Dallas to Montreal and then get off in New York, since New York is the hub for Dallas and Montreal. The cost is $193.50 less than a ticket from Dallas to New York would have been. The airlines end up outsmarting themselves.

Another popular tactic is back-to-back ticketing. A round-trip ticket between Seattle and Kansas City requiring a Saturday night stayover might cost $200. Without the stayover, the mid-week fare could cost as much as $1,000. So, some passengers buy two round-trip tickets between Seattle and Kansas City at $200 each, and then use alternate halves of each set of tickets to fly round-trip during the week without a Saturday stopover.

Herb Conroy, a Chicago businessman, was quoted as commenting: "The business passenger pays through the nose and we have to do whatever we can to even the score." By engaging in deceptive doubletalk when it comes to pricing, the entire airline industry has managed to alienate their best customers.

By not listening to and responding to the demands being made by today's consumer for fair treatment, the airlines missed the opportunity to build a relationship with the marketplace based on trust and real value. And, they don't stop there. Too often, their much-vaunted frequent-flyer-award programs become nothing more than me-too copies of one another and promotional cost centers. The chance to truly customize the relationship with the airline's best customers has fallen between the cracks in today's standardized frequent-flyer programs.

What is missing are daring initiatives that build loyalty by genuinely caring for the consumer's well-being rather than trying to get the better of him or her. The demanding new consumer attitude of the 1990s makes it imperative for all modern-day marketers to develop the "Caring and Daring" approach of the MaxiMarketing winners included in this book.

3. Rising Retail Control of the Selling Process

Big bold headlines heralding the "CLOUT!" of the retail giants ruling the marketplace appeared in *Business Week* just before the 1993 New Year's celebration got under way. The message was clear. Nowadays, producers of goods and services have little to celebrate.

Control of the selling process was slipping more and more into the hands of the big retail category killers. *Business Week* illustrated what manufacturers are up against with this reverse-success story: "The folks at Totes Inc. thought up a pretty nifty product. They took a heavy pair of socks, stuck rubbery treads on them to provide traction on slippery floors and called the result slipper socks. A year after introducing them in 1988, Totes was selling 14 million pairs a year. Kmart Corp. and Wal-Mart Stores Inc. alone accounted for as many as 1.5 million pairs.

"But not for long. Within two years both giant discounters had found suppliers that made knocked-off slipper socks for less. They dropped Totes—and lowered the price of their knock-offs 25 percent or more, to under $2 a pair."

You might think that Totes would never again want to deal with the likes of those voracious folks at Kmart and Wal-Mart. But you would be wrong.

Business Week reported: "These days, Totes executives figure their new products have a year at most, before these retailers crowd them out with lower-priced knock-offs. Says President Ronald Best: "Can I afford to deal with these guys?" The brutal truth: "You can't afford not to."

The new reality is a power shift to a privileged circle of merchants. More and more, they're telling manufacturers in every category what goods to make, how to price and promote their products, and how to structure their own organizations.

With marketing power so heavily on the side of Kmart, Wal-Mart, Staples, Toys 'R' Us, Home Depot, Circuit City, Costco Warehouse Club, Target Stores, Zellers in Canada, and all the rest of the big boys, there is hardly a business category that has not felt the change.

Canada Invades the United States. There is a visionary maverick retailer in Canada who has emerged as one of the leaders in the pitched battle between manufacturers and retailers. He is Dave Nichol, the defiant, irreverent, irrepressible president of Loblaw's, an $8 billion Canadian supermarket chain. What he has been accomplishing illuminates the enormity of the threat from store brands that is faced by the big advertised brands in the packaged foods field.

It was Nichol's genius to realize that a store brand need not grovel as a humble commoner in the realm of packaged food products. It can be positioned as royalty...not as a product of inferior quality compared to the more expensive advertised brands, but as one actually superior.

When Nichol joined the company as president in 1978, one of his first projects was a private-label brand selling well below the advertised brands. It was called No-Name, with the name printed in black on a plain yellow label.

But then he had the idea, which he frankly admits he got from the fabled British discount store Marks & Spencer, for a second line called "The President's Choice"—foods of higher quality and price than generics, personally developed or tested by Nichol, but still underselling the name brands.

For example, he introduced his "remarkable tasting" President's Choice Deluxe Macaroni and Cheese Dinner, for 49 cents a box. The price of the equivalent famous brand, Kraft Macaroni and Cheese, was 99 cents a box.

Next, he made his President's Choice line of products wildly successful by inventing his own advertising medium, *The Insider's Report*, which is said to reach 10 million Canadians each time it is published, as well as through his whimsical personal-appearance television commercials.

The company spends $12 million a year on product research, and 400 of the thousands of products they have developed have met the Darwinian test of survival of the fittest. New products can be developed and launched in as short a time as six months, compared to years for the big food manufacturers. Nichol is a Committee of One who can give a green light to a new product instantly.

Pointing to a bottle of Szechwan peanut sauce, a product he discovered in Bali, Nichol says, "If Kraft would bring this to market, they would go out and take it to Nebraska (or another test market), and they would spend hundreds of thousands of dollars and do all the demographics on it. If we like the way it tastes, we bring it to market. And then we let the consumer vote at the check-out counter as to whether it's going to stay or not."

"All the Ground Rules Are Going to Change." Make no mistake about it—Dave Nichol is a revolutionary who has thrown down the gauntlet to the big food manufacturers. "You have these enormous marketing costs built into the national brands," he told Prepared Foods. "That's the albatross around the manufacturers' neck....All the ground rules are going to change. You're going to see a massive shift in power from manufacturer to retailer in North America."

Soon, not satisfied with having merely conquered large parts of Canada, Nichol began to cast his gaze southward over the border to the United States. He launched a massive invasion by making licensing deals with a number of U.S. supermarket chains, so that they too could start selling President's Choice products, now named Master Choice in the United States.

Not long ago, our copy of the Sunday edition of *The New York Times* contained a freestanding advertising insert in the form of a glossy 20-page Master Choice magazine, put out by A&P on behalf of a number of chains it operates in the area. It is a combination of editorial articles, some but not all of which carry a selling message, pages of advertising for Master Choice products, and discount coupons.

Think about it! They are doing massive, glossy advertising of their own store brand, and discounting their own discount price. But the advertising is costing them a fraction of the cost of that many pages in a national paid-circulation magazine, thanks to lower retail rates and free distribution of the insert at their own supermarket locations.

The back cover of this store magazine shows a dramatic close-up of a can of Master Choice Cola, with the following ad copy:

> THE COLA WARS ARE OVER!
>
> Master Choice enters the fray and ends it. In an independent taste test of 13,000 regular Coke drinkers, Master Choice Cola outranked Coke and Pepsi 2 to 1. Let's toast to proof that better can cost less!

It's unthinkable to suggest that someday Coke and Pepsi might lose their overall global supremacy. For one thing, they have hundreds of thousands of other outlets worldwide besides supermarkets. But it is *not* unthinkable to consider that as public confidence in and satisfaction with Master Choice and other store-brand colas grow, still more supermarket customers might start trying them and make them the No. 1 colas in those supermarkets.

It could even become reverse chic to drink Master Choice Cola because it's not Coke or Pepsi. Don't forget that Wal-Mart's own cola, Sam's Choice, sold 40 million cases while Coke and Pepsi sales slipped slightly. Can Master Choice Cola be far behind?

"Coke and Pepsi, I think, have some real threats," says Dave Aaker, professor of marketing strategy at the University of California–Berkeley and author of *Managing Brand Equity*. "They sell every other week on special, it seems," he told *Marketing Week*, "but private label still comes in with this breathtakingly low price." (PS: Professor Aaker now drinks Safeway Select Cola. "The price is so low. And it tastes O.K.")

In March of 1992, an A&P spokesperson told *Supermarket News* that it planned to double the number of products in its Loblaw-supplied Master Choice line, which already numbered 120. And this is in addition to each chain's own private-label products, such as Waldbaum's, Kohl's, and Food Emporium's.

The Fight for Shelf Space Turns Brutal. Where will the shelf space for these new Master Choice products come from? Well, said the A&P spokesperson, it may be at the expense of other brands. "We find room usually by reducing sizes in other brands. On occasion, Master Choice will knock out a regional brand or even one of the other brands."

Tom Stephens, Loblaw's director of product development, puts it more bluntly: "The thing you're going to find in the nineties is that marginality is out. You're going to find a major de-listing of national brands in North America."

What must be truly disturbing for the multinational megabrands is that this dramatic rise in retailer power is happening not only here in America. *The Wall Street Journal* reports from Brussels: "Europe's big boys of retailing are pushing Mom and Pop into early retirement. In most of Europe, the number of small and medium-size stores has fallen drastically over the past five years....In Italy, where superstores were launched later than in most of Europe, Nielsen found that their number doubled between 1988 and 1992. The development was also swift in Austria where they rose by 50 percent in the same period."

In France, Holland, and the United Kingdom, the consolidation of power into the hands of a short list of all-powerful supermarket retailers is even more concentrated than it is here in the United States. All across Europe they are using this power to push their own store brands at the expense of private brands.

Business Week reported that the preference of millions of European shoppers for store brands over private brands is "creating what is probably the biggest postwar crisis that big brand marketers have yet faced. After years of watching store brands make steady gains in market share, the big multinational marketers are suddenly facing slow growth or worse, as the trend toward off-brand buying spreads from big Northern European nations, such as Britain, France, and Germany, south to Spain and Italy, where retailing is rapidly modernizing. Adding to the urgency is Europe's deep recession, which is driving shoppers to demand more value than ever. By some estimates, private-label goods now account for as much as 32 percent of supermarket sales volume in Britain and 24 percent in France."

In the global economic village of the 1990s, the alarm that sounds radical change is a universal signal.

Procter & Gamble—Fighting Back or Giving In? Faced with an increasingly costly retail-dominated marketing process, the mightiest packaged goods brand-builder in America, Procter & Gamble, finally decided to fight back.

P&G rocked the business world by introducing a new pricing policy. It amounted to a declaration of war on the old, deeply entrenched system of push-pull promotions dominated by the retailer. By the spring of 1992, P&G had cut the wholesale prices on nearly half of their products and announced their determination to pursue a total break with the past. The new policy was called "EDLP"—Every Day Low Prices. For a company known for its history of solid, deliberate growth, it was a strategic move of breathtaking daring.

P&G was determined to do away with what had become a wasteful, confusing, Byzantine pricing and promotions system. At one end it bribed retailers with so-called trade allowances and at the other end it bribed shoppers with periodic "sales" to pull goods through the supermarket distribution channel with temporarily reduced pricing.

P&G's trade promotion budget had swollen to more than $1.5 billion. It made sense for them to cut it out and pass the savings on to consumers in the form of lower prices while fattening company profits. The problem was that the supermarket chains would fight any such move because they stood to gain from the status quo.

The original idea of trade allowances was to stimulate sales by giving the grocers a special discount which they could use either to advertise the product or to run a promotion. Instead, many grocers would buy a huge amount "on deal" and stash it away. Later they could, if they chose, sell it at full retail price or more and pocket the saving themselves to increase profit margins instead of passing the saving on to shoppers.

During the 1980s, grocers spent millions of dollars building warehouses to store the huge inventories that resulted from this "forward buying." By 1991, as much as $60 to $80 billion worth of excess inventory was in their warehouses.

You can imagine how this system was driving product manufacturers crazy. They would get a huge order from a supermarket chain, and then have six months go by without receiving a reorder. Factories would run at top speed to fill the big order, then have to cut back and idle along at less than full capacity until the product went "on promotion" again.

In addition to these quantity discount deals, retailers were also demanding and getting "slotting fees" for allowing a new product to come in, "facing allowances" for prime shelf space, and "market development funds" for local advertising and instore displays which often were never spent but went straight into the retailers' pockets.

The more the retailers demanded these trade allowances from the brand marketers, the less money was available for brand-building advertising and timely promotions. Between 1981 and 1991, trade promotion allowances grew from 34 to 50 percent of the manufacturers' total marketing costs while media advertising expenditures plummeted from 43 to 25 percent.

It was a monstrous situation from the manufacturers' point of view. Push-pull promotional mania was weakening brand loyalty by training shoppers to favor savings over brand names and by cutting into advertising support for the brand. The supermarket chains were having it both ways—increasing profit margins and weakening the position of advertised brands against their store brands. If nothing changed, the chains would take total control of the market and ultimately reduce the manufacturer to the role of being in business only to serve the profit goals of the retailer.

Something had to be done. And P&G did it. But in effect they were only choosing the lesser of two evils. Yes, through their

EDLP policy, they put themselves in a better position to compete with lower-priced store brands and private labels. But by cutting prices across the board, they also cut into profit margins—and that in turn led to some painful downsizing of the company.

"Procter & Gamble Co., hounded by competition from lower-priced and private-label rivals, will slash 13,000 jobs, or 12 percent of its work force, and close 30 plants," reported *The Wall Street Journal* in July of 1993. "The sweeping retrenchment, the largest ever for P&G, is the latest sign that once-invincible makers of consumer brands are under pressure. Moreover, the move signals P&G's intent to increasingly use price as a weapon in the highly competitive consumer-products and food markets."

Of course, that doesn't mean that P&G is going to give up altogether in the fight to compete by building brand loyalty. They can't. To do so would truly mean the beginning of the end of their empire. But the big question now is, how can they maintain and build preference for P&G brands in a marketplace in which (1) brand-image advertising no longer works as well, and (2) there is no longer as much margin available for advertising expenditure?

A year or two earlier, P&G had already begun exploring new ways to get involved with the end users of their brands and to interact with consumers directly—the general direction followed by the MaxiMarketing winners profiled in this book.

One of P&G's key marketing executives, Robert Wientzen, manager of promotion and marketing services, wrote all P&G ad agencies asking to meet "to discuss our capabilities and our agencies' capabilities so we can have a better understanding of how we can use direct marketing." But before long, as might be expected from a corporation that never displayed a passion for consumer relationships in the first place, P&G downplayed individualized marketing by sending Wientzen, their direct marketing guru, over to Advanced Promotion Technologies as the new president-CEO of that partially owned point-of-purchase promotion house.

By the summer of 1993 it appeared that despite all of

Wientzen's early efforts, P&G's experimental forays into direct marketing seemed to be undercommitted and merely tactical maneuvers rather than a major strategic move like those of the winners examined in this book.

Nestlé of Switzerland Takes a Different Tack. For a more hopeful look at where the marketing of packaged goods (or as the Europeans call them, fast-moving consumer goods) may be going, you have to lift your sights from the embattled citadel in Cincinnati and focus on the Nestlé headquarters in Vevey, Switzerland. Nestlé is a multinational $80 billion Goliath of a company with a worldwide $3 billion advertising expenditure. More than half its revenues come from the food operation headed by General Manager Peter Brabeck. When the world's largest food manufacturer sets a new course, it's time to sit up and take notice.

In an interview given to *Marketing* magazine in the United Kingdom, Mr. Brabeck stunned the European marketing community with the announcement that Nestlé planned to build a global brand not just with advertising this time but on the basis of a one-to-one relationship with the consumer.

Nestlé has chosen the United Kingdom to be the laboratory for one of the biggest and boldest experiments in consumer brand building seen anywhere in the world—the launch of a coordinated worldwide consumer involvement strategy for the Buitoni pasta business they acquired in 1988.

Unlike P&G's hesitant dabbling with direct marketing, Nestlé would fight retail dominance with an all-out experiment in building a lasting relationship with the consumer beyond the mere sale of a product.

Why did Nestlé become the first megamarketing food company to embrace what we see as a MaxiMarketing approach as a major corporate strategy?

Here is Brabeck's answer: "The old advertising principle was that I am sender and those receiving the message will react. But what happens if they judge it and don't react? We will always need advertising to have a public appeal, but that alone will not be enough. The main thrust will be on one-to-one communication where you get a warmer and better response."

To discover how he is doing just that, see Chapter 8 for the Buitoni case history.

4. New Advertising and Marketing Realities

Business Week in their fall 1991 report gloomily headed "What Happened to Advertising?" asked this challenging question: "Why did a relatively mild recession trigger a depression in advertising?"

"To many marketers, the reason is as simple as it is scary. The recession has laid bare forces that are giving advertising a permanently diminished role. Cynical consumers are weary of the constant barrage of marketing messages. They're becoming less receptive to the blandishments of Madison Avenue."

Desperate to rise above this milling mass of clutter and be seen and heard by the public, advertisers and their agencies often strain for advertising so clever, so unusual, so entertaining that people will simply have to notice and remember. But this straining for effect frequently results in advertising which achieves entertainment value at the expense of sales results.

In October of 1991, Calvin Klein ran what was probably the largest single advertising insert in history: a 116-page insert in *Vanity Fair,* at a cost reported to be $1 million. No words to get in the way—just pictures of a model on a motorcycle and of an imaginary San Francisco rock concert. Six months later, according to *The Wall Street Journal,* the chairman of merchandising services at Federated Department Stores, Klein's best customer, reported that the ad "didn't have any noticeable impact on sales."

When Nuprin introduced its "Nupe it" campaign, it was widely praised and won a Gold Effie award for advertising effectiveness. But meanwhile, sales of Nuprin slipped 0.5 percent while the category was growing by 2 percent a year.

And surely by this time almost everyone in advertising knows the sad story of the battery-powered Energizer bunny who keeps going and going across other peoples' television commercials. He (or she?) made it to the Top 10 Best-Recalled commercials—but failed to make a dent in the market share of Duracell, the leader.

It's a New Brand Ball Game. At the 1992 conference of the American Association of Advertising Agencies, Interpublic Chairman Philip G. Geier argued earnestly, "The action we really need to take is an almost spiritual revival of our faith in brand advertising. We have no reason to hold back, because our mission is to build brands."

At first glance, this statement seems commendable and unassailable. But a careful rereading reveals an easily overlooked flaw in its logic. Where is the proof that today brand advertising really is the only way and the best way to build brands? Once this doubt is raised, it leads to the further question of whether advertising creativity to support a brand should be the overriding mission of today's ad agency, as the statement implies.

Just look at what we've observed in this chapter.

- The rising popularity of high-quality, low-priced store brands doing very well with little or no advertising support
- The increasing clutter of saturation advertising in all media, and the accompanying rise of indifference and skepticism toward advertising by the consumer
- The fragmentation of the media, and the ability of consumers increasingly to dodge television and radio advertising altogether by flipping and zapping or spending their time enjoying advertising-free entertainment
- The rising dominance of the retailer and the price wars that lead to a squeeze on profit margins and advertising budgets
- The approach of the electronic information superhighway and the growth of interactivity as the communication method of choice in the Information Age
- The mindset of many ad agency creative departments and

directors (and, alas, their clients), which too often tilts toward the creation of clever, startling advertising more likely to win advertising awards than to win new customers

Does all of this give you great confidence that a return to the grand old tradition of brand-building advertising* on "plain old television" is going to work its magic as it once did, and that today's creativity-driven advertising agency is well prepared to work this miracle?

Among the most open-minded advertisers, a different view started as a trickle in the 1980s, and began to flow freely as the 1990s got under way. It was that the answer was not simply to bombard the public with more and better brand advertising. Rather, it was to find out *who* and *where* your individual best prospects and customers were and collect this information in an accessible computer database—to talk directly to these people, listen to them, involve them, empower them, and serve them better. Advances in computer technology and electronic communication were making this new marketing mode both affordable and user-friendly.

With pressure on profit margins becoming an increasingly

*As we discuss the problems of advertising, we are keenly aware that we are guilty of great, though necessary, oversimplification.

The term "brand advertising" in itself implies a parity or near-parity product, a commodity (or a commodity service, like airline seats) that seeks to distinguish itself from other similar offerings.

But national advertising for branded commodities claiming some point of superiority over similar products represents perhaps as little as one-sixth of the more than $100 billion spent on all kinds of advertising in all media. The other five-sixths is devoted to retail advertising and to products and services which offer unique, newsworthy solutions to common problems or needs.

A great deal of this advertising is as effective as it ever was—when it can find and catch up with its target audience. But because it has become harder to find and cultivate the potential customer cost effectively, even advertisers of this sort will find our observations about the problems and solutions for brand advertisers to have relevance to their own problems as well.

It is also worth pointing out that, despite the examples we have provided of award-winning but ineffective ad campaigns, the sobering influence of the early 1990s recession seemed to be making some of the brand advertising on national television more sensible, down-to-earth, and sales-oriented.

common 1990s phenomenon, we began to see more double-duty advertising that builds brand image and asks for a response. MCI introduced their Family and Friends promotion with the biggest direct-response advertising campaign ever seen on prime-time TV, and General Motors followed by trading in their $50 million corporate image advertising for a double-duty advertising campaign to launch the new GM credit card.

But for most marketers progress is still in fits and starts. It has seemed almost as if advertisers and their agencies were being dragged kicking and screaming into the twenty-first century. They remain fond of the old way of doing business and are reluctant to give it up. This is true even as it becomes increasingly obvious that "the old advertising" just isn't working the way it once did.

If the rude awakening (or tocsin of doom, depending on your point of view) for advertisers required a radical manifesto, it was delivered on November 16, 1992, in a thundering *Advertising Age* opinion piece by Joe Cappo, the publication's senior vice-president and publishing director.

The article was sternly headed "AGENCIES: CHANGE OR DIE. Huge Marketing Revolution Upsets Old Rules." And it began with this wake-up call:

> If you are one of those advertising agency or media executives who have been quoted as saying that everything will be just peachy as soon as the recession is over, WAKE UP.
>
> This is no mere recession. What is happening in the advertising industry right now is a massive revolution that is changing the rules of marketing. If this kind of talk bothers you, then don't continue reading this article. It could be hazardous to your health.
>
> Those affected the most by the revolution will be traditional advertising agencies. They blossomed in the 1970's and 80's. They will become largely irrelevant before we leave the 1990's unless they change radically.

Cappo said that the revolution was taking place not only in the United States but in all affluent countries where advertising and media are well developed. It would just take a little longer for it to reach them. And he issued this startling warning: "*The trouble is that leaders of many mainline agencies don't recognize a revolution is in the works or, worse yet, they are trying to fight it. They are certain to lose the battle."*

What followed was such a penetrating analysis by so influential and knowledgeable an industry observer that it deserves a closer look. It helps explain why we felt this book was needed.

Cappo underscores much of what we have said here, adding to it the weight of the influence and authority of America's leading advertising journal. He identifies seven characteristics of the revolution, some of which we have already touched on in this chapter. They are:

1. The shifting of marketing dollars from media advertising to other forms of marketing, including sales promotion, public relations, direct mail, database-driven loyalty programs, catalog marketing, special events, sponsorships, trade promotions, and so forth. *Advertising Age* estimates that 65 percent of all marketing expenditures in the United States now go to these non-media sectors.
2. The shift of media buying from the agencies to in-house buyers or media buying services, or closer supervision of agency buying and "shaving commission percentages."
3. The splitting of mass media into smaller, more targeted buys. "Buying small isn't as profitable as buying big, so big agencies often ignore small or new media."
4. The vastly increased power of retailers. Their demand for fees to stock and display a marketer's product "siphons money away from advertising, and it isn't commissionable."
5. Advertisers bypassing their agencies and dealing directly with media in making deals for sponsorships, custom publishing, merchandising, and value-added programs.
6. Outsiders intruding on advertising matters. For example, Creative Artists Agency arranges the production of commercials for Coca-Cola without the involvement of the agency.
7. The rapid rise of database marketing, with its ability to collect dozens of data bits on hundreds of millions of consumers. This "is a long-term trend that will profoundly change the way advertisers sell their products."

Cappo linked these changes to the dramatic changes in the consumers targeted by advertisers. They are more difficult to reach through traditional mass media, smarter, more cynical about advertising, more knowledgeable about personal finance, and more health-conscious and environment-conscious.

> This is the new consumer that clients face. And clients have decided this new consumer must be approached in different ways that may or may not include media advertising. That is why marketing money is shifting away from conventional media. This is why agencies are in trouble.
>
> It seems that many ad agencies don't realize this. Yes, some are scrambling to get into areas that clients need. But it has mostly been a helter-skelter approach to the problem. They acquire a public relations firm, affiliate with a sales promotion agency, or merge with a direct response firm. But they never serve a cohesive meal. All they offer is a mish-mash of hors d'oeuvres.
>
> ...Indeed, most major agencies have decided to fight the trend rather than join it. You can hear their anti-revolutionary battle cries in speeches at association meetings and in op-ed articles by agency executives. They are hoping beyond hope that everything will return to the glory days of the 1960s and 1970s. It won't.
>
> ...Based on the long-term trends, if you do only media advertising, less and less of your client's marketing dollars will flow through your hands. You will become increasingly irrelevant. The marketing revolution is well under way. It will be successful. Over the next few years, the advertising business will change even more than it has in the last few. By the year 2000, the advertising business we know so well will have been transformed into something new.
>
> But this is not a dire prediction. It needn't spell disaster for you. It offers you an opportunity. You have two alternatives: Join the revolution and participate in the restructuring of one of our most important business functions.
>
> Or fight the revolution, fail to recognize the inevitable, and have your agency evaporate before the 21st century rolls around.

Whew! That's pretty strong medicine. And the fact that a top executive at *Advertising Age* felt it necessary to force it down their readers' throats is a revealing sign of how widespread the agency resistance to the marketing revolution has been.

Yet another indictment of the advertising and marketing establishment followed with publication of *The Marketing Revolution* by Kevin J. Clancy and Robert S. Shulman, former partners in what was the world's premier marketing research company, Yankelovich Clancy Shulman.

"The marketing revolution is coming because failure is self-evident," Clancy and Shulman wrote. "Even when they can measure return on investment—most marketing programs do not provide an acceptable ROI. They do not achieve their sales and profit goals."

Great Agencies Need Great Clients. However, it would not be true or fair to lay all of the blame for the resistance to the marketing revolution on the agencies, the media, and the research companies that profit from "plain old advertising," and none of it on the advertisers who pay the bills. Many advertisers, too, are guilty of yesterday's trade practices and are stuck in yesterday's way of thinking.

From our work as strategic marketing consultants for major corporations, and from our careful monitoring of advertising and business news, we have noted the following ways that companies often fail to meet the challenges and seize the opportunities of the new marketing era.

- Failure to shake off corporate timidity and orthodoxy, a desire to "play it safe" and follow conventional wisdom.
- Failure to give up their own infatuation with clever, creativity-driven advertising as the automatic solution to a brand-building challenge. "To have great poets, there must be great audiences, too," Walt Whitman reminded us. It also requires receptive clients before an agency can plan and win acceptance of an innovative marketing strategy. Every time you see silly or wasted advertising by an agency, remember that some client either demanded it or approved it.
- Failure to really care about the customer. For decades, advertisers got away with making quality and service claims not backed up by reality, "weasel wording" cleverly formulated to overpromise without breaking the law while forgetting about the customer after the sale was made. You can't get away with

that any more and hope to grow a brand. But not every advertiser has faced up to this new fact of life.

- Failure to care *enough* about the quality of the product. U.S. auto makers learned this the hard way, and have spent two decades fighting their way back.
- Failure to understand the new consumer, who is demanding to be involved, to belong, to be heard.
- Failure to understand that today a consumer product is four-dimensional, and the fourth dimension is what you do to care for the customer after the sale.
- Failure to understand that an in-house prospect/customer database is not a passing fad, it is the engine that will drive sales in the new information economy. But only if it is designed and used for true, customized, involvement marketing.
- Failure to rethink the marketing department table of organization to meet the new challenge. Too many companies today have advertising managers, sales promotion managers, direct marketing managers, and so on, each focused on a narrowly based function and all fighting to increase their share of the marketing budget pie. What is needed is a customer-focused marketing team that starts with a single manager in charge of reaching out to and aquiring new customers (whatever it takes to make that happen) and another manager with primary responsibility for customer care, maximized usage, and retaining loyalty (whatever it takes to make that happen).
- Failure to make advertising expenditures more accountable, by demanding measurement of actual responses and sales rather than relying on surveys of mere "recall scores" and "cost per retained impression."
- Failure to do away with an outmoded budgeting process which tries to cobble together an "integrated marketing" program out of what's left over after the traditional media advertising allocation has already been made.

This may seem like a gloomy indictment. Happily, it is not true of all marketers. As Joe Cappo pointed out, there are "a few exceptions" to the widespread failure to embrace true integrated, modern-day marketing.

This book is about the exceptions.

Here in the United States, and in every country in the world where advertising and marketing play an important role in the economy, remarkable breakthroughs are being achieved by companies taking full advantage of the new opportunities and the new imperatives. For them the 1990s is not just the decade of the rude awakening. It is the decade leading to a successful entry into the twenty-first century.

It is not too late for you and your company to learn from their successes.

It is not too late to be inspired by their real-world examples of the new power of "Caring and Daring," and to break free as they have done from the shackles of yesterday's outmoded practices.

It is not too late to stop wasting money on nonprospects and to start identifying and cultivating your best prospects and customers.

In examining the performance of the MaxiMarketing winners profiled in this book, we became aware of striking similarities underlying the business thinking behind the dramatic breakthroughs. We will identify and describe these keys to business success in the next chapter. You will then be able to recognize and learn from these models of excellence in the case histories that follow.

2
Seven Keys to Business Success Today

A travel guidebook tells you in advance how to get the most out of your journey. This chapter is your guide to our presentation of the MaxiMarketing winners in the following chapters. You will see how their innovations fit into a larger scheme of things and how their remarkable breakthroughs illustrate seven keys to success you may be able to use in meeting your own marketing challenges.

The companies you will visit in the following chapters anticipated the changed environment of the 1990s. In almost every case, they achieved startling results by going beyond the timid first steps other companies were taking in adjusting to the marketing revolution transforming business throughout the world.

These pacesetters were not content just to do what was rapidly becoming fashionable—such as adding a targeted direct-mail promotion to an "integrated marketing" budget or simply putting a toll-free phone number into their advertising. While there might be value in dressing up a traditional marketing program with such token "new thinking," at best these limited actions can only produce marginal improvement.

The MaxiMarketing winners you will read about in the following chapters are a breed apart. Just as the economies of the world were shifting to a new paradigm and so many marketers were falling behind, these companies moved to the head of the parade by marching to the sound of a different drummer.

Many of them went back to square one to rethink what business they were in—then moved beyond the standard advertising, promotion, and merchandising into new territory. In the process, they broke with conventional marketing practice and demonstrated the full potential of the nine MaxiMarketing steps we had first written about in the mid-eighties.

This time, we began by tracking down and analyzing outstanding performers around the world. We had no preconceived notions about why they were so successful, other than seeing how their operations appeared to illustrate many of the precepts in our earlier books.

Then, as the number of case studies grew, we were startled by the similarities that began to appear. Each company was a living example of how to apply some of the tactical steps of MaxiMarketing, but management in each of these model companies also went beyond MaxiMarketing in unanticipated ways that bore a surprising resemblance to events at other of the companies we examined.

Gradually we began to see the outlines of seven common denominators, seven keys to coming out on top in the decade of the rude awakening. These concepts reflected an overarching willingness to embark on daring new initiatives and a commitment to dealing with the consumer as an individual, rather than as a cipher, in the market as a whole.

By caring enough to *really put the customer first,* our chosen companies demonstrated how to gain ground on competitors who merely gave lip service to satisfying the customer. We knew that gaining an understanding of how our MaxiMarketing winners succeeded on such a grand scale, while competitors fumbled and stumbled, could provide valuable insights for management in today's difficult business environment.

Of course, not all of the observed companies were following all of the pathways to success we identified. Some of them did not have a need for a particular approach. But we did find each of the identified actions and attitudes being widely used.

So, before we spotlight the operations of the 24 front-runners in the following chapters, we will identify the commonalities of their extraordinary accomplishments. Then as we go inside each company, you will be able to spot these keys to success in action. In each instance, you can think about how what you discovered might have an impact on your own situation.

Here's your chance to learn from market leaders like Dell Computer, whose college dropout founder turned $1000 in personal savings into billions of dollars in annual sales...Nestlé's baby food company in France, where market share leaped from 20 to over 40 percent...Harley-Davidson, the American motorcycle manufacturer going from the edge of bankruptcy to not being able to keep up with the demand for its motorcycles today...MCI, the telecommunications maverick taking millions of long-distance customers away from AT&T and the other phone companies...The Amil Group, fastest-growing company in Brazil with a compound annual growth rate of 45 percent for the past ten years...Zellers, Canada's number one retailer with more than 60 percent of Canadian households signed up to participate in their Club Z frequent-shopper program...AMFB, financial services growing at triple the rate of their competitors in Malaysia...and other winners from North and South America, Europe, and the Asian Pacific region.

The spectacular success of any company is never the result of a single factor. There is far too much happening at any given moment in today's complex business environment—productivity gains, employee morale, refinancing of debt, new product developments, management reorganization—to assign full credit to any one business activity.

But, in every case you will read about in this book, you can be certain of one thing. Marketing innovation played a leading role in the company's remarkable achievements.

The seven keys to business success uncovered in our consulting assignments, interviews, and tracking of excellent performers can make a real difference in the future of managers who are open to considering bold moves of their own.

Key 1. Tell, Don't Sell: *The New Commandment of Information-Age Marketing*

A funny thing happened to consumers on the way to the 1990s. Deluged by a steadily rising tide of advertising for nearly a century, they found a way to fight back. *They stopped believing. Or even worse, they stopped paying attention.*

Of course, everyone didn't stop believing at once. Many consumers still are moved consciously or subconsciously to respond when exposed to advertising messages. Brand advertising still has the capability of moving mountains of goods and services—sometimes. But compared to the widespread unblinking acceptance of the past, more and more people began to turn off, skip past, or tune out mentally.

Says Peter Brabeck, the senior executive responsible for Nestlé communications worldwide, "There is no mass consumer any more, and people don't act just because someone tells them something."

When people shop for what they want today, they look and listen more intently than ever before, with the wariness and skepticism of veterans exposed to 100,000 advertising campaigns. "Over 60 percent of the people think there isn't any truth in advertising. That's an all-time low for advertising credibility," according to The Pre-Testing Company.

The antidote we found at many of the MaxiMarketing winners you will visit in the following chapters was the new commandment of Information-Age Marketing: "Tell, tell, tell, before you start to sell, sell, sell."

Nowhere are the dramatic benefits of this approach more apparent than in the field of personal investment and finance. And with good reason. Nowhere else can the customer lose so much if sold a bill of goods by a fast-talking high-pressure "expert," whether in print, on television, or in person.

There is a new generation of personal investors out there who are saying, "Don't give me your pitch, just give me the facts, and let *me* decide what to do with them."

The Fidelity Investments case history is a striking example of

Information-Age Marketing as practiced by the leader in the personal investment category. Fidelity started with $3.6 million in assets in 1943, grew to being 1000 times bigger by 1973, and is many times bigger than that today. They did it, in good measure, by responding to what the public was telling them about the information they wanted and the way they wanted it.

Unlike voracious old-time brokers, Fidelity almost never makes outbound sales calls. When the customer calls, a trained investment representative plays his or her computer keyboard like a Wurlitzer pipe organ to bring up on the screen a wealth of relevant factual information.

"We have five million customers," Fidelity told us. "We can't know them personally enough to give them great advice. *What we try to do is provide lots and lots of educational help so they can make their own decisions.*"

This emphasis on serving up the information a customer needs and wants is not entirely new in marketing. There have always been uncommon companies that put their customers' needs for fair, helpful, background information first. What is striking is the growing trend in that direction as advanced technology puts vital knowledge at the instant command of company representatives. Limitless amounts of information can be stored in a company's computers and be only a keystroke away from access by a friendly spokesperson responding to a prospect or customer.

In Canada, there is a $15 billion group of insurance and investment companies called North American Life that sells insurance the traditional way—use of image advertising to establish a brand name, and sales made by commissioned agents making phone calls and knocking on doors.

Recently, as you will read in the FNA Financial case history, North American launched a subsidiary dedicated to a totally different corporate strategy. In this major experiment, they wanted to see what would happen if "telling" was put before "selling" as the driving force in capturing business from a targeted segment.

Instead of giving prospects a sales pitch, the FNA Financial representative provides, free of charge, up to two hours of genuine, objective investment counseling by a trained, salaried financial advisor. The company representative accepts the customer's final decision without putting up a fight—even if that decision involves investing in a competitor's offering.

As FNA says to its prospective customers, "You are in control. We will give you the facts you need to make the best decisions and organize your finances the way you want." *What is really different is that they don't just say it, they mean it.* And you will be surprised to see just how well it's working!

The new subsidiary's salaried rookies, trained to provide objective information about insurance and investment options to targeted prospects, are outselling oldtime insurance agents who have five or ten times as much experience.

In the fast-moving consumer goods category, one of the reasons for Nestlé's big gains in the baby food category in France is a telephone information service staffed with licensed dieticians available ten hours a day, six days a week. The Nestlé mother's help line is strictly an information provider—its purpose is to tell mother what's best for baby, not to push the sale of baby food.

The Amil Health Plan people in Brazil go a step further. A plan member can call the Amil phone number 24 hours a day, and always find a medical doctor on duty. The doctor is ready to offer guidance on any health-related matter and, in an emergency, can provide what may turn out to be life-saving medical information. By demonstrating the company's caring philosophy in this special way, Amil adds a note of credibility to their advertising message: "We care about you."

Of course, the Information-Age Marketing key to success is not necessarily appropriate for solving every marketing problem. Denture wearers may not want to spend a great deal of time learning about denture adhesive. But, when it comes to providing the information consumers do want, most marketers remain guilty of putting "selling" ahead of "telling." They fail to understand the public's hunger for reliable assistance in an age of scepticism and the availability of an overwhelming number of choices.

Advanced information and communications technology has driven down the cost of telling the consumer everything he or she may want to know about almost anything you may want to sell. Low-key "telling" is going to increasingly replace high-pressure "selling" as the most effective way to get through to jaded consumers as we move further along in the shift from mass marketing to individualized marketing.

Key 2. Get Real: *The Art of Existential Marketing*

"A poem should not mean, but be," wrote the poet Archibald MacLeish.

The key to success for some companies is to change public perception of its brand not just by a different advertising message—but by establishing the product's *presence* in peoples' lives in exemplary ways. What you convey by what you *do* is more important than what you *say* in self-serving media messages.

A favorite advertising expression these days is "We Care." Yet, too often, the claim is not related to an alteration in how the product performs or the nature of the service provided, such as nurturing the morale of employees so they *want* to care. The end result is just another empty ad campaign promise.

What is needed are new ways of *doing* and *being* that break into public consciousness more effectively than advertising claims alone ever can. It is not a new idea. It is just one whose potential has been overlooked and whose time has come again.

Around the turn of the century, ad pioneer Claude Hopkins was hired as advertising manager of Swift & Company. One of his challenges was to move Cotosuet, a mixture of cottonseed oil and suet that was used instead of lard or butter in baking. Its chief competitor was Cottolene, the original product in the category. Cottolene had a big head start in sales which Cotosuet couldn't seem to overcome.

Hopkins went to the advertising manager of a retailer opening a new department store. They planned to have, on the fifth floor, a grocery department with a large bay window facing the street. Hopkins asked to have that window for a unique exhibit. "I will build there," he said, "the largest cake in the world. I will advertise the cake in a big way in the newspapers. I will make that the greatest feature in your opening."

On opening night, the crowds were so great that the police had to close the doors. Over the next week, 105,000 people climbed four flights of stairs to see the cake—there were so many people, the elevators could not carry them. Demonstrators offered samples of the cake. Prizes were awarded to those who guessed nearest to the correct weight of the cake, but they had to buy a pail of Cotosuet to enter.

Sales of Cotosuet zoomed. Then Hopkins repeated his triumph in many other cities. He led a traveling team of a baker, a decorator, and three demonstrators. They would go to the leading baker in each city and offer him the fame of building the cake if he would buy a carload or two of Cotosuet. Then, they would go to the leading grocer and offer to place the cake in his store if *he* would buy a carload of Cotosuet. Everywhere Hopkins and his team went, the event was wildly successful.

What was he doing? Was it advertising? Promotion? Public relations? Event marketing? We say it was all of this and more—it was Existential Marketing. Cotosuet broke through to public consciousness, not by what they claimed but what they did and how they did it. What followed was a new perception of the kind of company and product they were in the consumer's eyes.

In the decades that followed, this existential approach was little used because it seemed unnecessary. With the emergence of mass media, advertising was a much easier way to build a brand's recognition in the marketplace. Each new ad medium that developed was so exciting that people even seemed to enjoy and welcome the clever advertising. It was not so long ago that people actually went around humming and singing advertising jingles like, "Pepsi Cola hits the spot," or "Winston tastes good like a cigarette should."

But in this decade of the rude awakening—when suddenly there are alarm bells about the declining effect of brand-image advertising on a surfeited public—we are seeing a return by some of the smartest companies to "being and doing" as a key to marketing success.

One such marketer we discovered was Puget Sound Bank of Seattle. They set out to gain market share by doing something real and relevant rather than adding one more banking ad campaign to the bombardment in local media. Puget Sound Bank embarked on a bold partnership with local environmental groups to clean up the water and beaches of Puget Sound. Not just by sanctimonious preaching about the environment in their ads. But by a genuine shoulder-to-shoulder involvement with the community to make it happen.

They did it by making each transaction trigger a contribution to designated environmental groups.

They did it by encouraging bank employees and their families to turn out for Beach Clean-Up Day and inviting bank customers to join in.

They did it by putting collection tubs in the bank branches for discarded motor oil.

Puget Sound Bank demonstrated in a variety of ways that they genuinely cared about the quality of life their customers enjoy. "Getting real" about what was happening in their immediate environment did wonders for both Puget Sound Bank's share of mind and their share of market.

On a global scale, Nestlé Group management at their headquarters in Vevey, Switzerland, is seeking to radically redefine what packaged goods marketing is all about. They recognize that the power of traditional brand advertising is waning. But they have refused to join the stampede toward discounting of advertised brands as the only way to compete with economy-priced store brands.

Instead, they have decided to make their key to success a program for building credibility around what they do and who they are. Nestlé's Peter Brabeck says bluntly, "You can triple advertising spending, but if you can't establish a credible communication link with consumers, they won't act."

This big multinational marketer has invested $400 million in its new positioning for the Buitoni pasta brand. The first step in implementing the existential approach was the purchase of the Buitoni family villa in Italy. Nestlé has added product development and testing kitchens underground, so as not to disturb the charm of Casa Buitoni in its lovely Tuscany setting.

Another example we found of the power of creating a presence in people's lives beyond the purchase of the product is provided in The LEGO Company success story. LEGO Systems, Inc., is the maker of the famous plastic building bricks that dominate the construction toy category in America and Europe.

What is the essence of the fascination with the LEGO building system? Children of all ages can combine LEGO bricks and special pieces in an almost infinite number of ways to make almost anything the mind can conceive. (Just six eight-stud bricks can be joined in 103 million different configurations!)

So what better way could The LEGO Company find to demonstrate and dramatize that "LEGO Builds Imagination" than by building their own theme park in Denmark, with 42 million bricks joined to form animals, ships, trains, the Parthenon, the space shuttle Columbia, and an entire miniature village? Now they are planning to carry this same real-life experience to new theme parks in the United Kingdom and the United States.

Theme parks are only one part of the real presence of LEGO in the lives of children. There is also the invitation to join The LEGO Builder's Club packed into every set or the building competitions for each age level at all the places LEGO imagination can be seen in action and much more.

The largest shopping mall in the United States is one such place. The LEGO Imagination Center at the Mall of America located in Bloomington, Minnesota, works just like advertising. It says to people in concrete terms: Here is what you can do. It breaks through the clutter out there in the marketplace to 40 million visitors a year.

In the following chapters, you will see MaxiMarketing winners breaking through the public disbelief barrier by demonstrating that they are real, caring people worth knowing better. Whether it is Guinness lending a helping hand to tavern owners in Germany, the Amil Rescue Plan helicopter swooping out of the sky over Rio de Janeiro, or Shiseido in Japan showing women how to reach their appearance and beauty goals, "getting real" is replacing smoke and mirrors as the preferred means of communication in the 1990s.

Key 3. Stop Wasting Money on Nonprospects: *Database Marketing Comes of Age*

For nearly a decade, beginning in the mid-1980s, "database marketing" almost fit Mark Twain's famous comment about the weather: "Everyone talks about it, but no one ever does anything about it."

Some companies collected millions of names simply because it was the latest thing to do, and then treated the names as little more than a mailing list because they didn't know the first thing about customized marketing.

Huge external databases were available and true prospects were buried somewhere within them. But to analyze and manipulate the data required a substantial investment and confidence in the payoff, a confidence that few managers had in the 1980s.

Of course, there were some exceptional companies in the vanguard of the transition to database-driven marketing. But to most executives, focusing on a *segment of one* looked more like a far-fetched twenty-first-century fantasy than anything to take seriously in the here and now.

What changed all this and put the acceptance of direct marketing on a fast track was the slowdown of the world economy and the resulting pressure on profit margins in the early 1990s. Suddenly, the concept of stopping the waste in traditional mass marketing by turning to precisely targeted database-driven programs was an idea whose time had come. Individualized marketing is no longer just a promising futuristic possibility. Database Marketing has arrived.

Lorraine Scarpa, vice-president of marketing services for Kraft General Foods (KGF), in her address at the spring 1991 Direct Marketing Association Conference summed up the new attitude of big name advertisers when she declared: "Direct marketing works. It pays out. It makes money." And she continued, "Businesses that don't recognize its potential and its worth risk serious competitive disadvantage from those who have learned to incorporate direct marketing fully and creatively into their marketing mix."

At the time of the conference, KGF already had launched direct marketing programs for 20 different brands. Within 18 months, the number soared to more than 50 brand activities.

A turning point in the growing acceptance of database marketing was marked by a story in *The Wall Street Journal.* It pointed out that until very recently, customer databases used for billings, deposit records, and installment payment plans were stored in mainframe computers and were the jealously guarded kingdoms of the programmers who maintained them. Marketing managers who wanted to get into the database and search for particular types of customers had to stand in line and wait their turn.

But huge improvements in personal computers and data storage devices have now brought database manipulation to the marketing and product manager's desktop. High-end PCs with 2-gigabyte hard drives, capable of holding several million customer names, can now be obtained for around $10,000. And software to manage the data starts as low as $15,000. Data processing costs will surely continue to drop.

The *Journal* story told of the director of market research for a Tennessee department store chain who used her personal computer to identify 1400 customers who bought quality-brand dresses such as those by Anne Klein and Liz Claiborne only when they went on sale.

She found that when these customers didn't respond to the sale and waited for the second markdown, it cost the store $75 per person. So before the clothes reached that point, she spent $850 for a mailing to notify these customers in her database that their favorite designer labels were on sale. The two-day event increased volume on the dresses by 97 percent.

She was using The New Math of late-twentieth-century individualized marketing rather than the "cost per impression" math of mid-twentieth-century mass marketing. By that, we mean precise measurement of the cost of contacting an individual prospect or customer, a precise calculation of the affordability of that contact, and a precise measurement of the resulting present and future sales to that particular customer. She knew to the penny what the advertising produced.

In *MaxiMarketing,* one of the nine steps in the MaxiMarketing audit was "Maximized Accountability: Proving That It Works." But at the time we wrote that book, in 1985, Database Marketing was still in a primitive stage of development.

Retailers were notorious for their inability to relate advertising to sales to specific individuals: "We ran this big sale ad on Friday, and people bought those sale items on Saturday!"

Now retailers and brand advertisers alike can put an end to wasting money in buying nonprospect impressions rather than advertising to the most likely prospects. With an understanding of The New Math, you can spend less to sell more. In the following case histories, you will learn how this targeting is being done by our MaxiMarketing winners, including innovative retailers, brand advertisers, and service companies.

One of these retailers is NBO (acronym for "National Brands Outlet"), a $100 million discount menswear chain of 36 stores in the northeastern United States. You will read about how they became one of the first retailers to capture universal credit card information and turn it into a customer database of their own.

By becoming a database-driven retail marketer, NBO is able to apply the golden yardstick used by mail-order merchants ever since the 1970s—the measurement standard known as RFM. They can determine the value and importance of a customer in their 750,000-name database by the *Recency* of his or her last purchase, the *Frequency* of purchases, and the total *Monetary Value* of all the purchases over a given period of time. This makes it possible to identify and differentiate between the best and the worst customers in the database. Using strategies sharpened with The New Math, NBO keeps getting better at identifying, acquiring, and cultivating those customers who will return the highest profit margins.

The customer database is constantly being redefined and enhanced. By matching the NBO store data against the demographic information available from Donnelley Marketing's public database, they are able to determine the typical customer's likely age, income range, education level, length of residence, probability of having a child under 18 living at home, and more. Then with the application of predictive modeling, they can do mailings in partnership with American Express that go not only to Amex cardholders who have patronized NBO but also to other Amex cardholders, living in the NBO stores' trading areas, with profiles that match those of the NBO customers. Results have been extremely profitable.

FNA Financial in Toronto uses external databases to locate and contact their best prospects by mail and phone. They make excellent use of "cluster analysis" to determine which neighborhoods, which streets, and which blocks on those streets have the highest concentration of households matching their ideal prospect profile.

The same type of waste elimination selectivity is carried out for their newspaper advertising insert campaign. Each week, 5000 FNA advertising inserts are included only in copies of the local newspaper going to specific blocks selected for their high density of prospects—to be followed up within a week by 5000 phone calls to those targeted prospects seeking an appointment with the FNA Financial Advisor.

One of the most impressive examples of "less is more" Database Marketing that you will read about is the House of Seagram story.

Under the guidance of Richard Shaw, vice-president marketing communications, Seagram Distillers has been able to send delightful, image-building direct-mail offers to consumers known to be drinking competing brands.

With repeated testing and database refinement, Shaw's team is now able to calculate exactly how many months it will take to recoup the investment and start earning a profit from each conquest mailing.

In another move to make Seagram advertising more efficient and effective, Shaw made media history by going to the most suitable magazines for his brands and persuading them to put the Seagram ad only in subscriber copies going to readers who fit the ideal prospect profile. In a single stroke, the advertiser came close to tripling the cost-effectiveness of the advertising budget.

Real individualized marketing is here at last. You can choose to do it all on your own desktop computer, and play "What if?" games until the wee hours of the morning, or you can mine the prospect/customer data stored in the vastness of public and corporate mainframe databases.

Stop wasting misdirected marketing dollars. Think database. Or, better still, think "datamotion"—using the information in your database to single out the best prospects and customers for a variety of profitable interactions.

Key 4. Offer Gain without Pain: *Drive Competitors Crazy with Extra-Value Marketing*

Consumers want it all.

Under pressure from a slowed-down economy, consumer confidence is under siege today. The reaction almost everywhere in the world has been an unprecedented demand for value at the cash register. Hunting down a bargain and getting the best buy has become a sharpshooter's medal to be worn proudly.

Being cost-conscious is no longer a source of embarrassment, even among the relatively affluent. But at the same time, people are reluctant to give up the quality and service to which they became accustomed in better times.

In our previous book, *The Great Marketing Turnaround,* we noted the growing tendency of the smartest marketers to move beyond the Unique Selling Proposition (USP) of Rosser Reeves into gaining market share with an Extra-Value Proposition (EVP). The worldwide recession that followed publication of the book made Extra-Value Marketing a key to success for many of the businesses on our stellar performers list.

With marketers outdoing one another in pushing a cut-price Value Strategy, the way to drive the competition crazy is to develop an Extra-Value Strategy of your own that shifts the focus to a totally different playing field.

But there is no free lunch. How do you keep prices at a rock-bottom low, operate on a paper-thin margin, and still offer extra services, amenities, or rewards?

The answer is that you don't have to be the lowest-priced competitor to win in today's value-driven marketplace. Happily, most consumers seem to be willing to pay a *little* more in order to get a *lot* more.

So the best and the brightest of today's marketers are following this strategy: keep prices low but not necessarily the lowest, and find ways to offer value extras that the lowest-price competitors can't match.

In other words, it's time to defy the famous dictum of the fitness fanatics: *"No Pain, No Gain."* Offer your customers: *Gain Without Pain*—value pricing without demanding undue sacrifice. And then sweeten the deal with unexpected extras.

One of our profiled winners, Ryder Truck Rental, is a prime example. Marketing Director C. Mack says they don't try to compete on price alone. "Instead, our plan has been to create a position that's sufficiently attractive to justify a higher—though still reasonable—price. We do this by adding value—through convenience, reputation, promotions, and last but not least, image." You will hear the whole fascinating story of how Ryder used this formula to turn double-digit losses into double-digit profits.

NBO, the discount menswear chain, has worked to upgrade the plain pipe racks atmosphere of the typical off-price store without giving up plain pipe-racks prices. Says CEO Gene Kosack, "Before, our salespeople were basically traffic cops directing shoppers to the 40 regulars. We must provide our customers with more, whether that involves greeting them by name or spending an hour with them."

Private dressing rooms were installed in the upgraded stores, a rare amenity in off-price retailing. When it comes to alterations, NBO outdoes full-price department stores by having an on-site master tailor fit the garment to the customer and then make the alterations himself. Jim Frain, the marketing vice-president, told us: *"We are not going to make the customer suffer in order to save money."*

This is strikingly similar to what we heard at Dell Computer. Said Marketing Vice-President Tom Martin, "All the rest of the industry was focusing on performance at a given price. We offered low price without the pain you might expect when you pay a low price."

In Canada, the best-remembered advertising slogan in the country is that of Zellers, a leading discount chain of 266 stores: "The Lowest Price Is the Law." Yet despite their steady growth with that hard-hitting USP, they somehow manage to provide an EVP as well. One of the keys to their success is the extraordinary way they handle their Club Z frequent-buyer rewards program and make it a cornerstone of their advertising.

Each purchase at Zellers earns points toward free upscale merchandise in the full-color Club catalog—top-of-the-line items that provide a taste of luxury their customers might otherwise consider an unaffordable indulgence.

Unlike most frequent-shopper reward programs, usually treated as ancillary to the company's sales promotion efforts, Zellers Club Z gets top billing in TV advertising, point-of-sale signage, and the company's Annual Report. "Gain without Pain" is a way of life at Zellers.

The Extra-Value Proposition is not only a North American phenomenon. In Germany, Lexus luxury car owners are pampered with a dazzling succession of surprise gifts to retain their loyalty after they lay out $50,000 or so for the car of their choice. And, in Japan, Shiseido uses a "Gain Without Pain" marketing approach to sell more cosmetics than their number two and three competitors combined.

All these marketers are scattered along the price spectrum, from selling at the lowest prices in their category to near the highest. But they share the same key to success: *Offer Gain Without Pain.* They have made an important discovery, with an application for all marketers struggling to survive in today's cutthroat pricing climate.

Key 5. Bringing People Together: *Break Through the Clutter with Involvement Marketing*

It is a basic principle of psychology that experience reinforces learning. You could lecture students on the fine art of boxing for hours, but not until they had put the gloves on and tried a dodge and a feint for themselves would they really take in and understand what you had been saying.

So, in addition to Existential Marketing, another way to break through the clutter and boredom of advertising today is through Involvement Marketing—getting your prospects and customers to actually get together with you and each other and *do* something. Often this involves finding an appropriate interest you can share with prospects and customers. A marketing strategy that takes steps in this direction can make a deeper impression than advertising claims that skitter across the surface of the mind.

Despite some overlap between the two, there is an important difference between Existential Marketing, discussed earlier as Key 2, and the Involvement Marketing we want to look at now. Existential Marketing is what *you* as the marketer do to have your product or service experienced in the marketplace as a genuine, credible, favorable presence, not just an abstract advertising claim. Involvement Marketing is *what you get your prospects and customers to do*—an activity you get them involved in other than merely buying what you are selling.

When Claude Hopkins exhibited "The Largest Cake in the World," baked with Cotosuet, that was Existential Marketing. When he brought people together to taste a piece of the cake, and to compete for prizes by trying to guess the weight, that was Involvement Marketing.

In the same way, when The LEGO Company builds a theme park out of 42 million tiny plastic bricks, that is Existential Marketing. But when they invite kids visiting the park or the LEGO Imagination Center at the Mall of America to sit down and make something themselves out of LEGO bricks, that is Involvement Marketing.

When Puget Sound Bank employees and their families turned out for their own annual Beach Clean-Up Day, that was powerful Existential Marketing. It's one thing for a bank or any other kind of company to *claim* they care about the environment; it's quite another for the public to see with their own eyes the employees of the company actually doing something about it. But when the bank employees invited friends, customers, and environmentalists to join them on the beach and work shoulder to shoulder with them, that was Involvement Marketing.

FNA Financial gets their own financial advisors, their customers, and their prospects all involved with each other by buying tables at local women's fund-raising events and distributing the tickets both to their own executives and representatives and to their customers. A great deal of networking takes place among business and professional women attending these events, with business cards traded across the table. By making introductions for women who can help each other, FNA positions its executives and representatives as involved, caring, trustworthy colleagues rather than pushy salespeople.

From MCI forming Calling Circles made up of friends and family members to Toyota of Germany inviting Lexus owners to go on a ballooning trip or a gourmet weekend together, these MaxiMarketing winners have stumbled on the power of bringing people together with the advertiser and with each other as a key to business success.

Surely the ultimate in involvement, leading to an extraordinary feeling of community, are the local chapters of the motorcycle-owner club encouraged by Harley-Davidson and the regional and national rallies to which owners are invited.

When you can get tens of thousands of product owners paying you to attend a big party with beer, bands, and fun at your headquarters, as Harley-Davidson did in celebration of its 90th anniversary in 1993—and when your company personnel, from the top boss on down, come riding up on their own Harley Hogs to mix and mingle with the crowd—then you know you don't have to worry about Japanese motorcycle makers stealing your customers away from you. You have formed a real community of interest with your customers, one that image advertising in the media can reinforce, as Harley advertising does, but cannot create all by itself.

This is the magic of Involvement Marketing. And it is a key to marketing success destined to play an increasingly important role in the remaining years of this decade. As the clamor and clutter of thousands of advertising claims all around us become more intense, consumer resistance will continue to harden, making it ever more difficult to get anyone to pay attention to what your advertising is saying. Direct interaction centered on real customer interests is the best way to build strong, positive feelings.

But if you can encourage members of your target market to "reach out and touch someone," by phone or in person—that "someone" being you, the advertiser, or your other customers—you can break through the barrier in people's minds and form the most powerful kind of favorable impression of your product or service or store.

"Doing for" and "doing with" are two keys to success you'll be seeing more of in the 1990s.

Key 6. Care Enough to Put the Customer First: *Dramatic Demonstrations of TRC Marketing*

It is so easy for an advertising copywriter to dream up a great new campaign theme for a client that claims: "We listen. We care."

But to *really* listen to what your prospects and customers are asking for, and to *really* make the fundamental changes necessary to satisfy those needs, can mean shaking your company to its roots—or maybe even starting a new company.

A key to success frequently found at work in the companies spotlighted in this book is a corporate attitude we call Total Relationship Commitment, or TRC for short.

In a conversation at the Nestlé Baby Food headquarters outside Paris, Marketing Director Fabienne Petit summed it up this way: "I cannot speak with passion about my advertising but I am passionate about my links with the consumer—we are totally committed to our relationship with the parents."

"Passion" is a word you are not likely to hear very often at the Harvard Business School. But it is a word we heard used repeatedly by marketing directors and CEOs—people like Michael Dell of Dell Computer, Edson de Godoy Bueno of Amil, and Mike Keefe of Harley-Davidson—as they expressed their determination to do whatever possible, and at times the seemingly impossible, in the interest of the customers they served.

A striking example of TRC Marketing is seen in the Ryder Truck Rental story. Ryder began its turnaround by finding out what the consumer really wanted to take the hassle out of moving and then making substantial investments to deliver it.

Their marketing director told us, "We wanted our platform to be based on consumer needs, not hatched in a corporate office. The idea was that the consumer would lead us in our decision making, and sales would follow." Ryder's commitment to the rental customer goes far beyond the usual mail survey and standard number of focus groups.

Ryder went through an exhaustive and costly market research process they call "laddering." This involved climbing up the research ladder from a host of benefits on the bottom rung that consumer feedback said were important...to a handful of benefits they said were most important...then narrowing the list down to the one benefit people said was most important of all...and finally developing and researching the appeal of specific product and service features designed to deliver that benefit in the best way.

Once they knew how to go about "loving the customer," they attracted thousands of new customers who loved what Ryder was doing for them.

HSM Cultura in São Paulo, Brazil, is a TRC marketer. When the partners who run the company learned that left-handed people attending their seminars had difficulty writing notes on work sheets designed for the right-handed majority, they promptly made a change. Special handouts with observations placed on the page to accommodate ease of use by left-handed people were produced and distributed. "We endeavor to absolutely delight our clients and constantly find new ways of doing so," Harry Ufer, a partner, told us with justifiable pride.

The shining success of HSM Cultura in responding to customer needs in Brazil brings to mind the miserable failure of American automotive companies in Japan. Ford and General Motors still try to sell cars with the steering wheel on the left in a country where the standard is the British-style steering wheel on the right. It is hard to imagine a better example of not putting the customer's interest ahead of the seller's convenience. The result is an infinitesimal market share for the Americans compared to importers from other countries offering cars with the steering on the correct side for Japan.

Dell Computer went from a $1000 investment to billions in sales in record time, with a Total Relationship Commitment at the core of the company's business philosophy. Dell was the first in its field to become obsessive about taking care of customer needs in real time. If the rep on the phone can't solve the problem right away, he or she can access the Problem Resolution Database stored in the computer, where there's a good chance a similar problem and its solution have been entered previously.

If the complaint is one of several complaints about the same problem, a Dell marketing manager can walk about 130 feet across the floor to the people who designed the product. "Within five or six hours, engineering has fixed the design, and within two or three days the factory's got that change incorporated on the line." At a true TRC company, the consumer is the product designer's "personal assistant."

In talking with Peter Brabeck of Nestlé about the daring relaunch of the Buitoni brand we learned, "from the very first conception of how to present the product, Nestlé took into account the consumer's wishes and interests." Consumers wanted more than just another serving of pasta. Nestlé obliged with an opportunity to get acquainted with the authentic "Casa Buitoni" in the hills of Tuscany and an Italian lifestyle club for enhanced enjoyment of the wines, foods, and culture of Italy.

The Buitoni global strategy, as you will read later, is based on a profound belief in a radical new idea: a total commitment to the relationship with the consumer and a willingness to reexamine every aspect of the marketing mix in support of that commitment.

Listening. Responding. Passionately caring. You will see the TRC key to success at work in many of our MaxiMarketing winners' stories.

Key 7. Dare to Start Over: *Clear the Slate with "Square One" Marketing*

It is startling to note in how many of these cases a daring, successful new marketing strategy was born of necessity and represented a sharp break with the past. It is what we call "Square One" Marketing: pushing aside all of the old habits and sacred truths your company has lived by for years, and taking a fresh look at what changed circumstances require.

Too often when a product manager or an outside consultant comes up with a brilliant plan for getting closer to the customer or investing in a powerful marketing database to push an information-driven strategy, initial enthusiasm runs into the usual set of idea killers.

> "We don't have the money—it's all been allocated to the new advertising campaign or to generous trade allowances or to a blockbuster promotion needed to make this quarter's numbers in the business plan."
>
> "They (senior management) will never buy it."
>
> "We tried it before and it didn't work."
>
> "We don't have the people to get it done."
>
> "It's just a fad. It will fade away."

So the new move is either killed outright or starved to death.

There are a hundred ways to kill a challenging new idea that might have gotten the company moving in the right direction. Instead of focusing on what works about the innovative approach and then fixing the troublesome parts, management takes the easy way out. They analyze and critique the big idea and then stay with the tried-and-true. Trouble is, in the post–cold-war Information Society, what used to be tried-and-true may soon be down-and-out.

It's the reason why "Square One" Marketing is a key to success for so many of our MaxiMarketing winners.

In many of these cases, you will see that the company reached a crisis stage in which they were forced to reexamine basic premises of the industry in which they operated or to reexamine the assumptions on which their past achievements were based.

Unlike IBM, Sears, General Motors, and so many others in the 1980s, the companies we are writing about had the courage to go back to Square One and learn how to do it right.

After three consecutive years of decline in consumer truck

rental, Ryder established a separate division and made the basic shift from being product-oriented to being customer-driven. They put telling ahead of selling. They relied on real benefits you can touch and see rather than hyped-up advertising. They offered rental customers gain without pain. They cared enough to put the customer's interest ahead of immediate profit. They dared to go back to Square One and start over.

NBO's profits fell off in the recession, as department stores began slashing their prices on menswear to the discounters' level. Gene Kosack, CEO, realized that "the rules of the game have changed," and he had the steel nerves to order a radical restructuring of the company designed to meet the department store competition head-on. In retrospect what he did can be seen as a sound management decision. At the time, it was a risky leap of faith into uncharted waters.

When North American Life in Canada could no longer avoid facing the fact that many of their insurance sales representatives were costing more than they were bringing in, management acted boldly. Instead of merely tinkering with an outmoded selling system, they went back to Square One and built a brand-new subsidiary with a different strategy from the ground up.

When Harley-Davidson was close to bankruptcy in 1983, with their share of the market for superheavyweight motorcycles down from over 40 to 23 percent, a team of executives led a leveraged buyout to save the company. Then they embarked on a bold course of reinventing the company's engineering, production, and marketing. They transformed Harley-Davidson from a troubled loser into a soaring winner. Today, the company's production is sold out for months to come.

What saved all these companies was the willingness to break with the past and start over. Your company doesn't have to be facing disaster to profit from the examples provided by these MaxiMarketing winners. You can take your cue from a Latin saying chiseled over the doorway of a high school in the midwestern United States: "*Qui Non Proficit Deficit.*" Loosely translated: If you're not pushing ahead, you're falling behind.

If you happen to be the market leader, your continued leadership and your very survival may depend upon how daring you are in carrying out bold new customer care initiatives.

If your company is lagging behind, the case histories that follow may inspire the courage to think anew and take a leap of faith that can lead your company into a new cycle of growth.

Now it is time to move along to the stories of the 24 MaxiMarketing winners chosen to illustrate these keys to business success today—not only in North America but in all the developed and developing countries around the world. You will see for yourself how these innovators achieved outstanding results at a time when many businesses were stalled or slipping backward. And you will see many examples of the new power of "Caring and Daring" as the driving force in corporate success in the 1990s.

As you read these fascinating stories, ask yourself, "In what way might I adapt what is happening here to my own situation?" If you get a beginning idea, pause a moment to jot it down. It could be the seed of a dramatic breakthrough for you and your associates in the remaining years of this decade.

What we have given you in this chapter is only a guide for the journey, not the actual tour. We hope it has stirred your desire for a first-hand look at what the MaxiMarketing winners have accomplished and how they went about it. Taken together these product, service, and retail marketers selling to the consumer and to other businesses represent a spectrum of some of the best business thinking on five continents.

You will be meeting some wonderful people and we hope you will be stimulated by their success to make your own mark as one of the MaxiMarketing winners in the years ahead.

PART 2

MaxiMarketing Winners Selling Products

3
Michael Dell Sets the Pace for PCs

"The battle for supremacy [in personal computers] is over, and few will survive," proclaimed a cover story in *Business Week* in 1983. "The winner is...IBM." Computer guru Esther Dyson was quoted as advising entrepreneurs with small computer companies "to go into the restaurant business." But a young Texan named Michael Dell, a college student at the University of Texas in Austin, didn't know enough to be frightened off. Using $1000 in personal savings, he started selling computers out of his college dorm room at the age of 18.

Just 10 years later, editor Dennis Hatch was writing in *Target Marketing:*

> Any direct marketer who has traveled to the Maasi Mara in Kenya or the Serengeti in Tanzania and witnessed the bloody encounter of a fine old antelope being taken down by a pack of wild dogs can only think of IBM.
>
> ...IBM lost $4.97 billion for the year, the biggest loss in American corporate history. Job eliminations, which totalled 40,000 in 1992, are expected to reach 100,000 over three years ending December 31, 1993.

...Who are the wild dogs bringing down the poor old arthritic misshapen IBM? Dell Computer, for one...Dell has learned to talk to its customers, while IBM is talking to itself.

By setting an entirely new standard for selling PCs, the upstart Dell, more than any other company, forced their giant rivals Compaq and IBM to change the way they did business. It is one of the most astounding stories ever to unfold in America, still the land of opportunity. In fewer than 10 years, Michael Dell had run his business from a little college-dorm operation and $1000 in operating capital up to $2 billion in annual sales and was well along the path to hitting the $3 billion mark within a year after hitting $2 billion. Along the way, he not only changed the rules for how PCs are bought and sold but also showed how business is done and won in the decade of the rude awakening. Whatever may befall Dell Computer in the perilous next stage of cutthroat competition, nothing can detract from the remarkable record of those first years in business.

Behind Dell's scenario of little David versus mighty Goliath are lessons for all marketers—lessons about talking to, listening to, and caring for your prospects and customers, and about the daring leaps of faith necessary to reach a pinnacle of customer involvement that produced a decade of record-breaking growth and profits. Reading about how Dell did it, not as seen from the limited perspective of the stock analysts but rather with a view to illustrating the new power of "Caring and Daring," could be worth a semester or two at business school.

Even Then He Knew

When Michael Dell was growing up in Houston, he used to look at the impressive modern buildings going up along the Interstate 610 loop, and dream of the day he would have a business of his own in one of them.

He was wrong.

The dazzling building he ended up in is in Austin, not Houston. And he's not just a tenant. His company leases the entire building as its world headquarters.

Dell was a successful entrepreneur by the age of 12. He developed a mail-order auction catalog for stamp collectors, and netted his first $2000.

He was also fascinated by computers. In junior high school, he belonged to a computer club. At the age of 15, he took apart and put back together his first computer. He hung around in computer stores a lot. He noted that on a sale of $4000, the dealer kept $1500 and he wondered what the dealer was adding to the transaction that was worth $1500. Dell also noted that he often knew more about computers than the salespeople did.

In 1983 he entered the University of Texas at Austin as a premed student majoring in biology, planning to follow his father into medicine. But his fascination with computers and his entrepreneurial drive bubbled to the surface in his freshman year. He started buying excess-inventory computer components at cost from local dealers and reselling them as assembled computers at a profit to friends and colleagues. Soon he started buying stripped-down IBM's on the gray market*, "souping them up" with graphics cards and hard disks, and reselling them.

The Early Days of PCs Limited

By early 1984†, Dell Computer was operating part-time out of his dormitory room as PCs Limited and selling $50,000 to $60,000 worth of customized computers and components a month. The business was so exciting and fulfilling that Dell was having a hard time focusing on his studies.

So he made a deal with his parents. He would work full-time at his computer business during the summer. If he wasn't doing

*"Authorized Dealers" for major vendors such as IBM, Compaq, and Apple Computer had to agree to buy a certain number of units each month. Often, when they could not sell them all, they would secretly sell off their excess inventory to unauthorized dealers on the "gray market." A number of mail-order discounters got their start by buying computers on the gray market in this way and reselling them.

†Coincidentally, about that time, another college student dropped out of school to start a mail-order discount computer operation in an Iowa farmhouse. He was Ted Waitt, founder of Gateway 2000, today the next-largest direct marketing operation after Dell.

well by the end of August, he would forget about it and go back to school.

The rest is history—and what a history!

That fall, instead of going back to school, he kept working in the one-room office in town he had rented for his little computer operation. At first, he focused on assembling complete systems for local doctors, lawyers, and small businesses, and for agencies and college departments. His "factory" consisted of some friends working around a six-foot picnic table. Sales were $180,000 the first month. Then sales hit $265,000. After nine months, they totaled $6 million.

Next came a crucial decision. His little company stopped buying and reselling IBM computers and started designing and assembling their own, using off-the-shelf components. Dell himself put in many 18-hour days.

Young Dell Goes Direct

He started running "mail-order" ads—an accepted misnomer, since orders were placed not by mail but by calling an 800 number—in national personal-computer magazines. It was a natural next step for Dell to take, given his introduction to understanding the mysteries of "mail-order" as a 12-year-old direct marketer to stamp collectors.

The orders flowed in. Customers could call and configure their own computer, selecting the speed, memory, drives, and other peripherals they wanted. And by buying direct from the manufacturer, they were getting more computer for their money.

But the problems and complaints started flowing in just as rapidly. What about when the computer didn't function properly and the problem could not be solved by phone advice? It's no fun packing up a computer and shipping it back for servicing. For a small business to be deprived of its computer for days or weeks could be a disaster.

Looking back today, Dell recalls that he had two options. Either he could hire and train a national service force, which could prove to be almost prohibitively expensive for his little company. Or he could make a deal with a company that already had service personnel in the field, and teach them to service Dell computers. He chose the latter course, and was able to make such a deal with Honeywell (replaced later by Xerox).

His customers were delighted. Now, if they had a problem with their new Dell computer, they could call an 800 number and talk directly with someone fully knowledgeable and sympathetic at the manufacturer's headquarters. (Says Dell, "93 percent of the time, we are able to solve the problem right over the phone in about six minutes.") But if that didn't work, a Dell-authorized repair specialist showed up within 24 hours to take care of it.

Playing by His Own Rules

Dell's service set a standard the competition could not even approach. It was as if Dell Computer was operating in a new world of its own making. If you bought a PC from IBM or Compaq at that time, and if anything went wrong, you were at the mercy of the dealer. You got no help from the company whose name was on the machine you bought. And as business picked up, dealer service got worse rather than better.

Some, though not all, of the elements that account for Dell Computer's phenomenal success were now in place. Lower prices. Reliable customization. Direct phone orders from ads in computer-buff magazines. Instant service by phone or in person. Caring involvement with the prospect and customer every step of the way.

A neophyte in tune with the high-tech world into which he was born had laid the groundwork for a new high-touch way of going one-on-one with the customer, while the competition remained bogged down in the old, out-of-touch distribution system of the 1960s and 1970s.

By 1988, Dell sales had rocketed to $265 million and the company went public, raising $31.1 million through sale of 3.5 million common shares. The company was ready to take off into the stratosphere. With the possible exception of Michael Dell himself, few could have imagined just how far Dell Computer Company might rise. Demonstrating the shortsightedness and backward thinking that characterized professional seers reporting on Dell's progress in those years, *PC Week* wrote that "some Wall Streeters are concerned about Dell's long-term viability, citing the company's heavy reliance on the mail-order channel to sell its machines."

From $265 Million to $2 Billion in Four Years

The entire step-by-step story of how Dell managed to confound the experts and fight its way from $265 million to $2 billion in annual sales in just four years is too complex to detail here. It is a story of moves and countermoves by roving warriors on the new industrial battleground of electronic data processing and communication. The weapons were: speed in harnessing the next higher level of computer power, getting a price advantage, and the ability to take care of the customer after the purchase was made. We will mention just enough about this free-for-all to provide a number of insights into Dell's dazzling success that you may be able to apply to your own situation and to show how he outsmarted the competition by daring to do what had never been done before.

Michael Dell may never have read *MaxiMarketing* but he has demonstrated repeatedly how creating a customer feedback loop and building rewarding customer relationships can provide a priceless advantage in the battle for market share. He has never concealed what he believes is a key to his startling success: "By talking on the phone with thousands of customers every day we gained a priceless advantage," Dell has said, in contrasting what he was doing to Compaq and IBM at the time.

The Heavy Hitters Block the Way

When the personal computer was born in the early 1980s, mighty IBM had a huge head start with the knowledge, capital, and reputation developed in marketing mainframe computers.

With the single exception of the Apple Macintosh, IBM imposed its disk operating system of choice—MS-DOS—on the field. At the time, nobody took Apple's point-and-click simplicity and pull-down menus seriously. What the business world wanted was formidable businesslike commands typed out with Industrial Age precision.

But in a strategic error to be regretted later, "Big Blue" left the door open for IBM-compatibles or clones to be built by other companies. These look-alikes immediately began to spring up like garden weeds after a spring shower. The most aggressive copycat competitor was Compaq.

Rod Canion, the entrepreneur who launched Compaq in 1982, began to run rings around IBM in technical innovation. His fledgling company quickly established itself in both sales and reputation as the premium personal computer at a premium price. By 1988, when Dell was still a fledgling with $265 million in annual sales, Compaq's sales volume had soared to $450 million in just the second quarter of that year.

Ahead of Dell in 1988 stood IBM and Compaq barring the road to growth in market share. There was also the threat of Japanese and Korean manufacturers who had proved their electronics production wizardry in virtually monopolizing the VCR and camcorder markets. And right behind Dell, nipping at its heels, were a cabal of mail-order marketers with even lower prices than Dell was able to engineer—IBM-compatible merchandisers such as Gateway 2000, Northgate, Zeos International, and CompuAdd.

But each of Dell's adversaries had an Achilles heel. Each of them, along with the Wall Street analysts predicting the coming downfall of Dell, failed to grasp the powerful secret of success Michael Dell openly shared with anyone willing to listen.

Both IBM and Compaq were wedded to a retail distribution system that passed the buck on servicing to the dealer. The result too often was customer annoyance or outright rebellion at the treatment received. With their mass-marketing mentality, Dell's biggest competitors wasted precious advertising dollars on clever, self-serving advertising instead of providing the product information the market craved.

The Japanese and Koreans entering the market were whizzes at gearing up for large production runs of a standardized mass-produced model at a hard-to-beat price. But individual requirements and desires in the corporate and institutional market for computers change almost daily, and the exporters didn't have the understanding of the American market or the flexibility to satisfy that need. While leading the way in customizing production in other fields, the Japanese were totally out-classed by Michael Dell when it came to customizing the purchase of a computer.

The makers of bargain-basement IBM compatibles were beating everybody on price, even Dell. But to maintain their rock-bottom prices, they either couldn't afford to be lavish when it came to research and development and customer hand-holding or simply undervalued the importance of the customer relationship.

The March of the Maverick Marketer

So it was that Dell developed—or *evolved* might be a better word—a long-range maverick marketing strategy incorporating many of the strategic steps to success we have seen in the operations of the best MaxiMarketers. Dell's company would invest heavily in R&D,* not to impose new technological marvels on their customers but rather to find improved ways to satisfy the customer needs they were identifying on the phone every day. By 1989, they were spending $20 million a year on R&D and providing "gain without pain" to anyone looking for the best deal on a personal computer. They would keep their prices low, but not necessarily the lowest, on the ground that their customers would be willing to pay a little more than the lowest price in order to gain the superior treatment offered by Dell.

*In a chess move of breathtaking audacity for an expanding but still comparatively tiny computer manufacturer, in 1988 Dell captured one of IBM's star scientists, G. Glenn Henry, and installed him as director of Dell's product research. Henry had been an IBM Fellow, the company's highest ranking for scientists. "All my friends laughed," Henry recalls, when he told them he was giving up 21 years with IBM to join the upstart company of a 23-year-old college dropout. But Henry says he had become frustrated with IBM's way of doing things, especially its reliance on dealers. "I looked around and found that Dell actually had the formula for success."

Although it might have seemed absurd for a company with a minuscule share of the market, they would fight for recognition as one of the Big Three quality name brands, along with IBM and Compaq.

In 1988, Dell hired Chiat Day Mojo, which was subsequently spun off into Goldberg Mosier & O'Neil in San Francisco, as its advertising agency. The advertising strategy pursued during Dell's years of phenomenal growth is a prime example of the synergistic double-duty approach advocated in *MaxiMarketing.*

A barrage of hard-hitting copy positioned Dell as one of the "big guns" rather than a bargain-basement mail-order company. The image-enhancing campaign hammered away at the personal attention PC buyers could expect from Dell. While building awareness and brand image, the ads also pulled out all the stops to get a response by phone or mail.

Drawing on the renowned creative talents of Chiat Day Mojo, Michael Dell was determined to shed the image of being just another direct marketing discounter and to get the corporate world to take his company seriously as one of the major brands. At a time when Compaq had 8 percent of the PC market and Dell had perhaps 1 or 2 percent, Dell began to taunt and challenge the nation's second-largest PC maker.

It was as if a promising young heavyweight boxer decided that the way to win recognition as a major contender was to talk tough to the leading challenger (Compaq) for the world heavyweight title (held by IBM).

When Dell introduced its own laptop computers, it ran ads directly and savagely comparing their new model ("The Lap of Luxury") with the highly touted Compaq portable ("The Lap of Lunacy"). Furious, Compaq sued for misrepresentation. In 1991, Dell Computer was forced to alter its ad claims and pay Compaq an undisclosed sum.

Nonetheless, Michael Dell probably considered the legal expense of the case and cost of the settlement a worthwhile investment in advertising and public relations. For it accomplished something better than could be gained from paid advertising: reams of news stories mentioning Compaq and Dell in the same breath.

Targeting the Right Person in the Right Place

Michael Dell decided to concentrate almost his entire advertising budget in the magazines read by computer buffs. Before long, he became the dominant advertiser in the core publications read by the influencers who lived and breathed computer know-how at small, medium, and very large companies.

Dell grabbed the highly visible back-cover positions and still holds many of these positions today. In a single issue of *PC World,* against a barely perceptible single-page presence by Compaq, Dell would run a back-cover gatefold and eight or ten additional pages. (The big ad bucks for IBM and Compaq went into *Time, Business Week, Fortune,* and other showcases where their stockholders could marvel at the cleverness of the advertising.)

By outspending the competition where it mattered most, Dell's much smaller ad budget gained top share of mind and an avalanche of hot prospects from the prime audience targeted by the buff magazines. To the growing audience of computer specialty magazines, the small-time Dell operation began to look much more important than those IBM and Compaq folks talking to the wrong people in the wrong place about their high-priced and underserviced products.

The Direct-Response Edge

Most of Dell's direct-response advertising included a bound-in card offering the newest Dell product catalog. To get the free catalog, a respondent had to provide a great deal of information about herself or himself. For example: Name, Address, Title, Company, Type of Business, Approximate Number of Employees, Home Phone, Business Phone, Fax Number.

There were lots of questions on the response card, too: Which products are you most interested in? How many PCs does your company plan to purchase in the next 12 months? What do you plan to use the computers for? Are you interested in leasing? And on and on. Dell was one of the first companies in the world to understand what is often the primary function of the "new advertising"—the ability to gather valuable information about prospects who want to begin a dialogue with the company.

Were people really ready to tell Dell that much about themselves? You bet they were!

The cards came pouring in, and the tens of thousands of others who called the 800 number to request a catalog or order a computer by phone were asked the same questions. Dell built a database of vital information about each customer's business situation, making it possible to respond to each prospect and customer on an individual basis. PC buyers loved every minute of the special attention they were getting. Nobody had ever been this interested in them before.

When we asked Michael Dell what he saw as the special advantage his database gives him, he told us: "Of course, we use it for direct mail. But what it mostly does for us is provide a familiarity with the customer—a comfort level that personalizes the relationship. Customers who call are not just dealing with Dell Computer Corporation, they are dealing with people they are used to dealing with and who know about them and what happened when they called before."

The Next Surprise: New Channels of Distribution

Just when the big retail brands thought they had Dell pegged as strictly a mail-order merchant, Dell confounded them once again by opening its own alternative distribution channels. Dell turned to value-added resellers (VARS) and to mass-market computer and office-supply superstores and warehouse clubs.

Value-added resellers are consultants and integrators, such companies as Arthur Andersen or EDS, who go into a business to evaluate a need or problem and recommend solutions. The VARS act as a broker/consultant recommending the hardware and software required, while Dell provides direct technical support. Usually the VARS would load the software themselves, but Dell does this for them and picks up an aftermarket customer.

The new mass-marketing retail outlets such as Sam's or Wal-Mart have no interest in providing service once a Dell computer sale is made. As a result, they mesh perfectly with Dell's desire to take over the customer relationship after the sale.

By maximizing distribution with added channels (the final step in the MaxiMarketing model) that are willing to give up aftermarket sales and service, Dell greatly magnified its ability to grab new customers at the entry level and turn them into long-term buyers of Dell products and computer services.

Compaq and IBM Surrender

By the fall of 1991, it was clear that Compaq Computer's high-quality, high-price strategy was floundering. In a stunning series of events, one of the sharpest reversals in American corporate history became front-page news. Following Compaq's first quarterly loss, the press reported dismissal by the board of Rod Canion, Compaq's chief executive and company cofounder. By the first quarter of 1992, Compaq's profits were slipping dangerously, its earnings collapsed 60 percent from a year before. How the mighty had fallen!

Forbes magazine called it "a reflection of Compaq's struggle to contend with mail-order discounters." Compaq had gone from peak performance at the end of 1990 to a loss position just two quarters later and the slide was continuing. Forbes quoted Michael Dell reminding the world how he had forced Compaq's reversal: "If you think that Dell's just the low-priced computer, you've missed the whole point. We've done well because we came up with a better way to serve the customer." In our later conversation with Michael Dell, he emphasized over and over again his total commitment to a caring relationship with the consumer.

Finally, in June of 1992, after their share price had lost 25 percent in two weeks' time, came the inevitable next step. Compaq Computer Corporation announced plans to revamp its product, pricing, marketing, and distribution strategies. But the big shocker was the word that the company would develop a low-priced range of personal computers targeted at Dell, AST, Northgate, and other low-end competitors that had been eroding Compaq's market share.

And that wasn't the end of it. Compaq was expanding its field support and service organization by more than 50 percent and was planning to get into mail-order distribution. The new Compaq management had wisely decided to follow the trail blazed by Michael Dell and to move away from a hands-off relationship with the end-user toward the new hands-on MaxiMarketing paradigm.

In short order, IBM followed with their own capitulation. An IBM spokesperson said they would match Dell and Compaq on price by marketing a new line of low-priced computers with direct service and would go into the "mail-order" business, too.

Somewhere in Texas, a young man could pause for a moment to take pride in how much he had changed the assumptions of a major industry in so short a time.

Fortune magazine, in a cover story titled "The New Computer Revolution," saw a broader implication that went far beyond the selling of PCs."The pioneering experiences of the computing industry provide striking insights into the challenges managers in every business eventually must face," the article pointed out. "The way to win is to reexamine every cherished assumption and redesign entire organizations around customer needs. Anyone who hopes to escape the woozy inertia that disabled so many erstwhile giants of computing can benefit from the lessons—as well as the products—this industry provides."

Dell's moment of triumph was short-lived. The industry, with IBM, Compaq, and Dell now in the 1-2-3 market position for MS-DOS PCs, moved into a brutal price war and battle for unit sales and profits with the outcome still in doubt.

The View from Inside Dell Computer

"If you go back three or four years," we were told by Tom Martin, marketing vice-president of Dell Computer, "there's no doubt that our USP was a high-quality computer at an incredible price *that didn't force you to make any sacrifices.* All the rest of the industry was focusing on performance at a given price. We said, hey, instead of giving you just 1 percent more performance, we'll give you 101 percent of performance at 70 percent of the cost. We offered low price without the pain you might expect when you pay a low price. You could call our USP painless gain."

"Now," he went on, "the 30, 40, 50 percent price differences are gone [due to price wars]. And so attention is shifting to other variables—service, support quality, ability to take care of the customer throughout the complete purchase cycle. Before, we offered low price without the 'pain' associated with low price. Now we offer these other benefits—an astonishing level of customer care without the 'pain' often experienced when the customer tries to get the service he deserves."

For instance, there is the customization benefit. "If you go to a reseller to buy a Compaq machine, they can put any hard drive you want in it, any monitor, fill it with any amount of RAM you want," Martin pointed out.

"So from a customization standpoint, I don't think we have a huge advantage. Where I do think we have an advantage is that frequently the reseller doesn't have the engineering support staff to make sure that all of the products will work properly together, to test them, to build the diagnostic software routines, and to actually conduct the test on the finished product. We can offer customization without the traditional pain of customization."

You can take it from Tom Martin that Dell is going to go right on finding daring new ways to take the pain out of buying a personal computer. Providing "gain without pain" is a key to business success Dell will continue to pursue in the future.

The Dell Telecomputing Lifeline

"Hello, Dell?" At the heart of Michael Dell's marketing success is an electronic marvel that is transforming the world we live in and the way we work today.

No, it's not what you think. This modern-day wonder is more than 120 years old.

We're talking, of course, about the telephone.

Dell coupled the telephone with another marvel you would expect to find there, the computer, to scale new heights in customer convenience and satisfaction. When you call Dell's 800 number, the person you talk to is not your typical low-pay, mindless telemarketing phone operator. The phone representatives at Dell first get five weeks of classroom training, and then another full year of helping out and making outbound calls to substantiate leads, before they are allowed to take customer calls. In addition to their technical training in computers, they are also taught how to listen.

Dell trainees who are finally allowed to join the exalted ranks of their 1000 highly trained phone reps enjoy another important advantage. In addition to all of the knowledge and training stored away in the memory cells of their own brains, they also have the advantage of a larger, more reliable "brain"—the information stored in the computer sitting in front of them.

Once you as a customer are entered into the Dell database, every call you place gets red-carpet treatment. With a few keystrokes, your rep can call up on the screen your complete transaction and company history—who you are, what you do, when you first inquired, when you bought, what you bought, your previous thoughts on system configuration, your technical concerns. The rep can see at a glance what equipment you have, what your repair history has been, and can make sure that what you are ordering will be appropriate to your needs and will work well with what you already have.

If you're calling Dell for technical support, your rep may be able to solve your problem by immediately accessing and examining a sophisticated database of product details and graphic illustrations of key components. Thanks to the instant availability of this information, the company claims that over 90 percent of the problems they receive can be solved over the phone within six minutes. (Most customers say that if they are lucky, they can expect a dealer to solve their problems over the phone only 20 to 30 percent of the time.) If your questions to the Dell representative are too tough or too technical, you'll be transferred to a more knowledgeable technical expert—and then, as a final resort, a service rep in the field will be at your office the next day.

In its outline, there is an uncanny resemblance between this marriage of phone and computer and that used by the Fidelity Investment reps, who sit in front of a computer screen and instantly access—as needed—vast amounts of information about the customer, the Fidelity product offerings, and the latest business and financial news. Dell and Fidelity are stunning examples of how the marriage of telecommunications and computer technology is creating a dazzling new "telecomputing" channel of communication—propelling the power of one-to-one customer handling into possibilities barely imagined a decade ago.

Application of telecomputing communication to meet customer needs in the health-care industry, the automotive industry, the airline industry, and even the packaged goods industry as shown by the Nestlé "Allô Diététique" service will proliferate as the "informationalization" of the marketing process proceeds. Are you exploring the possibilities for your business category?

Different Strokes for Different Folks

Dell has organized its sales and support staff into teams or "cells." Each cell is made up of three salespersons, three technical support persons, and two customer support persons. If you're a large customer or a VAR, you will be assigned to a cell that will be responsible for satisfying your every computer need.*

If you're a small business or a home computer user, you won't ordinarily get the same person on the phone every time you call Dell. However, you can ask for—and probably get—your usual rep if that is the way you prefer to do business.

If you are identified as an executive in a larger business or a government agency, you will get the full business-to-business treatment from a dedicated salesperson. Half of Dell's sales are produced by field salespersons following up business leads.

If you're a government agency, you will talk to a government-computer specialist who knows that what you buy must be at a price acceptable to the General Services Administration and

*Dell has used this cell model to expand strongly into international sales, which now account for about a fourth of the company's sales volume. Since the company launched its international operations in 1987, operating subsidiaries have been established in the United Kingdom, Germany, France, Sweden, Italy, Finland, the Netherlands, Ireland, Spain, Norway, Mexico, and Japan. Dell recently opened offices in Poland and the Czech Republic. In each country, a wholly owned subsidiary, run by locals and made up of sales and support cells, is able to deal knowledgeably with the country's differences in language, customs, government regulations, and business needs.

who is familiar with the terms, conditions, and operating procedures for dealing with government purchasing requirements.

The listening, learning, and noting done by the phone rep, augmented by the artificial intelligence capability of the rep's computer, stimulates constant improvement in product and service in at least four ways. The system doesn't always work perfectly, but it is a model of how a customer feedback loop can improve overall performance.

- Each technician is able to profit from the problem solving of all the others. As Dell ad copy explains it, "Calls made to Dell Technical Support are entered into our system. If our technicians run into a problem they can't solve, they access the Problem Resolution Database. Chances are a similar problem—and solution—have been entered in the past."
- The constant feedback from customers, along with the built-in link between manufacturing, sales, and service, permits quick identification of faulty parts or design glitches and correction of the faults on the production line. "If we get more than a few complaints," explains a Dell marketing manager, "I go about 130 feet to the people who design the thing. Within five or six hours, engineering has fixed the design, and within two or three days, the factory's got that change incorporated on the line."
- Constant analysis of the 15,000 phone calls received each day assists the company in spotting trends early and developing products or services to meet the fast-changing demands of the marketplace.
- Since every computer is built to order, there is no excess inventory of older models to be marked down and cleared out before a new model is introduced.

Daring to Do More Than Expected

Dell's unwavering dedication to the customer was expressed in this way by Joel Kocher, president of Dell USA: "The customer is god—not just king." Newly hired Dell employees, average

age 28, are indoctrinated in and live by the company's "24-7" philosophy—that is, the company spends 24 hours a day, 7 days a week, doing whatever it takes to satisfy the customer.

Tom Martin told us that "when a customer has a problem, our goal is to stop at nothing to solve that problem." He gave the following example: "A couple of months ago, somebody was ordering a PC and for whatever the reasons the product was slated to ship on the last day that would work for the customer. It was a Friday as I recall. The customer had to have it that day, but we don't have same-day delivery from Austin. Conveniently enough, in this case, the customer was in Houston. And so the sales rep drove over to the factory, pulled out the system—which is no mean feat in terms of paperwork because the system is supposed to ship by a common carrier—put the system in her car, drove to Houston, and then found the customer to make the delivery."

This behavior is in marked contrast to the uneven, often inadequate and lackluster service and support provided by most dealers retailing IBM and Compaq PCs. Is it any wonder that word of mouth from Dell customers kept building market share through the eighties and into the nineties?

"Is Anybody Listening?"

That was the title of a wise little classic of management communication written many years ago by William S. Whyte and widely ignored ever since. What Whyte argued was that successful communication is a two-way street—that your subordinates won't listen to you or can't hear you if you're not listening to them.

We have already seen how intently and profitably Dell listens to its customers. In fact, the company slogan is, "When you talk, we listen."* Sometimes this means the listener is Michael Dell himself, who is known to drop in on customer service calls from

*Contrast this with the problem that hobbled IBM in the late 1980s and helped make Dell's rise possible. According to a story in *The Economist:* "In 1987 IBM's chairman at the time, Mr. John Akers, set up meetings between his top managers and his biggest customers. The results were not flattering. Customers lambasted IBM for arrogance—its unwillingness to listen and inability to adapt to customer needs....Instead of sweating blood to help customers, runs the most common complaint, IBM tries to bully them into doing things the Big Blue way."

time to time to get a feel for what his customers like and dislike. He told us, "There is no substitute for the unwashed and unbleached words of the customer. It's a reality check you need because the world changes all the time."

We asked Dell if he takes time to pick up the phone himself now that his company has become a multibillion-dollar operation. His answer: "I have a phone in my office set up just for listening in. When I am at my desk, I still turn it on and just listen."

At Dell, listening to the customer goes hand in hand with everybody, from the boss on down, listening to each other. But how? Can you imagine a lowly employee in a big hierarchically organized corporation going over his or her supervisor's head and writing a memo of suggestions or questions to the CEO? Or even committing the sin of merely carboning the top boss? That would be an unforgivable violation of the sacred rule of going through channels. On the other hand, if you obediently write only your supervisor, that may be as far as your ideas get.

But, at Dell, there is a forum where employees can meet and exchange ideas with Michael Dell and each other at any hour of the day, any day of the week. How? Why, by a method totally appropriate to a new-age computer company: E-mail!

Through Dell's E-mail, people in the company can post any comment, question, or news for any interested parties. Says Michael Dell, "Electronic mail allows communication very quickly and easily. If a buyer in Dell Japan wants to tell the guys in product development about new technologies over there, he can write the memo on the bullet train and send it by E-mail and we have it in minutes."

And through this same medium, the founder is able to conduct "Mike's Fireside Chats," a forum in which employees can question him and he can provide long, thoughtful answers. Michael Dell is able to constantly communicate to everyone in the company the zeal for quality and service that have been essential to the company's success.

What does all of this have to do with marketing? The answer is—plenty! It may seem beyond what most practitioners think about when the subject of marketing comes up but it is at the heart of Dell's business success.

Everything a company does is linked to everything else. You can't have great advertising, promotion, and merchandising without a corporate culture that puts the customer's interest first.

Michael Dell's caring enough to listen to reps leads to reps listening to him. That in turn helps create reps who are genuinely passionate about listening to the customer. Claiming to listen to the customer is hardly a new idea in marketing. But claiming to listen and daring to use the power of caring to really do it—and to do it with rare sensitivity and understanding—that is the cornerstone of the achievements chronicled in this book.

The Battle Rages On

After the new management at Compaq Computer Corporation started competing with Michael Dell and the other low-priced marketers on their own turf by cutting prices and launching a direct marketing operation, Dell counterattacked with a hard-hitting ad campaign of its own.

One advertisement positioned Dell as the "INNOVATION LEADER" versus Compaq as the "IMITATION LEADER." The ad listed 14 Dell "firsts" beginning with "selling direct in 1984" and "offering a 30-day no-questions-asked guarantee." Shown opposite in each case was listed where "Compaq follows" or is "Not yet there."

We'll let the body copy of the ad speak for itself:

> For 8 years, Compaq scoffed at Dell's idea of dealing directly with our customers.
>
> They stood on the sidelines while we ignited a computer revolution, catapulted into the Fortune 500, notched up over $2 billion in annual sales, and swept the customer satisfaction polls.
>
> Finally it dawned on Compaq that maybe a direct relationship with customers is a pretty good idea. So they copied us.
>
> The trouble is, it's just a copy.
>
> While Compaq has barely installed their phones, we get an average of 15,000 calls a day. With all this input, we can come up with new innovations.

It wasn't long before the battle for the direct-order portion of the market picked up speed with the mailing of the first Compaq and IBM mail-order catalogs. *PC Week* commented:

> While corporate customers are more willing than ever to buy PCs direct, they say IBM and Compaq Computer Corp. haven't done much to woo them from established direct-response players such as Dell Computer Corp. and Gateway 2000 Inc.
>
> IBM and Compaq, which are still learning the mechanics of the direct-response business, are primarily offering a limited set of low-end products that lack the features and power required by corporate customers. Moreover, because they don't want to anger their traditional resellers, the hardware giants tend to steer corporate buyers to traditional channels by not granting volume discounts...

But these were only the opening moves. As the pace of price-slashing and direct-selling competition intensified, Dell now finds itself fighting off savage competition from both above and below.

In the spring of 1993, the three largest price competitors at Dell's heels—Gateway 2000, AST Research, and Packard Bell—together had a greater sales volume than Dell. Gateway 2000, their lower-priced mail-order competitor, passed the billion-dollar-mark in sales.

IBM "liberated" its PC business by making it a separate $7 billion company, named IBM Personal Computer Company. According to the new entity's president, Robert Corrigan, within its first 40 days, IBM Personal Computer launched 83 new products, and in the first quarter of 1993 racked up solid sales gains. (The parent IBM Computer Corporation's losses of $285 million for that period were caused mainly by the continuing collapse of mainframe sales, which fell by a staggering "high double-digit percentage.")

And how was Compaq Computer Corporation doing after finally listening to and responding to the marketplace? A year after Eckhard Pfeiffer took over the reins at Compaq, he could triumphantly report quarterly sales of $1 billion (an annualized rate of $4 billion a year), a 50 percent increase, and a profit for the quarter of almost $50 million.

Dell Stumbles on the New Playing Field

After forcing Compaq and IBM to play by their rules, fast-stepping Dell Computer fumbled by misjudging the growing market for small notebook computers. Profits in the first quarter of 1993 were down by half to $10.2 million, even though revenues rose more than 80 percent to $672 million.

In a *New York Times* interview, Dell's president Joel Kocher explained, "We grew from a $500 million-a-year company to a $2 billion concern. This year revenues are expected to reach $3 billion. That explosive growth has strained Dell's systems for managing everything from inventories to product forecasting.

"Our desktop business is great," Mr. Kocher added. "In the first quarter desktop sales doubled. There's nothing wrong with the Dell business model. We just need to put the right products in the model."

The whole history of Dell until now suggests that Kocher is right. Never underestimate Michael Dell and the company he has built around his understanding of the market and his passion for cultivating the relationship with his customers. But Dell's stumble on the way to hitting the $3 billion mark only underlined how quickly fortunes can shift in the personal computer business.

By the summer of 1993, the savage PC price wars had wounded yet another company: Apple Computer Inc., once thought to be in a league of its own. *The New York Times* reported: "The value of Apple's stock plummeted by 10.6 percent, after the company predicted that its earnings would fall because price-cutting had eroded the company's profit margins." Apple's shares lost more than 19 percent of their value in a week's time as a result of the price cuts by Dell, Compaq, and IBM that forced John Sculley to eliminate much of the price premium Apple had been able to charge for Macintosh computers.

While Apple's profits slid, Compaq's lower-priced models and souped-up service produced good early 1993 numbers. Sales rose by $189 million over the previous period with a $1.2 million increase in pretax profit.

IBM intensified its direct-sales effort with the mailing of more than a million 80-page catalogs carrying for the first time the full range of IBM personal computer lines along with numerous non-IBM accessories and software. The battle for the 20 percent of the market that already preferred to shop direct was picking up momentum.

The Jury Is Out

By the time you read this, who knows which computer company will be winning the latest round? Marketing know-how, manufacturing efficiency, new technology, and a fickle public will all play a role in the raging battle for growth and survival.

And even if Dell Computer were to declare bankruptcy in a year or two, which is wildly improbable, the company still has written a "Caring and Daring" success story that students of marketing will gaze at in awe for years to come.

Michael Dell has one strength going for him that the stock analysts have never fully understood. Deep down in his psyche is the experience that shaped him as a teenager. He may have come a long way from selling stamps by mail as a 12-year-old but the mindset absorbed in those days is still with him. Michael Dell, the boy-wonder marketer, will always have the kind of gut-feeling for customer involvement and dialogue that is the hallmark of the MaxiMarketing winners in today's fiercely competitive business arena.

When we asked Michael Dell what differentiated his company from the competition during the years of its spectacular rise, he replied: "We have a tremendous passionate commitment to taking care of the customer. That passion absolutely is the difference."

But how, we wanted to know, do you convey that passion to the people who work for you?

"First of all, it has to be practiced within the company by the people at the top. It's not something you show on a chart or a piece of paper you send out and say, 'Just do this.' It becomes the DNA of the business. It becomes *what we do* because it's *what we are*. I think that what you were saying about 'caring and daring' absolutely makes sense."

4
Harley's HOG Heaven

"Getting close to the customer" became part of the lore of business management in the eighties, thanks to Peters and Waterman's million-copy best-seller *In Search of Excellence.* It was a powerful idea that some companies took to heart and went on to expand into a forceful and profitable competitive edge. But, for too many companies, it became little more than setting up a customer-complaint hotline and doing customer-satisfaction surveys.

When Harley-Davidson executives say they have a passion for getting close to the customer, they're talking *really* close. Like sharing beer and hot dogs with fellow bikers at a motorcycle rally, or roaring down the highway with them on an Ultra Classic Electra Glide.*

An important aim in the new marketing is what our colleague Richard Cross has termed "customer bonding." But how many companies do you know whose customers bond so strongly with a product that they have the corporate logo tattooed on

*The discussion in these pages will be confined to the Motorcycle Division of Harley-Davidson, Inc. The company also owns the Holiday Rambler Corporation, a leading producer of premium recreational vehicles and specialized commercial vehicles, acquired in 1986. The company hopes to build up this division by using many of the same marketing techniques that have worked so well for Harley-Davidson motorcycles, such as company-sponsored clubs and activities and emphasis on lifestyle. But these luxury vehicles, selling for $100,000 or more, were hard-hit by the recession, dragging down overall company earnings. Holiday Rambler finally began to turn around with a small profit in 1992.

their bulging biceps, as many Harley-Davidson motorcycle owners do? Or who can invite their customers to a nice little 90th Anniversary celebration, as Harley-Davidson did in 1993, and have over 66,000 of them buy $10 tickets?

For an "advanced course" in customer loyalty, we recommend picking up a copy of *The Five Degrees of Customer Bonding* by Richard Cross and Janet Smith. You'll learn how the smartest companies climb beyond mere brand awareness into the rarefied atmosphere of enduring customer relationships, forming a close-knit community of like-minded people, and benefiting from the explosive power of brand advocacy.

Surely the story you are about to read, how Harley-Davidson went from a troubled loser to a soaring winner, is one of the greatest single examples of the "Bringing People Together" key to success ever seen in America.

Don't be concerned that the marketing of Harley-Davidson's humongous motorcycles may seem to have little to do with what happens in your own category. What you will be discovering is a way of thinking that has universal application.

Later in this book, you will see how a packaged-goods company, with a marketing challenge at the absolute opposite end of the spectrum from selling a gleaming $10,000 machine, is breaking new ground by following many of the same applications of MaxiMarketing principles behind the success of Harley-Davidson.

What a Difference a Decade Makes

Harley-Davidson went from teetering on the brink of bankruptcy in 1982, as a result of production problems and a flood of Japanese imports, to beating the Japanese and becoming the $1.2 billion "king of the road" 10 years later. It is a brilliant example of the art of keeping your old customers resold and letting them do much of the job of winning new ones for you.

The extent of the turnaround was just short of miraculous. In the United States, their share of market for superheavyweight motorcycles (those with engine capacity of 850 cc and up) had collapsed from more than 40 percent in the mid-1970s to 23 percent by 1983. But by the late 1980s, Harley-Davidson had more orders than they could fill and were backordered for months ahead.

Share of market bounced back to 63 percent by 1989 and continued the climb to 68 percent of the market three years later. Rapidly rising overseas sales were expected to hit over $300 million in the early years of this decade. It is a dramatic comeback that is the climax of a company history which started over 90 years ago.

Harley-Davidson began in 1903 at a 10-foot by 15-foot shed located in the backyard of the Davidson home in Milwaukee.

The scene is depicted in a night shot in one of the company's many striking ads evoking the romance of motorcycling. An annoyed housewife stands silhouetted at the back door of the house, waiting impatiently while dinner is getting cold. On the dimly lit door of the nearby shed we can see in crude hand lettering, "Harley-Davidson Motor Co."

The copy is reminiscent of the Wright Brothers tinkering with their flying machine. In just a few words, it tells a great deal about the love of cycling that permeates both the company and its customers...

> 90 years ago, four men decided to take a motorcycle ride. There was only one catch. They had to build it first.
>
> So Bill Harley and Arthur, Walter, and William A. Davidson rolled up their sleeves and got to work.
>
> After countless gallons of midnight oil and who knows how many missed meals, the first Harley-Davidson motorcycle rolled out of the "factory."
>
> At the time, they had no way of knowing that they had created much more than a motorcycle. That machine was the start of a commitment, a powerful relationship between rider and motorcycle that continues to this day in garages across America. If you've been there, no further explanation is necessary.
>
> So here's to anyone whose mom ever yelled because you were spending too much time with a motorcycle.
>
> And here's to the four men who were able to build a machine so powerful, it became a way of life.

The sign-off print line running across the bottom of the ad also says a great deal about the company:

We care about you. Sign up for a Motorcycle Safety Foundation rider course today. Ride with your headlight on and watch out for the other person. Always wear a helmet, proper eyewear and appropriate clothing and insist your passenger does too...

The Company That Grew with America

Production at the fledgling company grew steadily. In 1909, they introduced a more powerful motorcycle with a V-twin engine that is still the company's standard. The engine had double the power of its predecessors, carrying riders at the then unbelievable speed of 60 miles an hour. It gave Harley-Davidson a big edge over the more than 150 competing brands of motorcycle.

The company's history has been intertwined with America's history for almost a century. Military use of motorcycles in World War I gave manufacturing an important boost. By the end of the war, 20,000 Harley-Davidsons had been called into action.

The Great Depression was devastating to the U.S. motorcycle industry. Only two manufacturers survived—Harley-Davidson and Indian. (Indian folded in 1953, leaving Harley-Davidson as the sole surviving U.S. motorcycle manufacturer.)

In World War II, motorcycles again played an important role. The company built and shipped more than 90,000 machines, and earned the Army-Navy "E" award for excellence in wartime production.

After the war, civilian demand for motorcycles exploded and business boomed. In 1960, the company merged with the American Machine and Foundry Company (AMF).

Then in the early 1980s Harley-Davidson found itself in deep trouble. Under the pressure of expanding production, product quality had slipped. There were buyer complaints of oil leaks and excessive engine noise. The defect rate on the manufacturing line was 50 percent. Meanwhile, Japanese manufacturers like Honda and Kawasaki had invaded the U.S. market with lower-priced, well-made, heavyweight machines. And demand was hurt by the first major recession since World War II.

All these factors converged to drive the company to the edge of bankruptcy. But 13 members of the Harley-Davidson management team thought they saw how to turn the company around. (As Mike Keefe, marketing manager, wryly explained it to us, "Just as hanging concentrates the mind wonderfully, so does losing millions of dollars.") They purchased the company from AMF in a leveraged buyout that put decision making in the hands of executive managers who understood the lifestyle of motorcyclists because they were cyclists themselves.

Vaughn L. Beals, Jr., the new chairman who had put his personal fortune on the line, set about beating the Japanese at their own game. He turned to the teaching of W. Edwards Deming, the American who had led the Japanese into quality management, and put Deming's principles to work for Harley-Davidson. Just-in-time inventory, statistical control of production, and the workers on the line monitoring the quality of their work became a way of life for the new management style in Harley-Davidson's downtown Milwaukee plant.

But just as the revitalization program was beginning to show results, the new owners of Harley-Davidson were dealt another heavy blow. Japanese manufacturers did not limit production of heavyweights in the face of declining demand and dumped their surplus inventory on the U.S. market.

In 1982, Harley-Davidson was able to prove threat of injury to the International Trade Commission. As a result, President Reagan imposed additional tariffs on imported Japanese motorcycles for a five-year period.

The government action gave the American company the breathing spell it needed for its new policies to take hold. Total Quality Management on the factory floor knocked the defect rate down from 50 percent to 1 percent. By 1986, Harley-Davidson had overtaken Honda in sale of superheavyweights.

Early the next year, in what seemed like a supreme act of confidence, generosity, or bravado, the Milwaukee management petitioned the ITC to remove the tariffs on Japanese imports a year early! (Actually, there was method in their madness. Management believed that the more the market is expanded by all makers, including the Japanese, the more riders there will be who will eventually want a Harley.)

We have told this story of the company's rise, fall, and rise again as a necessary prologue to what follows. Without first overcoming the quality gap against the competition, the effectiveness of Harley-Davidson's relationship-building strategy would have been fatally flawed.

Getting the product and the relationship right tripled their share of the U.S. market for superheavyweights in less than a decade. They trounced the Japanese competition, at a time when U.S. electronics manufacturers almost gave up altogether and American auto makers were forced to demand limitation of imports or see their competitive position totally destroyed.

The Machine That Became a Way of Life

The meteoric rise of the new Harley-Davidson cannot be explained in terms of manufacturing excellence or sociological trends alone. One must also look to a dazzling demonstration of what it means to go beyond the usual marketing process and create the kind of customer bond few companies have ever achieved.

At the heart of this legendary success is a consistent vision, a brilliant expression of what the company is selling: not only a machine, but a way of life.

In his classic *How to Write a Good Advertisement,* direct-marketing pioneer Victor O. Schwab recounts the story of how Dr. Samuel Johnson had auctioned off the contents of the old Anchor Brewery in London some 200 years earlier. "We are not here to sell boilers and vats," Dr. Johnson boomed out, "but the potentiality of growing rich beyond the dreams of avarice."

He also told of how Daniel Webster is supposed to have auctioned off a friend's farm in New Hampshire. "Neighbors," said Webster, "we're not auctioning Tom Brown's 34 good milk cows...or 80 acres of fine land...or a sturdy home that's seen 20 winters. No, I'm offering you the chance of biting into a red apple with the juice running over your lips...the smell of new-mown hay...clear mountain stream water on your table...the crunch of snow under your feet...and the best neighbors in the world."

In the same way, Harley-Davidson is not selling engineering specifications, although those are certainly mentioned. They are selling a mystique. A great adventure. A brotherhood and sisterhood. A personal statement. A love affair. A social opportunity. A fountain of youth. A way out. A lifestyle. And they have been wildly successful at supporting this message with bold initiatives in fostering a caring relationship with owners of their motorcycles.

We talked at great length with Mike Keefe, the Harley-Davidson marketing manager, about how the product has become so much more than a form of transportation and how he can maintain an incredible 90 percent customer loyalty rate. Nurturing this unusual customer relationship breaks down into five major components:

1. The Harley Owners Group activities
2. The shoulder-to-shoulder and eyeball-to-eyeball contact between management and customers at rallies
3. Free "sampling" of the product, in the form of free demo rides at major motorcycle events
4. The reinforcement advertising
5. The HOG dealer involvement

"Our Greatest Tool for Getting Close to Customers"

The Harley Owners Group happily has as an appropriate acronym, HOG. It fits the group perfectly since Harley owners have affectionately referred to their machines as HOGs for years. (We recently saw a Harley with a license plate whose digits began with the letters HOGGIE.)

The HOG Club was formed in 1983. The first year of membership is given free to new owners of a Harley. After that, annual dues are $35. The annual renewal rate is 68 percent. Membership has grown steadily from 35,000, the number of bikes sold the first year, to 200,000 members worldwide 10 years later.

Keefe rates HOG his No.1 channel for customer communication: "At HOG rallies, the company CEO, president, manager of HOG, and any other high-level people who happen to be there will stand up in front of a room, and any question (except new-product questions) is fair game. If there is a particular problem, they will take it up on a personal basis afterwards."

Keefe explained that keeping Harley owners actively involved with their motorcycle and out on the open road is his biggest challenge. If you stop using your Harley after the first flush of enthusiasm passes and the novelty wears off, you aren't likely to trade it in for an improved model in coming years. You aren't as likely to buy Harley clothing and paraphernalia, a significant and growing profit center for the company. Most important, you won't be out there impressing your friends and neighbors with the joys of Harley ownership and persuading them to go out and do likewise.

HOG membership is no superficial add-on. It is at the heart of Harley-Davidson's motorcycle business. Peggy Lamb, manager of member services for the club, describes the mission of the club vividly in terms of what it seeks to avoid: "having a person buy a Harley and a month or two later having second thoughts. You know, 'Gee, I don't know where to ride. There's nothing really going on. My friends aren't really into it. I wonder if I made the right purchase decision.'"

Not to worry. The HOG member benefits and the activities encouraged in the club magazine do their best to convert members from mere ownership to joyous fanaticism.

With the growing trend in the 1990s toward relationship marketing, running a customer club for buyers of your product or service is becoming almost *de rigeur.* But far too often these so-called clubs are half-hearted, trivial efforts, offering a meager package of benefits—a trite newsletter, discounts on future purchases, insurance (at purported but not necessarily genuine savings), self-liquidating premiums, a plastic wallet card, and so on. They don't fool anybody into feeling that he or she is a member of a real club.

But the Harley club is a "HOG" of a different color. The Harley Owners Group offers a carefully engineered program of deep involvement for members. It is true that many of the club's features arise from the unique nature of the product and the members' feelings about owning a prestigious motorcycle. Still, it is a model of profound member involvement and ingenious rewards which can be profitably studied by marketers from other product categories.

In certain ways, joining HOG is curiously reminiscent of joining the Boy/Girl Scouts or enlisting in the Armed Forces and being rewarded by priceless comradeship, exciting field trips, the right to be awarded badges or medals for achievement and a chance to "be the best you can be."

Here is a rundown of the benefits and activities listed in the membership handbook:

- *ABC's of Touring.* This is an awards program comparable to a ham radio operator seeking to log reception of a record number of international call letters combined with a kind of real-life geography game. You earn a point each time you prove with photos that you and your Harley were in a village, city, county, state, national forest, or country whose name begins with a different letter of the alphabet, plus additional points for proof of attendance at state and regional HOG rallies. Collecting 20 points wins you a pin; 30 points, a pin and a bandana; 46 points, a pin, a bandana, and an ABC's of Touring hat (wow!). The grand prize winner gets a $500 gift certificate. The next twelve ranking entries win items of cycle gear.
- *Emergency Pick-Up Service* reimburses members who are at least 50 miles from home and require towing service.
- *Fly and Ride* enables members to rent a Harley at 10 popular touring centers in the United States plus locations in Canada, Australia, and Germany. Wherever you go, there's a Harley waiting for you.
- *H.O.G. Travel Center* is a travel agency that books airline flights, car rentals, and hotel rooms for members.
- *Insurance Program* offers reasonably priced coverage (in most states) of your Harley and accessories through a wholly owned company subsidiary.
- *Mileage Merit Program* awards pins, patches, and engraved plaques for different levels of mileage recorded within a specified time frame.
- *Ten-Year Member Recognition* is a patch awarded for being a HOG member for ten consecutive years.
- *$1000 Theft Reward* is promised for information leading to the arrest and conviction of anyone stealing a member's

motorcycle. Members are provided with a theft reward decal for their machines to discourage thieves.

- *Touring Handbook* comes in three different editions—North America, Europe, and Australia/New Zealand. Each edition contains detailed maps with special notations of all cities that have Harley-Davidson dealerships and other valuable touring information. The handbook also has such useful data as climate charts, listings of city tourism bureaus, various special events, national parks, and customs information.
- *Tuition Reimbursement* in the form of a credit coupon worth up to $50 is provided to members who successfully complete an accredited Motorcycle Safety Foundation rider training course. Such members also receive a pin with the "Safe Rider Skills" logo.
- *"The Enthusiast,"* published three times a year, is a magazine which has been entertaining and informing Harley-Davidson enthusiasts since 1916. It is the oldest continuously published motorcycle magazine in the world.
- *"Hog Tales"* is the official publication of the Harley Owners Group, published six times a year. It is a cornucopia of news and photos of past events, calendars of coming rallies and events... self-submitted photos and bios of members...group photos of local chapters...a "Hog Tale" by a member telling of a riding adventure...and a list of all the members in the Mileage Merit program, grouped by the mileage category they have achieved. Instant fame for everybody who likes it (and who doesn't?). And in an "Ask Charlie" feature, experts answer members' questions about mechanical problems.
- *Local HOG Chapters* sponsored by Harley-Davidson dealers are "a great way to meet new friends, participate in chapter activities, and have lots of fun."

Note the two themes which predominate: Activities! Activities! Activities! and Recognition! Recognition! Recognition!

Almost everybody yearns to be "somebody." *Hog Tales* and the other benefits make sure that you almost certainly will be, one way or another. Mike Keefe told us that 90 percent of HOG members say they intend to buy another Harley. "We may lose some. But once you get on a Harley, you'll stay on a Harley. It's a very comfortable, very forgiving machine. The emphasis is more on enjoying the journey than getting anywhere in particular. And that's exactly the feeling we complement with the HOG membership experience," he explained.

"How to Win Friends and Influence People"

The first local HOG chapters were started in 1985. There were 33 of them the first year. Today, there are over 750 worldwide. These local participation centers are a dramatic example of how far Harley-Davidson will go to get involved with owners in a way that almost has no parallel. How many other companies do you know that encourage purchasers of their products to get together with other owners in the same area?* If you buy a Harley and don't have anyone to ride with, you can join your local HOG chapter and meet new friends who share your interest and enthusiasm.

A membership invitation folder vividly captures the fun, the excitement, and the satisfaction of chapter membership.

> The ride of a lifetime. Eighty cubic inches of Milwaukee iron thunder coming to life. Could anything feel more right than a morning ride on a Harley-Davidson?
>
> You're about to find out. Because at the end of this ride is a scene both new and familiar: a parking lot full of people and Harley-Davidson motorcycles.
>
> It's your first local chapter meeting of the Harley Owners Group.
>
> H.O.G. exists for one reason: to make the Harley-Davidson experience even better. Walking through the denim and leather, you're among friends you've never met. Everyone's talking motorcycles. Everybody's swapping stories. Catching up. You can participate in everything from road trips to service seminars. Or not. It's up to you.
>
> The chapter's Road Captain explains the upcoming ride for MDA. Somebody else has pictures of the Hydra-Glide he's restoring. And the whole place vibrates with the sound of V-twin engines.

*One of the rare parallels we can think of is the subscriber-discussion groups started by the magazine, *The Utne Reader*. At last report, there were 20,000 dues-paying members of Utne Neighborhood Salons.

> On this fine Saturday morning, while most people are washing windows and mowing yards, the brothers and sisters of H.O.G. have different priorities. And while they're all fiercely individual, they're all genuine Harley. Through and Through.

Honestly, now—doesn't that make you feel like letting your lawn grow shaggy while you hop on a Harley and roar down to a local chapter meeting?

Hi, My Name Is Harley. What's Yours?

Our studies of successful companies tell us that consumers want to *like* the companies they buy from. One important element in winning customers is the company's openness and responsiveness to customer feedback.

Many of the winners we write about in this book have highly sensitive and sophisticated customer-feedback mechanisms. But Harley-Davidson is one of a kind in demonstrating just how close a billion-dollar company can get to its customers.

It is completely staffed by motorcycle enthusiasts, from the president down to secretaries and mail-room clerks. That's a company tradition going back to 1909, when Walter Davidson won the highest score ever for an AMA event, a record which still stands.

Today, President Richard Teerlink rides a Harley every day. And Keefe talked with pride about what happens at Harley rallies: "When there is a gathering of thousands of cyclists, we don't hire a promotion firm to stand at the literature tables, answer questions, and show off new models, as the Japanese manufacturers do. Harley-Davidson executives, managers, engineers, lawyers, and secretaries hop on their Hogs, ride to the rally, and personally represent the company there."

Try It, You'll Like It

"Free samples" of the Harley-Davidson experience play an important role in Harley's current sold-out status.

In 1987, Harley executives found an old trailer sunk to its axle in mud. They jacked it up, painted it black, named it "Black Beauty," threw 15 motorcycles on it, and started taking it to rallies to offer demo rides.

Since then, more than 80,000 motorcyclists attending major motorcycle events, many of them owners of competitive brands, have taken advantage of the company's offer to test-ride a new Harley.

The company's Demo Ride fleet is staffed entirely by employee volunteers from all areas of the company. They use the experience to gain a better understanding of the products, the customers, and the potential customers.

These demo rides are an important customer-feedback mechanism. The vice-president of engineering talking to a bunch of people who just rode the new "soft-tail" is going to find out if those people like it or not. There is always a comment table for inviting and collecting written comments; these are typed up and distributed throughout the company.

Left-Brain and Right-Brain Creativity

"Advertising helps but ads are probably fifth or sixth on the list," we were told by Mike Keefe. "The leading reason people tell us they buy a Harley is advice of a friend or relative. It's hard to talk with persuasive advertising to someone who's spending $5000 to $15,000 on a toy."

Nevertheless, Harley-Davidson advertising is the sort that gives creativity a good name: spectacular superrealistic color photography with a right-brain emotional punch, combined with gently humorous left-brain copy that captures the Harley-Davidson mystique and idealizes the Harley way of life.

Keefe said that about 45 to 50 percent of purchasers come from owning a competitive bike, and undoubtedly the advertising does play some part in influencing this decision. An even more important function of the advertising, he pointed out, is its effect on people who have already purchased a Harley and want to feel reassured that they did the right thing.

As he put it, "People can buy the bike and be enjoying it, but what I want them to be able to do is explain their enjoyment. And also, when they read these ads, to say, 'Yeah, that's just the way I felt, without really realizing how I was feeling at the time.' I would say that 50 to 60 percent of our advertising is designed to reinforce the buying decision and also to reinforce the ability of owners to articulate their feelings."

He compares it to his own personal experience with automobiles. "I bought an Audi Quattro because I fell in love with it. And *then* I went out to read everything I could find about it to prove I made the right decision."

Although most Harley owners are mild-mannered business and professional people by day rather than ominous Hell's Angels, the ads celebrate the defiance of herdlike behavior and the marching to a different drummer that their motorcycles represent to them.

For instance, one ad shows a Harley and a pup tent at dusk in an empty desert landscape. It is headed, "WE DON'T CARE HOW EVERYONE ELSE DOES IT." Then notice how the copy that follows artfully blends product talk with celebration of shared emotional and spiritual values.

> As you go through life, it's easy to do what everyone else does. It's easy. And boring. We prefer to go our own way. The Harley-Davidson Electra Glide Sport is a prime example of that. As touring motorcycles go, it is simple. Simple is not a word normally used to describe a touring machine. But keeping it simple allows us to work on things that truly make it a better motorcycle. Like relocating the battery and oil tank to make room for new, larger saddlebags with more secure lids, latches, and locks. While making sure that the Sport retains its classic good looks. We don't care if everyone else is loading up their bikes with every new-age gizmo they can find. At Harley-Davidson, we believe that motorcycling is about individuality. If you're of a like mind, you're welcome to ride along.

On the surface this seems to be merely an advertisement for the Sport model. It seems to fulfill Keefe's purpose of making new buyers of the Sport feel good about their decision. But upon reflection, you can see that in both words and picture the ad also is saying something about what it means to be a Harley-Davidson owner, regardless of the model you own.

There is subtle flattery in the copy which makes you feel good about being a Harley owner whether you would ever really camp out alone on the desert or not. You feel like at least you're that kind of guy, and your Harley tells that to the world. (We use the word "guy" in its gender-neutral sense, since one of Harley's fastest-growing market segments is women.)

Keefe says his favorite ad shows a young man in a T-shirt, and tattooed on his arm is the Harley bar, shield, and eagle logo. The headline: "When was the last time you felt this strongly about anything?"

A "Caring" Company Cares for Dealers, Too

In studying winning MaxiMarketing companies, we observed again and again that *caring* seems to be indivisible. That is, the same caring attitude is a seamless web covering customers, employees, and dealers alike. At Harley-Davidson, this outlook has been formalized in the company's vision statement that notes its "commitment to continuously improve the quality of profitable relationships with stakeholders (customers, employees, suppliers, shareholders, governments, and society)." To emphasize this view of employees as "stakeholders," the company's Annual Report in 1992 included in fine print the names of every one of its 5800 employees.

As far as the dealers are concerned, Mike Keefe told us, "We had to realize that our dealers were our partners, and we work very hard at building the relationship with them rather than treating them just as factory customers. And we do that in a lot of the same ways that we build relationships with Harley owners. For example, Town Hall meetings. Every summer, four or five of our top people go out into the field, and conduct a Town Hall meeting with dealers in every one of the 30 districts in the country."

At these meetings, the Harley-Davidson top guns start by giving a short presentation of some sort. Then it's question time, no holds barred, so they can find out what the dealers' issues are and try to resolve them on the spot when possible.

A Dealer Advisory Council is elected by the dealers themselves and meets three times a year to advise on such things as co-op advertising plans. There is usually an annual incentive trip for the top dealers, where several hundred dealers and their wives mingle with Harley-Davidson executives and develop genuine friendships with them. As Keefe himself says, "Some of my best friends are now dealers. We develop very deep, and I suspect, lasting friendships."

One reason this sensitive cultivation of dealers is important is that the local dealer must be inspired, encouraged, and persuaded to be more than just a retailer. He is also the company's local Troop Leader or Scout Master, helping local customers enjoy The Harley Experience.

As Keefe explains it, "There's a pattern of things that you try to get them to do: hold meetings at the store, hold open houses, have rides every weekend, etc. Goofy little stuff, but stuff that deepens the relationship, shows his customers that he is a human being who likes to ride motorcycles also.

"If you go to a Honda dealer—I don't mean to knock Honda, but he'll try to sell you a snowblower, a lawn mower, a motorcycle—it's kind of like your center for internal-combustion engines. You go into a Harley dealership, and it's nothing but motorcycles, it's a world of motorcycles. I think that's a big difference. And if that guy who's your dealer is out riding with you on Saturday morning, going up for doughnuts and coffee, the store becomes kind of the center for motorcycling activity. Of course, he sells more stuff that way, which makes him happy, and the customers get to know him by his first name."

It's not like selecting a car dealer, where all you care about is price and maybe convenience of location. Harley owners will often ride 25 or 30 miles out of their way in order to do business and schmooze with a particular Harley dealer with whom they feel especially compatible.

Harley-Davidson Country

Doing business with your Harley dealer is an ongoing experience, because it includes shopping for Harley-Davidson MotorClothes and other paraphernalia. Peripheral sales represent an important profit center for both company and dealers. As Keefe admits, "It's fun to wear big black boots and black leather jackets and helmets and goggles. It's fun to dress up."

The oversized 60-page catalog of MotorClothes (which are available only at the dealer's showroom) contains much, much more than just jackets and boots and helmets. It goes on and on—chaps and denim vests and pullovers and socks and gauntlets and kids' clothes. There are hip bags and shoulder bags and shaving kits and hats, jewelry and mugs and watches, sunglasses and collectibles and Christmas cards. It's almost like forming your own country.

The Japanese motorcycle manufacturers have tried to do all of the things that have contributed to Harley-Davidson's spectacular success, including the rallies and the clubs and the demo rides, but have not been able to do them as well. Says Keefe, "I would like to see them do better. The better they do, the better we'll do. We could certainly use more motorcyclists, so I would welcome their success. Their problem is that they still look at it as a business, which of course we do too. But we also look at it as fun and a *passion* and kind of our reason for living."

A *passion!* (Italics are ours.) Perhaps, if one word can best describe what is needed to go beyond marketing—even beyond MaxiMarketing—to confound the competition, it is bringing genuine passion to your "Caring and Daring" initiatives.

Not every marketer has the good fortune to be charged with selling such a fun product as a Harley-Davidson motorcycle. But no matter what business you are in, you and your own company can find inspiration in the Harley story—a powerful example of the payoff from a corporate commitment to passionate involvement in everything from product development to employee morale to customer and dealer relationships.

At Harley-Davidson, once again, we see the effect of "Super-Synergy"—the interaction of all the components of the marketing process and actions that go beyond the usual. The management interacting with the dealers and the customers. The dealers interacting with the customers and the management. The mystique in the advertising helping to promote the sale of the MotorClothes and paraphernalia—and the merchandise, much of it logotyped, helping to promote the mystique. The local chapters, with their dealer-sponsored rides and events, bringing owners to the dealer and stimulating the sale of Harley-Davidson clothing and accessories—and owners walking and riding around in their Harley-Davidson gear influencing their friends to become part of this dashing clan.

Looking back at what the Harley-Davidson management has achieved in one turbulent decade, there is much to admire. At the top of the list, we would put their willingness to take risks, to learn from mistakes, and relentlessly to pursue the corporate vision of rare harmony between the company and its customers.

Perhaps what is most impressive is the way in which they have made the purchase of the product the beginning of the real relationship rather than the end of the selling process.

Their customer database is not simply an excuse to send out periodic mailings and promotions. It is a launching pad for bringing together everybody who cares about the motorcycle-riding experience and for reinforcing the joys of HOG membership.

Harley-Davidson has gone far beyond what most companies think the new one-to-one marketing is about—and the results show what can happen when the full potential is realized.

5

LEGO Conquers the U.S.A., Brick by Brick

For an earlier generation, the familiar modular toy of childhood was Tinker Toys. Out of a large cylindrical box spilled multi-holed wooden spools and quarter-inch wooden dowels that could be joined together in an almost infinite number of ways to form carts, windmills, crude animals and people, and so on.

Tinker Toys have survived, but just barely. They tended to be a onetime purchase. To an easily bored child, the novelty soon wore off. There was a limit to what you could do with Tinker Toys, and the final construction was not very representational.

Recently, by searching the shelves of a large Toys 'R' Us store, we were able to locate one lonely Tinker Toys cylindrical carton, filled with spools and dowels now made of colored plastic.

But in 1949, a new kind of modular toy was born that has literally conquered the world of toys. It is sold in nearly 670,000 shops in some 125 countries. Over 300 million children around the world have played with these little objects. A statistician with nothing better to do has calculated that the world's children spend some 5 billion hours a year with them. Worldwide sales are estimated to be $1.7 billion. In an industry driven by short-lived fads, the manufacturer has had, as we write this, 19 consecutive years of growth.

We are talking about the array of products built around the ubiquitous, irresistible LEGO© Brand building bricks.

In the United States, within the last two decades the LEGO Company has gone from being found in 30 percent of all homes with children under 14 to 7 out of 10 homes.

LEGO Systems, Inc., the company's U.S. division, has been experiencing a steady compounded growth averaging 15 percent a year. The company is satisfied with that, and you would be too if you felt in your bones, as they do, that this growth was destined to continue. "I can feel it," we were told by Richard Garvey, the marketing director. "The brand is growing like an amoeba."

The word "amoeba" was aptly chosen. For one of the things that struck us repeatedly as we examined the entire American operation is that it is like a living organism. Each part, each activity, supports and in turn is supported by all of the others. We were astonished and impressed by how The LEGO Company is so rich in so many innovative manifestations of a "Caring and Daring" corporate culture.

If you are an investor, you would do well to buy stock in this company if you could. But you can't. It is still a privately owned family business based in Denmark.

The success of the U.S. company is intertwined with the global strategy of the parent company, The LEGO Group. Both must be examined to fully understand and to fully appreciate the LEGO miracle.

Together they have exhibited a whole palette of brand-building components:

- Long-range vision of an ever-expanding marketplace presence
- Daring to carry consumer involvement far beyond the purchase of the product
- Obsession with quality in manufacturing and service
- Devotion to dialogue and listening to the customer
- Identification by name and address, and profiling, of the best customers
- Genuine caring about people, children, and the environment

It all adds up to something for which we have coined the

phrase "Super-Synergy"—a synergistic blend of technology, methodology, and strategic planning in which each separate activity or product in the marketing system supports and strengthens the others.

Ole Kirk's Passionate Belief

The LEGO Company was founded in the Danish village of Billund by a Danish carpenter, Ole Kirk Christiansen, the grandfather of the current president, Kjeld Kirk Kristiansen. It was 1932, and Ole Kirk and his few employees had no joinery and cabinetry work. So he turned them to making toys. He named his toys LEGO, from the Danish words "leg godt," meaning "play well." (Happily and coincidentally, it turned out that "LEGO" also means "I put together" in Latin.)

Ole Kirk was a man who apparently held a passionate, deeply felt belief that "The best is not good enough for children." It is a view that profoundly influences The LEGO Company's corporate thinking right up to the present time.

Injection-molded plastics made their appearance after World War II. As a result, in 1949, the company was able to introduce the first binding brick, with studs on top that made it possible for them to be easily snapped together or pulled apart.

LEGO bricks were not a dramatic instant success. The public was slow to accept toys made of inexpensive molded plastic instead of good, old-fashioned, tooled wood.

The big breakthrough came in 1958, with the introduction of a brick with studs on top and tubes underneath. This provided greater versatility. Just six 8-stud bricks could be put together in 103 million different ways! The new design also provided greater stability, and made possible structures almost literally of any size and shape. (The current world's record for the highest LEGO brick structure is a tower built in Switzerland in August of 1992. It was a tower 20.61 meters high, about the height of a seven-story building.)

Sales took off. By the end of the 1950s, LEGO bricks had become one of the most popular toys in Europe.

An early reason for the LEGO success was their fierce commitment to producing a quality product. The company was practicing Total Quality Management long before it became fashionable to do so. This was prompted not only by the corporate creed but also by the product requirements. The brick's uncanny way of snapping together and pulling apart, known as "clutch power," is the result of a painstaking manufacturing process that is legendary in the toy industry. The allowable variation in the diameters of studs and tubes is only 0.02 mm or about 0.00089 inch. The molds are made of hardened steel and polished to a high sheen with diamond dust.

The U.S. company president, Peter Eio, told us that five years earlier, they had only 600 rejects per million units. Now they were down to a mere 30 per million. Their goal: zero defects.

They don't farm out anything in the manufacturing process, not even the packaging. In that way they control the quality of everything directly.

Creating an Entire World, Brick by Brick

It took a visionary company to decide to build a whole theme park that would include breathtaking recreations of villages, animals, ships, trains, the Parthenon, the space shuttle Columbia, etc., all fashioned out of 42 million of those little tiny bricks. A scale model of Mount Rushmore, made from 1.5 million bricks, had to be assembled by crane.

Since LEGOLAND© Park opened in 1968 in Billund, it has become the most popular tourist attraction in Denmark outside of Copenhagen. More than 20 million adults and children have passed through its gates. Everywhere in the park, along with the exhibits and rides and other attractions, there are millions of LEGO bricks to play with.

Now the company is planning to open a theme park outside London in 1996 and one in the United States in 1999, each to cost an estimated $100 million. This sum is even more impressive when you consider that all LEGO development is self-financed.

But by this time management has enough experience with the original LEGOLAND Park to know that one theme park, apart from its stand-alone profitability, is easily equal to five years' worth of paid advertising in its effect on brand preference and sales.

From False Start to Overwhelming Brand Acceptance

The LEGO Company's first foray into the U.S. market was not encouraging. By 1961, The LEGO Group was still a relatively small and undercapitalized company. The only U.S. avenue they chose was a licensing agreement with Samsonite, the luggage manufacturer. But Samsonite merely sold the bricks by the pound, doing little to package or market them, and over ten years managed to chalk up no more than $4 million in sales all told. As a result, The LEGO Company in 1972 bought back the license and undertook to build sales in the United States with their own efforts.

"We had our work cut out for us, and it was definitely an uphill battle," says Garvey. "In the U.S., the LEGO approach was a questionable concept. Kids were simply not asking their parents for it."

The strategy they adopted was to build a brand franchise through advertising and relationship-building activities, and to develop line extensions which would bracket young people from the pram almost all the way to the high school prom. They started with zero brand identity in 1972 and now are one of the best-known product lines in the United States, according to Total Research Brand Equity.

Garvey believes that it is urgently important to establish a strong brand before the outbreak of the fast-approaching video revolution, when every household will be able to receive 500 TV channels or more. "Once you reach that point," he says, "if you don't have a brand image, it's going to be almost impossible to create one."

Garvey came to The LEGO Company from Quaker Oats, bringing with him a packaged-goods marketer's ingrained respect for the importance of establishing brand equity. He says the company won't hire marketing people from the toy industry because toy people are too interested in products and not enough in the marketing process.

This thinking has stood The LEGO Company in good stead in fighting off competition. In the 1980s they lost legal battles to prevent other toy companies from making interlocking blocks, but have still managed to maintain unquestioned leadership. Says Garvey, "Lots of me-too products come and go....A new one comes, another one dies off, replaced by another. But competition has always been a good experience for us. It makes us examine what we are doing."

"What Business Are You In?"

The self-examination process is an important element in LEGO's steady growth. It has forced them to think about what business they are in. In *MaxiMarketing* we talked about the importance of "The Law of the Situation," a term invented in 1904 by Mary Parker Follett, the first U.S. management consultant. This commandment requires your company to ask itself, "*What business are we in?*" Mary Follett's client was a company that thought it was in the window-shade business. But citing The Law of the Situation, she persuaded them that they were actually in the light-control business, expanding their horizon immensely.

The LEGO Company considers that it is not in the toy business but rather in the child-development business. This has already led to some important activities and line extensions, while others are still on the drawing board.

Future expansion might include, for example, modular children's furniture so kids could change their rooms around as easily as they reassemble their LEGO bricks.

Then there is the possibility of nationwide LEGO Child Care Centers. The prototype, established for LEGO employees and other local parents at the company's U.S. headquarters in Enfield, Connecticut, combines typical infant, toddler, and preschool care with a program for school-age children that permits them to build working LEGO models and control them with Apple IIgs computers.

LEGO management understands that child development encompasses the child in all of us! So, as you might expect, they have successfully tested a line of LEGO construction sets designed especially for senior citizens. As the population ages, it could become a significant growth segment.

The New Way to Build Brand Equity

An important key to the company's U.S. success in brand building is that they understand, as too many brand marketers do not, that acceptance of a product or service is no longer crucially dependent upon what you communicate in your media advertising. *It is everything your company says and does that touches the lives and hearts and minds of your prospects and customers.*

In the United States, LEGO Systems is currently spending about $22 million a year on advertising, heavy for a toy company. But this is only one part of the living organism of everything they do—the myriad of interactive involvements.

What is significant is that each component builds interest in and supports all of the other parts—just as your body's heart pumps blood to the brain and the brain sends nerve signals to the muscles, including those of the heart.

The DUPLO® Preschool Line creates an early familiarity with and affection for LEGO bricks that paves the way for continued interest and brand loyalty all the way through childhood to the early teen years, when devout "LEGO MANIACS" are ready to tackle the highly sophisticated Technic line.

The DACTA® Line for Schools wins educational respect and credibility for the company and its products in a nonexploitive way while expanding its product line.

The LEGO® Theme Parks, existing and planned, excite a child's imagination with the limitless possibilities of LEGO brick construction while also serving as a valuable profit center. It's another example of how "Bringing People Together" in an unusual way puts the product into a category all its own.

The LEGO Shop-at-Home Catalog, offering direct sale of some 200 products, scoops up additional sales from buyers too busy to go shopping or frustrated by incomplete store inventory, and undoubtedly stirs young users to dream of their next LEGO construction project.

The LEGO catalog is one more example of how a MaxiMarketing winner can maximize distribution by adding the direct-order channel to their saturation coverage of retail outlets.

The LEGO Builders Club was launched in 1989. In-box literature and outgoing mail offer membership to "LEGO MANIACS" for $7.95 a year. It is believed the club now has 100,000 members, a respectable but not huge number, but typical of the company philosophy of growing "The LEGO Way"—developing an outstanding service and letting interested people find their way to it in due time.

Club members get a newsletter, a magazine, contests, offers of special merchandise not available in stores, even a special mailing of Happy Birthday greetings and offers at the member's birthday time.

Keep in mind the reinforcement at work in these member mailings, the synergistic interaction with other components of the LEGO marketing system. The Winter 1992 mailing to club members accomplishes all this:

1. Advertises the LEGO Imagination Center at the Mall of America (see page 111) on the front cover of the Club magazine, *Brick Kicks*
2. Displays photos of "members' masterpieces" inside and invites members to send in a photo of their own impressive LEGO creation
3. Announces new LEGO toys, thus stimulating store traffic
4. Contains a members-only mail-order offer of a Sky Patrol set *not available in stores*
5. Calls attention to the special opportunity to collect free LEGO Stunt Club models by buying special marked boxes of Kellogg's Froot Loops, Apple Jacks, and Smacks breakfast cereals, and includes a coupon good for 50 cents off a Kellogg's cereal purchase.

In this one mailing you can see how LEGO uses their one-to-one relationship with their core market—those willing to pay $7.95 for membership—to demonstrate a commitment to bringing fun and new challenges into the lives of dedicated "LEGO MANIACS."

This is not your usual hesitant, toe-in-the-water club put together by marketers going through the motions of "staying in touch" with end-users. It is an extension of the passion for pleasing the customer at the heart of LEGO's involvement with the heavy users who become LEGO advocates.

The LEGO Imagination Center at Mall of America, in Bloomington, Minnesota, located in a dramatic four-story courtyard, is an open structure composed of giant "LEGO" beams, columns, and arches. It contains large models of dinosaurs, spaceships, and circus performers; play areas where children can build their own LEGO models.

The Imagination Center also is the location of LEGO's first retail store. It is a great success even though it was not part of the original plan for the exhibition center. When they considered adding the store at the last minute, many within the company opposed the idea because of concern about retailers' reaction. But time has vindicated the decision. We were told by Peter Eio, "All LEGO retailers in the immediate surrounding area are experiencing sizeable increases in LEGO sales."

Eio sees the store and mall exhibition as "working just like advertising. It says to people in concrete terms—here is what you can do. It breaks through the clutter of the marketplace to 40 million visitors a year."

Copromotions with carefully selected, prestigious promotional partners. Companies like Kellogg's and McDonald's offer LEGO toys as sales incentives, provide free advertising for the LEGO brand, and feed new names and addresses into the LEGO database.

LEGO Model Designers, "big kids at play," are full-time staff professionals who bring the skills of architecture and sculpture to the creation of breathtaking LEGO models for permanent and traveling displays. Their "real" creations advertise the potential of LEGO bricks as powerfully as any promotion or media advertising possibly could.

LEGO WEAR apparel for kids, all bearing the LEGO trademark, was conceived when parents started calling up asking where they could buy the clothes worn by "Jack the LEGO MANIAC" in the LEGO TV spots. Here again is the dynamic of mutual support, with the toy brand supporting the apparel sales and the apparel helping to advertise the brand.

The LEGO Database of LEGO customers and prospects is destined to play a key role in the company's future growth. It is fed by the variety of advertising and promotional activities that capture names and addresses, and as it grows, can serve as a springboard for an expanded line of toys and for introducing new nontoy products. As new toys from all manufacturers come roaring down the spillway each year, many retailers simply may not have the shelf space to carry a full inventory of all LEGO toys and the database will become a vital selling channel into the home.

To market the DUPLO line for preschoolers, The LEGO Company prepared and distributed, through giveaways and magazine bind-ins, some 13 million copies of an eight-page parents' guide to interactive play and a coupon good for a child guidance video. Parents could either mail in the coupon with a proof-of-purchase label or get the video free at any of some 500 Toys 'R' Us stores if they made a minimum $10 DUPLO toy purchase. Around 50,000 videos were distributed in this way and the DUPLO database got an infusion of new names.

Said Kerry Phelan, director of marketing for the DUPLO brand, "We are looking at direct marketing to represent a bigger part of our marketing mix in the long term. If we start building a database for children at the DUPLO age, we can keep a dialogue with them throughout the whole system of play."

And Garvey said to us, "I've told my marketing people that in 10 years a full 50 percent of the advertising budget will be directed to direct marketing."

The LEGO "Colloquy" with Customers is cited by President Peter Eio as an important part of the company's success. LEGO builders love to tell The LEGO Company about their triumphs, and management loves to hear from them. Many LEGO users take photos of their creations and proudly mail in the photos. Each month the company receives "tens of thousands" of spontaneous letters, and each letter-writer gets a customized reply. Direct involvement with the end-user is the way of life at LEGO.

Says Garvey, "We have ombudsmen to reach out to customers. We love complaints. If we don't know something's wrong, how will we know to fix it? We try to make it as easy as possible for customers to communicate with us. We have a staff of 20 consumer correspondents completely dedicated to and at the service of the consumer. We consider it a key element in the marketing mix."

LEGO Building Competitions are held in many countries. Young builders in three age groups send in photos of their constructions, and the winners are invited to compete directly at regional and national competitions. National winners usually get a trip to Billund, Denmark, to compete with other national winners.

In 1992, 32 children from 11 countries competed for the "LEGO World Cup" titles. Just imagine all the free publicity this program generates in hometown newspapers. For LEGO, the "Get Real" key to business success just comes naturally.

The LEGO Promise to Planet Earth, a program to practice the three *Rs*—Reduce, Reuse, and Recycle—is another reflection of the sense of caring that seems to permeate the corporate culture. It begins with the product itself, the little plastic bricks that are endlessly usable and reusable, never wear out, and can be passed on to younger members of the family. The company works constantly to reduce the amount of paper and plastic in the packaging, and does as much of its printing as possible on recycled paper using biodegradable vegetable inks. Throughout the company, employees collect, sort, and recycle paper, metal, and plastic. A computerized energy management system automatically shuts down light, heat, and air conditioning when they are not being used.

A "Green Wave" Committee, made up of LEGO employees from all over the world, was created to explore new ways the company can do its share to protect and preserve the planet. A widely distributed educational poster by LEGO Systems combines good citizenship and good business. It suggests 20 ways to build a better planet and also sets forth The LEGO Promise.

The LEGO Prize for Improving Conditions for Children (another demonstration of caring!) is an international award that seeks to recognize extraordinary efforts and contributions toward improving the conditions under which children live and grow. It is now worth 1 million Danish kroner annually, awarded to one or more candidates proposed by LEGO companies from all over the world.

By now you can begin to see what it takes to gain 70 percent penetration of households in America for a simple little toy. What it takes is all the quality built into the product and, as important, all the intangibles that fulfill the ultimate potential of what the product can become in the imagination of the children and their parents.

"The Next Disney?"

The provocative headline on a story in *Adweek's Marketing Week* about LEGO Systems in the spring of 1992 read: "The Next Disney." To many it may have seemed like an absurdly audacious claim.

But when you see how this MaxiMarketing winner dares to get involved with customers in so many innovative ways, in the United States and around the world, you might begin to think anything is possible.

Talk about growing great oaks from little acorns! The smallest LEGO basic building brick is no bigger than an acorn. But in large part, because management understands the power of breaking through the noise of the marketplace with an overwhelming succession of bold, caring initiatives, this little plastic acorn has grown and will continue to grow into a mighty worldwide business empire.

6
The House of Seagram: Into MaxiMarketing and Beyond

When we wrote *MaxiMarketing* in the mid-1980s, we outlined a new approach to marketing that we felt was necessary to meet the challenge of the glaring inefficiencies of mass marketing. But when we looked for examples of what we called MaxiMarketing, we really couldn't find any advertisers who were doing everything that we advocated. It was too early in the individualized marketing revolution that was just beginning to take place.

In order to illustrate what we were talking about, we had to construct a kind of multicolor patchwork quilt. We cited a variety of examples of companies that were doing different pieces of the new marketing and doing them well. From these fragments, we were able to piece together a complete picture of what we then saw as the nine-step MaxiMarketing process.

But even as we wrote, there were a few companies that were quietly getting ready to steal a march on their competitors by making a wholehearted commitment to this new way of thinking about the marketplace. One of them was The House of Seagram.

In 1986, Richard Shaw, at that time marketing vice president of the 375 Spirits division of Seagram, wanted a new challenge and saw a great opportunity in the rising tide of direct-relationship marketing.

He got started by sending a mailing for Glenlivet scotch to outside lists. It was "a disaster." But it was a beginning. He had taken his first step on the learning curve. As direct-marketing veterans could have told him, when you are doing accountable advertising, you can learn as much from your failures as from your successes.

Seagram started putting together its own in-house database of the names, addresses, and brand preferences of consumers of alcoholic beverages, so that the company could target by mail users of their own and competing brands.

By 1988, Shaw was appointed to head a small department at the newly organized House of Seagram division, referred to modestly as the "direct mail" department, and mailings were going directly to consumers to promote retail sales for 12 Seagram brands.

By 1990, when we wrote *The Great Marketing Turnaround,* Richard Shaw was the vice president for direct marketing and the Seagram database had grown to 6 million names.

Now, as we write this in 1993, the Seagram database has grown to 10 million names. That's close to 25 percent of the drinking households in the country. Annual Seagram expenditure for direct, one-to-one interaction with end-users is approaching $10 million. A significant portion of the Glenlivet ad budget is now devoted to direct and interactive marketing, and each year the results "keep getting better."

Seagram's daringly successful moves into one-to-one marketing obviously are not the work of Richard Shaw alone or entirely of the direct marketing department for that matter.

At Seagram, management believes that direct marketing is basic to marketing communications and it is treated as seriously as the company treats the general advertising so vital to building brand image.

In all of the programs described on the following pages, the product group has been integral to the development of the thinking process leading up to the direct marketing campaign.

Product management is responsible for each brand and the marketing communications team works with the product group to make each new database application happen.

Going "Direct" Goes Worldwide

Today, Shaw is vice president of marketing communications with his "direct" responsibilities folded into overall brand activity. To carry out the corporate management commitment to establishing a network of shared direct marketing experience worldwide, Shaw travels the world working with the marketing team in each region and key country affiliate. He has been given dotted-line responsibility on the organization chart for Seagram one-to-one marketing development in the Asia Pacific, European, African, and Latin American regions.

Seagram is determined to rapidly expand database-driven marketing to their operations outside the United States. In each country, the Seagram subsidiary will decide what strategic information is needed for their own database in order to develop the most effective local marketing campaigns.

As far as we know, this is the first multinational consumer marketer with a coordinated corporate effort to move toward individualized marketing wherever they have a presence in the world. And it is the first example we have seen of an organizational structure set to make it happen.

Of all the companies we have examined or heard about, what Seagram has accomplished and is currently working on comes closest to doing everything—and more—that we talked about in *MaxiMarketing.*

- We wrote about the importance of *targeting,* and Seagram has singled out and communicated with users of competing brands with uncanny precision.
- We urged seizing advantage of new *media* opportunities, and Seagram has blazed a trail in using the established media in startling new ways.
- We advocated maximized *accountability,* and Seagram man-

agement can tell you with considerable accuracy the cost of acquiring a new user from a promotion and the precise date for the anticipated return of the investment.

- We stressed the importance of *awareness* advertising that would appeal to the whole brain—both the right brain which controls creativity and intuition and the left hemisphere which controls logic and language. Seagram's direct mail has brilliantly combined the elegance of high-style image advertising with the smooth readability and persuasiveness of the best direct-response advertising.
- We proposed maximized *activation,* which would involve the consumer without using brand-cheapening discount promotion. Although Seagram's programs have done some cash rebate offers, more often they have offered artful rewards and memberships which strengthen the brand image.
- We explored the *synergy* in multiple-duty advertising. Today, Seagram direct mail and some of its print advertising does triple duty. It deepens a favorable brand image. It induces a response which leads to cultivation of the relationship with the consumer. And it feeds customer information into the in-house database, by including questionnaires on the response card as often as possible. Some of the direct mail also performs a fourth duty: it obtains the names of friends of the recipients.
- We pointed to *linkage* which builds a bridge between the advertising and the sale by sending more advertising to interested inquirers, and today media advertising which calls for direct-mail follow-up is an essential part of the House of Seagram marketing program.
- We said that greater sales could be achieved from combining *Brand Image* and *Database Development* than either alone could achieve, and Seagram has managed to maximize both database marketing efficiency while enhancing image-building efficiency in its marketing programs.

The Break with the Past

To appreciate what Seagram has accomplished, it is important to place what has happened in an overall historical perspective of liquor advertising and promotion.

One good definition of a parity product in food and drink is that if you were blindfolded, you couldn't tell the difference between one brand and another. (Years ago, *The Wall Street Journal* conducted a blindfold test of soft drinks with a panel of consumers. Not only could many of the panelists not taste the difference between Coke and Pepsi—some couldn't even correctly distinguish a cola drink from ginger ale!)

In many categories, popularly priced mass-market distilled spirits pretty much meet this definition. As a result, liquor companies have tended to seek a common way out of the predicament of parity products—namely, they use the power of clever associations and fashionability to create a brand preference in the consumer's mind.

Over the years this has produced an endless stream of vacuous—but, nonetheless, sometimes successful—creative efforts by advertising agencies to make a certain liquor brand stick in the bottom of your mind and at the top of your list.

Increasingly, however, there are signs that the public is becoming jaded and bored and that this traditional method of brand-building is losing its effectiveness.

Image Advertising Still Works—Sometimes

Of course, the ways of popular fads and fashions are mysterious, and now and then controlled lightning still does strike.

A prime recent example is Absolut vodka. In 1980, Absolut was a tiny vodka brand selling about 12,000 cases a year. They launched a series of magazine ads playing verbally and visually on the word "Absolut." Recalled a company executive, "We weren't selling just another vodka. *We wanted to make this a fashionable product, like perfume.*" [Italics ours.] Each year there were more clever variations, as well as expensive talked-about novelty ads with a built-in music box or snowflakes or a jigsaw puzzle. By 1990, Absolut was selling 2.7 million cases a year and had become the No. 1 imported vodka.

But for every success such as Absolut, there are probably several dozen liquor campaigns that don't "move the needle" at all. Nonetheless, the ads keep running and the advertisers keep hoping that they will hit pay dirt.

Even Seagram has followed this path in advertising its major premium brands. Shaw concedes that it would be more difficult for direct marketing to "move the needle" on a major brand like Seagram's V.O.

Why? Because the further your sales move up to being a mass parity product, the more efficient mass advertising becomes. In other words, if almost everybody drinks either Coke or Pepsi, then advertising that blankets almost everybody is comparatively very efficient, with much less waste. There are other ways to approach these mass-market products using MaxiMarketing principles, but Shaw declined to comment on the specifics of what he has in mind at this time.

For Seagram's big-selling Extra Dry Gin, controlled lightening did strike in 1992. Seagram ran a very successful ad campaign based on sheer cleverness.* In a spoof of the theory of some academic critics of advertising that many ads have hidden subliminal images and messages, the ads asked, "Can you find the hidden pleasure in refreshing Seagram's Gin?" And the accompanying photo would show liquor swirling in a glass with a vague representational image to be glimpsed or imagined there if you looked closely enough.

It seems to have contributed to Seagram's gin selling 4.1 million cases that year, up 2.8 percent from the previous year, making it No. 3 in distilled spirits sales, while seven other brands in the top ten had flat sales that year.

But when it comes to selling pricey premium liquors that most people can't or won't pay a stiff sum for, or are not in the habit of drinking, then the efficiency of mass advertising falls off rapidly. Even in the glossiest upper-class magazine, too many advertising dollars are wasted on nonprospects. For example, only 6 percent of the adult population has had a glass of scotch within the last 30 days. So, at best, your potential sales may not be large enough to support an advertising campaign with enough insertions to make a sufficient dent in awareness among the small group of prospects.

*It is interesting to note, however, that even here, in a campaign that did not involve direct marketing or direct response at all, there was a distinct element of involvement—so often an important ingredient in advertising success today. The reader got involved in trying to detect the images hidden in the swirling liquor.

For maximum efficiency, you must focus on identified users. Since, overall, the market for distilled spirits is not growing but shrinking slightly, it means that your brand can grow only by locating and identifying drinkers of competing brands and winning them over.

Such a challenge is made to order for direct relationship marketing. But most premium brands have been slow to realize this. Richard Shaw saw the opportunity and has exploited it to the maximum.

He has moved "beyond MaxiMarketing" with guiding principles of his own, related to precepts stated or implied in our first book. These include:

- *Interaction deepens impression.* Most advertising is a one-way communication between an active sender (the advertiser) and a passive receiver (the consumer). But once you get the consumer to do something—make a call, send a card, make a choice—you have dug deeper into the consumer's consciousness. Or as Shaw puts it, *"Creating a cognitive action intensifies the impression."*

  Seagram received startling confirmation of this in a split test for Chivas Regal that included an interactive involvement device, an envelope—with a reply card inside—tipped onto the magazine page. Gallup Robinson research measured the PNR (proven name registration) effect of the ad with the interactive device and found that it was far more effective than the creative ad alone in registering awareness.
- *Less is more.* Highly targeted direct mail derived from knowledge of individual prospects and customers in a proprietary database is actually a way of getting more sales from smarter, more targeted advertising. Now, Shaw has pioneered in pushing this dynamic into magazine advertising in a revolutionary way, as you will see.
- *It pays to be unselfish.* Imagine helping your dealers advertise and sell brands that are *competing* with yours. Yes, that is what Seagram is now doing with its innovative dealer direct-mail program. Sounds crazy, but there's a method to the madness.
- *Response isn't everything.* At the time we wrote *MaxiMarketing,* we argued for the effect on the buying attitude of direct-mail

recipients who do not respond but are nonetheless favorably impressed. But that early in the one-to-one marketing revolution, not enough advertising research had been done to prove that we were right. Now Seagram has been able to substantiate that the awareness generated among all recipients of the mailing must be factored into the equation.

- *The lion can lie down with the lamb.* In many companies, the brand-image advertising advocates and the direct-response advertising advocates are at each other's throats. The image people don't want their beautiful ads spoiled by the addition of "horsey" 800 numbers and reply coupons. While, at the same time, the direct-response people hate to see money "wasted" on unmeasurable image-building advertising when it could be spent on responsive advertising and follow-up that locates and cultivates prospects identified by name, address, demographic profile, and buying behavior.

  The reality is that both camps have legitimate claims and interests. Shaw has developed ways to satisfy them both—to get cost-efficient responses from interactive ads and direct-mail pieces so elegant, so urbane, such a delight to the eye and mind that they are an image-maker's dream.

Due credit must be given to the superb creative work of the direct-response ad agencies Seagram has used: Bronner Slosberg Humphrey for Chivas Regal scotch, Crown Royal Canadian whisky, and Martell cognac, Ogilvy & Mather Direct for the Glenlivet (for which it won a DMA Gold Echo Award in 1989), and FCB Direct West for Mumm Cordon Rouge and Mumm Grand Cordon Champagnes.

Now that Seagram has addresses and profiles of 10 million liquor consumers, marketing management is finding it more cost-effective to bypass mass media altogether in promoting an expensive "limited-edition" product.

$100 Bottle of Champagne Free—Sort Of

For instance, in 1993, when the Seagram Classics Wine company wanted to promote the sale of its 1985 *tête de cuvée Mumm Grand*

Cordon Champagne, at $100 a bottle, the only advertising medium used was direct mail. But what direct mail!

The elegant mailing was sent to just 10,000 affluent prospects carefully selected from the database. Inside a gold-embossed, linen presentation case, the recipient found a signed, limited-edition serigraph interpretation of the Grand Cordon label, created by French artist Hélène Coty (a no-fooling fine artist, who happened also to be the agency's associate art director), and printed on museum-quality, acid-free, archival paper.

The accompanying letter, printed on vellum, imparted the glad tidings that a free bottle of this $100 champagne had been "set aside in your name, here in the cellars of Champagne Mumm." The only catch in this deft tongue-in-cheek offer was, of course, that you had to pick up your free bottle in person—in Reims, France. Or, if that was not convenient, you could send back a card for a list of nearby retailers where you could buy a bottle.

They expected perhaps 200 responses. According to a story in *The Wall Street Journal,* they got back nearly three times that many—and 170 people actually asked to have a free bottle held for them in Reims!

"Won't You Linger a Little Longer?"

These artful direct-to-the-home Seagram campaigns add something else that is new to liquor advertising. For want of a better phrase, we will call it the Linger Factor.

There is good reason to believe that the longer the consumer can be induced to linger with your advertising communication, the deeper the impression it will make. Brand-image liquor advertising has ranged all the way from one campaign where the copy consisted of just a single word—"Yes"—to extremes of cleverness and graphic association with fleeting images that go beyond almost any other advertising category. But the problem has been that today's sophisticated readers have better things to do than "ooh" and "aah" over advertising copy about a parity product.

We believe a significant accomplishment of Seagram's mailings to the individual user is that they have overcome this problem by giving the reader reasons for lingering longer, allowing the advertising impression to sink in deeper. All the skills in the copywriter's toolbox are used to snare and hold the reader for one minute...two minutes...three...four...five.

For instance, consider this letter in the royal purple envelope of The Society of the Crown, one of a series of mailings. It begins:

> Dear Friend:
>
> In the spring of 1939, Britain's King George VI and his Queen visited Canada. It was an historic occasion, since no reigning British monarch had ever before crossed the seas on such a journey.
>
> To mark the day, a very special bottle of whisky was presented to the royal couple.
>
> The bottle was nested in a rich purple pouch that closed with a golden drawstring. On the pouch was woven the image of a jeweled crown. The bottle was intricately cut with dozens of facets and corked with the carved replica of a second crown.
>
> But it was the whisky itself which made the gift truly fit for a king and his queen. The finest in all of Canada was what it had to be.
>
> And it was called Crown Royal.
>
> In the years that followed...

Do you see what we mean by the Linger Factor? Don't you want to keep reading? The mailing draws you in like a Venus's flytrap, and holds you until you swear you'll never settle for a different brand next time.

There is an embarrassment of riches in the panoply of marketing programs that Seagram has developed since 1986. We will focus on just three breakthrough programs that deserve special attention: the Crown Royal direct mail because of its pioneering use of predictive modeling and the New Marketing Math to stop wasting money on nonprospects; the precedent-shattering Seagram database-targeted magazine ad insertions; and the new program for dealers that is extending the benefits of accessing the Seagram database to retailers.

A Crowning Achievement: Making More, Spending Less

In Chapter 3 of *MaxiMarketing,* we constructed a theoretical model of a mailing plan for promotion of an expensive brand of liquor. We said that for mass-marketers accustomed to thinking in terms of reaching and influencing millions of magazine readers and television households, the traditionally small percentages of response from a targeted direct-mail effort may not seem worth the bother. But we predicted that in the new marketing, less would become more.

We showed how, once you had a viable marketing database, direct mail could be used to reach your competitor's customers profitably with an entirely new technique for calculating the return on the advertising expenditure.

In our hypothetical example, we pointed to four factors that set this new approach apart from the usual sales promotion mailing or advertising insertion. They were:

1. Zero waste circulation
2. Potent, persuasive, brand-advertising copy
3. Calculating the effect of the mailing not only on respondents but also on nonrespondents and friends of respondents over an extended period of time
4. Respondent data captured for addition to the database

In 1990, four years after we wrote about what we believed could happen, Seagram launched a direct-mail campaign that turned our hypothesis into a resounding reality. The product being promoted was Crown Royal, the most important profit maker of the House of Seagram in the United States.

Seagram decided to launch a carefully researched campaign aimed at winning over 3500 users of competitive Canadian whiskies and of Jack Daniels. All four factors we cited in our theoretical MaxiMarketing model were employed in the Crown Royal program.

Three different mailings were sent to the same 150,000 names over a five-month period, all designed to tempt users to try Crown Royal. The first mailing enclosed a whimsical tongue-in-cheek modern fairy tale and offered a pair of Crown Royal on-the-rocks glasses as a premium for proof-of-purchase. The second used a playing-cards theme, and offered two sets of Crown Royal playing cards. The third mailing was a self-mailer with a sweepstakes offering a chance to win a stay at your own "castle" in the Bahamas, Acapulco, or Bermuda, as well as a pair of free highball glasses. The mailings were a dazzling demonstration of image enhancement, response stimulation, and "cognitive action" that "intensifies impression."

Using the most reputable pre- and post-research techniques, Seagram measured the "slippage" as well as the number who responded. ("Slippage" is their name for the recipients who did not respond to the mailing offer but who are directly influenced to make a purchase by the mailing.) They found that for every person who redeemed the offer, there were two additional buyers as a result of the mailing. In our theoretical model prepared four years earlier, we had a more modest "guesstimate" of only *one* nonrespondent buyer for each person who responded.

Response rates were only the beginning of the result analysis. As recommended in our example in *MaxiMarketing,* Seagram measured the long-term buying experience of each convert. Management wanted to know the answer to that all-important question: What is a new customer worth? They now have the answer.

The final conversion rate (the percentage of triers who became repeat buyers) of 54 percent and the actual number of bottles sold per person was incorporated into the breakeven analysis. As predicted in our model, the direct-mail campaign also did wonders to increase awareness of the brand among the 150,000 prospects who received the mailings and did not respond. The House of Seagram researchers showed unaided brand awareness among nonredeemers going from 14 to 23 percent—quite a result for a series of just three mailings. Among these consumers, the program reinforced Crown Royal's favorable brand image in the areas of high quality, prestige, "giftability," and impressive packaging. The Crown Royal direct-mail recipients were all solid-gold prospects, which meant that the dramatic improvement in their unaided brand awareness was also solid gold.

Also as expected, the impact on friends of respondents was an important factor in the overall success of the campaign. Shaw reports that lists generated from referral names perform at three to four times the norm. The goal of the campaign was to win over 3500 of the Royal Crown competitive brand users and to earn back the entire investment in the mailing within two years. When all the numbers were in from the test campaign, Seagram had attracted more than 3500 new customers, and the breakeven point was reached in 2.3 years.

The usual mass-marketer tiptoeing into individualized marketing would have stopped there and called it a good day. But not Seagram. The following year, 1991, Seagram went beyond the steps outlined in our hypothetical example by applying an exotic new capability just beginning to fulfill its promise when *MaxiMarketing* was published in 1986. Seagram created a mathematical response model that produced a list of the specific names and addresses of those people in the database who were most likely to respond to future offers and go on to become some of their best customers.

Armed with this refined ability to stop wasting money on non-prospects, the team set out to convert an additional 5000 users of competitive Canadian whiskies and of Jack Daniels to the Crown Royal franchise and get an improved payback outcome.

Using predictive modeling, the database names were classified into 20 groups arranged from the greatest likelihood of response down to the least likely. "The focus of the mailing was to target the highest scoring cells, groups 1–4," Shaw told us. "Representatives of groups 5–20 were included, in modest quantity, in order to validate the performance of the model."

Following this model, Seagram was able to select 150,000 well-targeted prospects for the second round of testing. The 1991 program called for mailing with minor revisions the same three packages used in 1990, and the goal was to double the response rate of about 3.5 percent achieved the first time.

The series of three mailings in 1991 to the top four cells pulled an astonishing 8 percent response, actually slightly *better than double the previous year's result* and just about what the predictive model had forecast. The new era of addressable, accountable advertising foreseen in the final chapter of *MaxiMarketing* five years before was now the operational norm for the House of Seagram.

When Seagram factored in the 2 to 1 "slippage" ratio previously established, the actual number of converts (respondents converted to steady customers) produced by the mailing soared to almost 25 percent. The 1991 campaign result surpassed the breakeven levels necessary to pay out in two years by a comfortable margin. When the Crown Royal direct-mail program was further extended and refined in 1992, it achieved an astonishing nine-month payback rate.

Today, The House of Seagram has an ever-growing database and ever-increasing sophistication in how to analyze and use the knowledge accumulated over the years. The investment in a daring new one-on-one targeting strategy—while competitors continued spending their communications dollars on the same old, wasteful, scattershot media buys—has given Seagram a decisive marketing advantage.

In recent years, Shaw told us, Seagram has sold off many of their lower profit-margin brands to follow a corporate strategy of focusing on their premium, most profitable, brands. Many of these famous-name brands have experienced record growth in just three years.

This is especially impressive in view of the dampening trend of overall reduction in distilled spirits sales—what Shaw calls the "environmental and cultural issues."* Each year, since the mid-1970s, fewer people participate in social drinking of distilled spirits (liquor) and there is less consumption per capita.

*It is also impressive to see how Seagram has dealt with its social responsibility in this new cultural environment.

At the start of the 1992 holiday season, Seagram placed a heavyweight media schedule behind a blunt ad suggesting that drinking responsibly sometimes means "not drinking at all."

Seagram has been running so-called responsible drinking ads since 1934 and is a big supporter of the Century Council, a group of brewers and distillers who work with cities on discouraging underage drinking and driving when drinking. This corporate policy is in sharp contrast to tobacco manufacturers continuing to maintain there is no connection between smoking and cancer, despite the weight of 40,000 studies supporting a contrary view.

Advertising professionals working at the general agency or with the pacesetting Seagram database operation can feel good about the balanced approach. It is also worth mentioning that there are genuine differences of opinion among medical scientists over whether drinking in moderation is harmful to your health or actually sometimes helpful; but there is no difference of opinion in the medical establishment conclusion that smoking, in any amount, can be harmful.

I Want You, Dear Reader, and Only You

Early in the 1980s, R. R. Donnelley & Sons fired the first shot of the revolution in the way the magazines of the future will be assembled and distributed. They introduced a method of selective computer-controlled collating called *selectronic binding* that made it possible for different individual readers to receive different mixes of editorial and advertising pages.

Farm Journal was the first big user, customizing its editorial content and advertising pages to the special needs and interests of each type of farm operation, based on information provided by the subscribers. Before long, issues of *Farm Journal* were coming out in as many as thousands of different versions. The computer would tell the high speed press what to print in each copy.

Soon a few other magazines—*American Baby, Games, Modern Maturity*—experimented with customized advertising content. They were followed at the beginning of the 1990s by Time Warner magazines, *Time, Sports Illustrated, People,* and *Money,* offering to sell advertising bound only into copies going into a certain subset of their subscriber base. These selections were based on databits about the subscribers in the magazine's own database.

In 1992, Richard Shaw persuaded Seagram management to seek to move selective binding a step further. Seagram would go to certain desirable magazines and say, in effect, "Yes, we want to buy and pay for advertising exposure only to selected readers of your magazine—but it must be *our own selection* of names, not your 'ready-made' selections. Now you tell us what is the minimum circulation you are willing to sell us—what premium you are going to charge—and what extra production costs we will have to absorb."

It took a year to pull it off. Only a marketer with Shaw's persistence, vision, and enthusiasm could have accomplished it. Some of the magazines refused to consider the idea, or grudgingly offered only a limited test. Shaw had to put together a task force including representatives of the Seagram ad agencies involved and overcome the predictable resistance to this new way of thinking.

Working with a consultant, Myles Megdal of Marketing Information Technologies, Seagram management matched the Seagram file with names in the subscriber databases of the magazines that agreed to try it by using a predictive modeling equation based on a proprietary system. They employed a *GAINS* chart—descending to each new level of a less likely match until they were able to find enough desirable subscribers to make the insertion worthwhile within the minimum circulation set by the publication.

They were then able to put together a multimillion-dollar buy, using seven magazines in the first year of implementation. Three brands were advertised. The creative part was the same as what they would have used in any magazine campaign. The only variable was the selective binding. They purchased 36 percent of the circulation of one magazine and reached 88 percent of the target group. Ordinarily, they would have had to purchase 100 percent of circulation to reach approximately the same target.

Shaw estimated that he got a four-times lift in efficiency, greatly exceeding in value the additional cost per thousand charge by the publication for binding selectively. He had effectively found a way to reach his best prospects with three advertising insertions for what it had formerly cost to reach them once. For the first time, the efficiency of direct mail's ability to select an individual prospect had been combined with the much lower cost of media advertising.

You would expect a mad rush of cost-conscious advertisers to follow in Seagram's footsteps. But, despite the lightning changes taking place in communications, the mill of the gods of marketing still grind exceedingly slow. It will probably take years before other major advertisers fully realize the significance of this development and put to use their own prospect-customer database to make selective binding in print media work for them too.

Nevertheless, the handwriting is on the wall. Sooner or later many other advertisers will feel compelled to follow the trail Seagram has blazed. They, too, will start telling magazine publishers that they want to stop wasting money on nonprospects and to start paying only for advertising sent to real prospects in their product category.

Opening the Database to Dealers

In 1992, Seagram took another giant step. It gave liquor retailers "access" to the names in its database.

It is a proven fact that one way to promote directly to individual users and help your dealers at the same time is to provide the dealers with tested direct mail they can send to their own mailing list of customers.

There's one big problem with that, however. Most small Mom 'n' Pop stores are unsophisticated marketers. They don't even have a mailing list of customers. And even those that do, are not capable of direct mail much more advanced than sticking postage stamps on hand-addressed sale flyers and dropping them in the nearest mailbox. Even the large chains are not much better, because they are just not accustomed to thinking in terms of database marketing.

In *The Great Marketing Turnaround,* we told the story of how this problem was dealt with in the jewelry field. An enterprising marketer named James Porte boosted sales for his jewelry manufacturing employer, Michael Anthony Jewelers, by reaching out a helping hand to their retailers. He showed them how to start collecting the names and profiles of customers, and offered to maintain this data for them in Michael Anthony's master database and to do slick readymade mailings for them.

Now, in the liquor category, the House of Seagram has taken this idea a step further. In 1992, they announced an innovative holiday promotion program that put the power of the Seagram marketing database at the service of their dealers.

The dealers didn't have to design their holiday mailings. Of course, they could do that if they wished, working with Seagram's highly qualified suppliers. Otherwise they could simply select a preformatted self-mailer design and name the brands and offers they wanted included. (Since the dealers were paying all the direct-mail costs themselves, obviously they would want to feature other brands besides Seagram's.)

The dealers didn't have to supply any of their own customer names, although they could do that also if they wished. Instead, for a list-rental charge, Seagram would select from its own master database all the names of people residing in the zip zone(s) in which the dealer was doing business.

The dealer didn't have to handle any details of getting out the mailing. That would all be taken care of by Seagram's designated suppliers, Dallas Graphics or Direct Solutions, who would afterwards provide the dealer with an official U.S. Postal Service Form 3602 verifying the drop.

An optional money-saving-offer panel to be presented by the customer to the store's cashier was suggested for each mailer, so that the dealer could see and count visible results from what he did with the mailing.

Naturally, the self-mailers would include products by Seagram competitors. All Seagram asked was that out of a total number of 34 products featured, at least 7 of them be House of Seagram Distilled Spirits and at least one be Mumm Champagne or Mumm Cuvée Napa.

It is typical of Shaw's entrepreneurial spirit and daring to plunge into a new area, learn from his mistakes, "get the bugs out," and do a refined, expanded, more successful effort the following year. This is in refreshing contrast to a common corporate practice we have observed of setting up a team to study a project to death while the world races on past them.

In the first year, 1992, Seagram signed up a few retailers for whom they mailed a total of approximately half-a-million pieces. As a result of what they did, along with a concerted effort by the trade-channel marketing group and field-sales team, some big chains became interested in taking part the following year. The things Seagram learned that first time out left them better prepared to deal with a greatly expanded promotion.

For everybody who was involved that first year, it was a win-win proposition. As Shaw pointed out, "By truly making it possible for the retailer to increase his marketing effectiveness, we are able to justify receiving 20 percent of the space in the retailer's mailing for House of Seagram brands while representing only 10 percent of market share." In post-promotion research, 74.5 percent of the retailers who took part had a positive opinion of the program and 72.5 percent said they would do it again.

Seagram has shown how a branded-product company can come out ahead by really caring about its retailers, and helping them sell competing products, as well as the company's own brands, to identified users in each retailer's trading area.

Doing More Than Enough

By now, many marketers have added some form of targeted direct mail to their marketing mix. But that sadly is about as far as they have gone in the MaxiMarketing process. What Seagram has demonstrated is the power of implementing multiple "Caring and Daring" initiatives—the pattern we have seen in so many of our MaxiMarketing winner case studies.

It is not just doing something right that moves the needle. It is doing "more than enough"—getting lots of new individualized actions right is what takes market share away from the competition or sends sales volume off the chart.

Seagram pioneered the technique of building a vast proprietary consumer database and putting it to profitable use.

Seagram found a way to eliminate the waste in media advertising and is experimenting with new ways to add a response element.

Seagram has gotten closer to their distribution by offering a genuine helping hand and sophisticated database-driven marketing know-how.

From what we have seen, it is very likely that they will go right on finding additional ways to attract new users and retain the loyalty of current customers. We would estimate that only a very small percentage of product marketers with end-user databases have approached the sophistication of Seagram's "less makes more" predictive modeling.

What Seagram has accomplished demonstrates the enormous profit potential for any marketer in analyzing the increasing flow of consumer data available in their own computer memory. We are only at the earliest stage of the new capability to make Information-Age Marketing an extraordinarily efficient business-building tool.

7

Nestlé Baby Food: Scoring a Perfect "7" in France

We have said and written that the kind of creative ingenuity heretofore lavished on mass advertising is now needed for the creation of trailblazing marketing strategies.

This is not as easy a concept to grasp as might appear. One does not ordinarily think of a strategy as being a piece of creative work in the same sense as a TV commercial. Yet what can be more creative than a daring leap of imagination leading to a whole new way of looking at a problem and how it might be solved?

We found such an example of imaginative strategy-formulation at a company headquarters located in a Paris neighborhood. There, the baby food division of Sopad-Nestlé in France, has made huge gains in market share in competition with the Bledina brand, a subsidiary of BSN, the $18 billion European fast-moving consumer goods powerhouse.

When we put the yardstick of the seven keys to business success in the 1990s up against the Nestlé program, it scores a perfect "7." What you see is a startling glimpse into the future of building brands in ways that avoid the suicidal path of price discounting and the strategy of depending upon advertising alone to gain consumer preference.

Traditionally, brand building for packaged goods has been a three-dimensional process:

Dimension 1: The *height* of the impressions on consumers—the sheer extent of the advertising bombardment achieved by the purchase of advertising time and space in the various media

Dimension 2: The *depth* of the brand awareness achieved, based on the power of the image or sales argument in the advertising

Dimension 3: The *width* of the distribution and the muscle available to push the brand to a prominent place on the shelf at the point of sale

Now, Nestlé Baby Foods in France has added a fourth dimension of brand building: breaking through the clutter of the marketplace with *Involvement Marketing,* by moving into the lives and activities of prospects and customers as a genuinely helpful, caring, trusted companion.

Fabienne Petit, the marketing director, told us that she has a *passion*—that word again!—for making life better for the parents of babies. Her creative strategy has played a vital role in sweeping Nestlé past Gerber into a close second behind Bledina, while piling up an astonishing gain of almost 24 share points.

Here is what Nestlé did to make it happen.

Le Relais Bébé

In France, just about everybody takes off for a long vacation in the summertime. The pace of business life slows to a crawl, as almost everyone seems to hit the road at the same time. Well-maintained campgrounds abound throughout the country. As a result, the whole family can pile into the car and roam around France or head for Spain and Italy for not much greater cost than staying at home.

But if you are traveling with a baby still in diapers, going anywhere by car may not seem the fun it was before the newcomer joined the family. Nestlé came up with the answer—a way to dramatically improve the quality of life for any parent and baby on the road.

They provide rest-stop structures alongside the highway where parents can feed and change their baby. In eight locations along the main travel routes, a sparkling clean *Le Relais Bébé* awaits and welcomes the family. It is an attractive roadside building painted in the familiar blue and white Nestlé colors and adorned with the lovable Nestlé baby food symbol, their blue teddy bear "Ptipo."

Imagine yourself as the parent of an infant and reading this inviting copy in a Nestlé brochure:

> With a baby, the road is sometimes long and when feeding time comes or baby gets cross, one dreams of a quiet place to stop without leaving one's route.
>
> This year you can count on Relais Bébé Nestlé to be at your service along the principal autoroutes of France.
>
> These places are fitted out for mothers and their babies. You will find a warm welcome waiting, the assistance and advice of the specially trained hostesses...and everything you need to change and feed your baby.
>
> Different baby food selections will be proposed to you, each specially recommended by Nestlé dieticians, for little ones from 3 months up.
>
> The baby will be served free of charge no matter what time of day: cereals for breakfast, little dishes for lunch or evening, a snack of desserts, cookies, fruit juices....from a "menu" that is complete and well suited to each stage of development.
>
> These rest stops for babies have been created to make your vacation travel more agreeable. So leave home worry-free; the Relais Bébé are easy to find and easy to reach, to ease your passage going or returning. They are at your service from June 26 to August 31.

Each summer, 64 hostesses at these rest stops welcome 120,000 baby visits and dispense 600,000 samples of baby food. There are free disposable diapers, a changing table, and high chairs for the babies to sit in while dining.

Can you picture any traditional, image advertising with pictures of apple-cheeked babies and misty-eyed mothers that could possibly have as profound an effect on a parent's attitude toward Nestlé as a stop at *Le Relais Bébé?*

Says Marketing Director Petit:

> *Le Relais Bébé* has important benefits for Nestlé.
>
> For one thing, it is a genuine showcase of brand image. Nestlé is the only mass-marketing brand to have such a presence on the highways.
>
> In addition, the strong customer service aspect of the operation relayed to journalists enables Nestlé to obtain numerous free write-ups in magazines.
>
> But it is above all the quality of a contact of more than 20 minutes with the mothers that distinguishes this operation. At the key moment of the baby's meal, Nestlé through its hostesses finds itself in direct contact with the mothers in a consumer-brand relationship that is quite unusual.

Just think of the word-of-mouth advertising value these rest stops generate when the family members return home from the trip and tell friends about how they were treated. If each parent who makes a stop at a Nestlé highway oasis shares the experience with just two or three friends who have babies, Nestlé is reaching several hundred thousand prime prospects with an unforgettable message.

"Allô Nestlé Diététique"

In all Nestlé media advertising, direct mail, and packaging, parents are invited to call the toll-free number for its free baby-nutrition counseling service, "Allô Nestlé Diététique."

Any time during ten hours each day, six days a week, a concerned parent in France can call and get free advice from one of Nestlé's licensed dieticians about what's right for baby. These trained counselors inform, listen to, advise, and reassure more than 20,000 mothers a year.

Nestlé receives over 500 thank-you cards and letters a year from mothers who use the service. It is more of Petit's "tell, don't sell" approach to winning market share. When asked why she spends so much money on activities unrelated to making an immediate sale, she answered: "I want to win the hearts of France's new mothers by offering the information and help they need during the early months of motherhood, rather than the sales pitch they usually get and ignore from baby product manufacturers."

Help at Every Stage of Baby's Development

Nestlé maintains and constantly updates a database of 220,000 new mothers with the names and addresses extracted from maternity records. The first mailing contains a reply card on which the new mother can fill in baby's name and indicate interest in receiving further mailings. This file is then used to send six direct-mail packages, personalized with the first name of the baby at key stages of development in the baby's new life. Mailings are sent at three months, six months, nine months, first birthday, eighteen months, and two years.

Although the word "package" is often used in direct-mail terminology to denote any mailing in an envelope, each of the six mailings in the series really is a package, bulging with goodies. These envelopes include not only samples of baby food and promotional coupons but also a blue cutout of the Nestlé teddy bear that can dangle over the crib, and information cards with tips from pediatricians on what to expect as baby develops.

The first-birthday package contains a wonderful gift, Baby's First Book, *"Bon. Assez Dormi!"* ("Sleep Well") The pages are printed on heavy cardboard and feature the adventures of a little blue teddy bear named "Ptipo"!

To help celebrate the big event, there is also a chocolate cake mix, a birthday candle in the shape and color of the Nestlé blue teddy bear, and a recipe card telling how to bake the chocolate birthday cake using Nestlé baby cocoa for the whole family to enjoy.

There is a very special Mother's Day mailing that offers a rose for Mama from a local florist as a gift from Baby and a loving postcard with a "handwritten" greeting from Baby to Mama (courtesy of Nestlé):

> Happy holiday, Mama, how I love you!
>
> Since I do not know how to write, I have asked the little Nestlé teddy bear to send you this card to say to you that you are the most beautiful Mommy in the world and that I love you madly.
>
> I give you a kiss as big as a mountain.
>
> Your little baby, getting bigger every day!

Petit told us: "We receive hundreds of thank-you letters from mothers delighted with the Mother's Day and birthday mailings. It's most unusual in a country where people usually write to a manufacturer only if they have a complaint."

She believes there are four key elements that have been decisive in the brand's success:

1. The tone of the mailings, which is affectionate and personal
2. The progressive evolution of the message, so that as the baby grows, Nestlé is there at the right time with the right products and the right message
3. The helpful, informative content of every communication in putting "genuine help" ahead of selling Nestlé products
4. The companionship Nestlé provides at critical stages in the development of the baby

What about the Competition?

While Nestlé has been gaining more than 20 percent of the market, what has the competition been doing? We learned from Mme. Petit that "the leading brand is trying to copy our direct marketing approach but they only have two mailings."

From what we have seen, the Bledina mailings do not come close to what Nestlé has achieved in warmth, originality, and ability to hold the mother's interest. What is most startling about the competitive response is that all through the sensational rise of this MaxiMarketing winner, Bledina baby food has been outspending Nestlé baby food by as much as 7 to 1 when it comes to image advertising. The competition does a lot of TV and not much direct marketing. Of course, such a method makes no sense in trying to reach cost-effectively a narrowly targeted market of mothers who represent a niche of only 7 percent of the national population.

If ever there was an example of one advertiser wasting money on nonprospects while the other uses targeted marketing to eliminate the waste, this is it. "They use a lot of money to touch people that are not interested at all in their products. We prefer to do direct," comments Petit.

Now that you have received a glimpse of the Nestlé Baby Food marketing program, you can see how it scores a perfect 7 in applying the keys to success we set forth in Chapter 2.

Key 1: Tell, don't sell. The offer of helpful, caring information is at the heart of everything they do.

Key 2: Get real. Nestlé is not just a faraway, impersonal, baby food factory. It is a warm, caring presence in the lives of the French mother. Everywhere she turns there is Nestlé—free professional advice on the phone, a real birthday present, a welcome highway rest stop with free baby food and fresh diapers—even a remembrance on Mother's Day.

Key 3: Stop wasting money on nonprospects. Petit's direct relationship with mothers assures Nestlé's senior management that every dollar she spends is reaching the target.

Key 4: Offer gain without pain. All of the benefits Nestlé offers—the file cards with baby care tips, baby's first book, the birthday cake, the phone service, the highway rest stops—are part of Nestlé's Extra-Value Marketing strategy.

Key 5: Get people together. The friendly dieticians who chat with parents calling Allô Nestlé Diététique and the 64 hostesses who greet them at the highway rest stops provide direct involvement and personal interaction with tens of thousands of prospects and customers. And the parents who sit at the picnic tables outside the Nestlé highway rest stops and chat with other parents become part of a community of Nestlé Baby Food advocates.

Key 6: Care enough to really put the customer first. This is strongly conveyed in all the marketing programs. "It is the marketer's job today," says Petit, "to search for techniques where you can bring real service to the consumer, so that they get the feeling that you are really helping them and not just trying to make them buy your product. I think it's a new way of succeeding with the new consumer in the coming years."

Key 7: Dare to start over. While there was no dramatic rescue from bankruptcy such as we saw in the case of Harley-Davidson, the Nestlé baby food division in France certainly exhibits a sharp break with the traditional dependence on TV advertising typically followed by brand advertisers.

We see once again, as we did with the LEGO brand, a "Super-Synergy" in which each part of the overall program supports and strengthens the others. The direct mail and the ads in magazines directed to mothers invite people to call Allô Nestlé Diététique; common questions and misunderstandings gleaned from calls to Allô Nestlé Diététique are answered in the ads; and the mailings contain information cards about *Relais Bébé.*

The Results Keep Getting Better

We told part of the Nestlé story, up to 1990, in *The Great Marketing Turnaround:* how Nestlé shot past Gerber in France to become the No. 2 brand there, zooming from a 20 percent share of market to 30 percent in just four years. Was the early success an aberration or a harbinger of a new model of excellence?

The story just keeps getting better. The most recent market research survey of 1000 mothers showed an approval rating of 97 percent for the Nestlé direct mail and 94 percent for *Relais Bébé.* Now, as this book goes to press, the Nestlé share of market has climbed to more than 43 percent—close to a 24-share-point rise in less than seven years. It is an astonishing gain in a category where a shift of one share point is big news in the business press.

We know that, in the end, each marketer must arrive at a unique strategy to reflect the unique situation in which the company operates. But there is much any marketer can learn from the Nestlé baby food experience in France.

Certainly, the fact that the product is sold to a very narrow segment of the population contributed to the success of using an individualized customer focus. However, if you think such an approach is only suitable for sharply defined niche markets, stay tuned. The next part of the Nestlé story may prove even more surprising than their MaxiMarketing success in France.

8

A Daring Change in Direction from Corporate Nestlé

The giant multinational Nestlé Corporation, headquartered in Vevey, Switzerland, is the largest food company in the world. To engineer a change of direction in an organization of this magnitude is a formidable challenge.

Peter Brabeck, Nestlé's chief marketing strategist and general manager in charge of several Strategic Business Units—source of more than half the company's SFr54.5 billion sales turnover—has set himself such a task.

In November of 1992, *Marketing* magazine in the United Kingdom reported the first news of a bold Nestlé experiment. Corporate management intended to build a global brand on the basis of a one-to-one relationship with the consumer and make the United Kingdom the test market—an unprecedented move for a major packaged goods marketer.

"In his view," wrote *The Financial Times* of London after interviewing Brabeck, "Nestlé is increasingly threatened by isolation from the market, and *its brands imprisoned in a 'ghetto' from which advertising provides no escape.*"

As we have discussed earlier, there are now fewer and larger retail chains wielding enormous power, and they are able to control, limit, and even eliminate advertised brands in their stores in order to favor their own private-label brands. Meanwhile, the fragmentation of the media and the increasing consumer resistance to advertising messages is making it increasingly difficult, if not impossible, for an advertised brand to break out of this "prison" merely through the power of stepping up the advertising volume.

Yes, the big brands and the big stores have become partners and competitors at the same time. And Brabeck is determined to restore the balance of power of the manufacturer's brand—by finding a brand-building method that is right for the decade running up to the twenty-first century.

The Road Nestlé Chose

Basically, Nestlé had three choices.

1. Discount, discount, discount. Compete with store brands on price by putting most of your marketing dollars into promotional couponing and trade allowances, draining money away from brand-building advertising regardless of how this weakens the brand over the long run.
2. Follow the P&G model in America and move to an EDLP (Every Day Low Price) strategy. By eliminating burdensome trade allowances and doing away with the on-and-off bargain-pricing cycle, P&G hopes to level the playing field. If successful, they believe that their brand-building advertising expertise will then make them king of the hill once more. But the assumption is based on a defining role for advertising that is no longer the reality it once was.
3. Build powerful, direct, personal communication with the consumer that adds value to the product, and start exploring alternate means of distribution.

It is the third route that Brabeck has chosen. Brabeck believes that "we will always need advertising to have a public appeal, but that alone will not be enough. The main thrust will be on one-on-one communication where you get a warmer and better response."

When asked to elaborate on this view, Brabeck told us: "We believe in credible communication, something different from what advertising by itself can do. We must use advertising to establish a dialogue with the consumer—a bridge between two partners that continues to establish the brand image and also to get a response starting a meaningful relationship. What you call double-duty advertising."

In the *Marketing* magazine article, he commented: "We're confronting a consumer who wants a personal relationship with a brand but who wants that brand to be publicly known."

"Rubbish," replied the marketing director of one of the giant retailers in the same issue. "Consumers want a relationship with products they buy—in terms of quality, etc.—but a personal, brand relationship is twaddle."

Who is right? Our money is on Brabeck.

Buitoni as the Marketing Laboratory

In a huge decentralized business empire such as Nestlé, fundamental change cannot be imposed from the top simply by issuing a decree.

So Brabeck has undertaken essentially the same approach we will see in a later chapter at North American Insurance of Canada: namely, develop a prototype (as North American did by establishing FNA Financial) and use its success to inspire and guide future development at the rest of the company.

The brand chosen for test-tube development was Buitoni pasta, and the primary market chosen was the United Kingdom, although Buitoni product managers in other countries would also become involved almost from the start.

The Buitoni brand was already the market leader in dry pasta in the United Kingdom, but the rapid rise of store brands there convinced Brabeck that new thinking would be necessary to retain that leadership and to ensure success of a new line of fresh pasta.

The significance of this move was not lost on British marketers. Under a huge banner headline, "Nestlé adopts the personal touch," the British trade publication *Marketing* began their story this way:

> Nestlé has chosen the U.K. to be the laboratory of one of the biggest and boldest experiments in consumer brand building yet. In a radical move designed to sidestep the power of both media owners and retailers, the world's biggest food company plans to build a global brand on the foundations of a one-to-one relationship with its consumers.

A Dramatic Example of Existential Marketing

Buitoni Pasta really was developed by somebody named Buitoni. The brand had its historical roots in the tiny Tuscan village of Sansepolcro.

The company was founded there in 1827 by Giulia Buitoni, affectionately called Mamma Guilia by all. She was a woman of vision and courage, and the first to realize that the best pasta is made with durum wheat semolina. Although large supplies of this semolina were available only in the Puglia region, 600 kilometers to the south, she dispatched horse-drawn carts on a regular basis for a round trip that lasted some 40 days!

Recently, on Via Firenzuola in Sansepolcro, site of Mamma Giulia's first "factory," the city council dedicated a plaque commemorating that long-ago beginning in 1827.

Brabeck discovered that the Buitoni family villa was still standing. In a master stroke of Existential Marketing, he acquired it and had it restored and rebuilt to serve as the brand's own world headquarters, Casa Buitoni. The entire shell of the building was lifted up in order to lay new foundations and build subterranean offices, and then was set back into place.

The restored building houses the company's first research center to focus solely on one brand, plus a public relations unit, kitchens, and sleeping accommodations for 20 people. It opened its doors in October of 1992, and 165 journalists were invited to attend the opening celebration. Later it plans to offer two- or three-day residential courses on Italian cooking.

"With the Casa, we can establish almost our own private

medium," explained Brabeck. Here is what he shared with us about the concept:

> The priority for its restoration (which took two years) was given to safeguarding the spirit, look, and emotions attached to a real home and, of course, its distinct Italian authenticity. In fact, this was the home of Guiseppe Buitoni, who lived in it for some years prior to World War II.
>
> Although "Casa Buitoni" is functional in terms of ongoing P.R. activities and Experimental Kitchen research, the general aspect of the house is that of a family home. This is because visitors should be made to feel as if they're being personally welcomed into the home of the Buitoni family.
>
> This pleasant, warm, and sharing welcome is of high strategic importance, as the total Buitoni communication is centered around it. Therefore, "Casa Buitoni" is the symbol and heart of our Buitoni business worldwide.
>
> If you make a pretense of what a brand stands for and consumers realize it, then you've made a big mistake. We are spending a great deal of money to build upon the authentic brand heritage by actually doing things to strengthen the Buitoni tradition and not just talking about it.

Part of the concept was the attraction that warm, sunny, vital Tuscany has always held for inhabitants of the Western world, especially those of the cloudy isle of Britain and the chilly lands of Northern Europe. "Do you know the land where the lemon trees bloom?" wrote Goethe, yearningly, in Germany. "There! There must I go!"

The Casa Buitoni immediately became part of the new Buitoni packaging, which bears an oval "seal of quality" with a picture of the building and the words, "Dalla Casa Buitoni, 1827."

Concurrently, the marketing manager of the Nestlé Food Division in the United Kingdom, Duncan MacCallum, launched an ad campaign built around the Casa Buitoni connection. Each of a series of full-page ads in women's and cooking magazines introduced the repositioned Buitoni brand and took the reader step by step through a pasta recipe in order to "share Buitoni's passion for pasta" and "share the Italian love of food." A panel in the ads and the closing of the new television commercials invited people to call for a free 20-page recipe booklet.

Building a Launch Pad for the Casa Buitoni Club

The names of people who request the recipe booklet were collected in a state-of-the-art relational database. In a short time, Nestlé enrolled 100,000 members, the target number management originally considered large enough for the next planned step, the launching of The Casa Buitoni Club. The Club is at the heart of the marketing strategy.

Club members receive a magazine filled with recipes, articles, and features that draw the members into a like-minded community of people interested in the mystique of the Italian lifestyle at its best. Nestlé plans to offer club members an opportunity to win trips to Casa Buitoni for cooking lessons and participation in product development.

"In the Italian foods market, unless you are Italian, there is a hell of an education job that needs to be done, on a product-by-product basis," MacCallum told us. "There's only so much you can do in terms of mass media approach, only so much you can communicate, and then you need to go down to the one-to-one level in terms of explaining to people what a good risotto rice dish is, or why fresh pasta and sauce works so much better than a standard ready meal or something you could get in the frozen food cabinet." (Key 1: tell, don't sell!)

This is exactly what we were writing about and advocating six years earlier, in 1986, in the chapter on "Maximized Linkage" in our first book, *MaxiMarketing*. We said then:

> In today's increasingly demassified marketplace, the role of mass advertising is destined to change. Instead of influencing "everybody" in the media audience, a more proper function for it may be to attract, interest, sift out, identify, gather together and communicate with the comparative few who are the immediate prospects for what is being advertised.
>
> Then what happens next becomes as important as what has gone before. The curiosity of this minority is converted into a firm buying intention by additional advertising and promotion of equal quality, sent directly to the home of the interested prospect.
>
> We call this form of advertising "linkage." It links the up-

> front advertising to the sale with additional arguments and benefits which the up-front advertising didn't have space or time to include.
>
> Giving this follow-up process more serious attention and funding must—and will—become an important part of the marketing strategy of the smartest companies.

By this yardstick, Nestlé would have to qualify in our eyes as one of the smartest MaxiMarketers today.

In the same chapter (on "Maximized Linkage"), we also talked about the urgent need to reorganize marketing management structures in order to put somebody in charge of "loving the prospect" and somebody in charge of "loving the product." Peter Brabeck seems to have effectively combined these two functions in his global role.

In *MaxiMarketing* we predicted that the concept of "Lifetime Customer Value" which had always been a driving force in classic direct marketing would become an important factor for all marketers in the coming telecomputer era. Now, compare that with what "MaxiMarketer" Duncan MacCallum of Nestlé U.K. was telling us about his packaged-goods marketing program.

> We didn't want to go out and buy a list. We wanted what we call quality names. For Buitoni, we want consumer lifetime value. Once you have got them on your database and you are regularly corresponding with them, if you continue that, you are talking about a long-term, lifetime commitment to a brand rather than just a one-off promotion. Within the food industry, this is something that we believe is relatively new. The industry has tended to do a lot of short-term promotions, with no further correspondence. Our intention is to get the names and then continue to update them with the Buitoni Club connection.

MacCallum also was enthusiastic about the value of the database in introducing new products. For instance, when they introduced Buitoni Risotto in August of 1992, as an experiment they mailed out 5000 packs to targeted prospects in the database. "We had a response of around 25 percent, pretty high, and this encouraged us."

The First Indication of Strategic Sucess

The Buitoni database already contains information on each respondent's age, sex, and region, and more details are sure to be added in the future. An example of the potential power of Buitoni's new strategy was provided during the launch of Buitoni Fresco, a new line of fresh pasta and sauce.

Because of too many products fighting to get space in the refrigerated compartments, the refrigerated area of the grocery store and supermarket is one of the most difficult places to get distribution in the United Kingdom. For this reason, MacCallum explained to us, when he was planning the introduction, "Buitoni fresh pasta is unlikely to go nationally to every single store group, because they don't have the chill cabinet space; it is more likely to be regional. Fresh pasta is very much eaten in the south of Britain. So we can do a mailing for Buitoni Fresco to the south. We can mail to our database of customers who we know are within the catchment area of the stores involved."

Later, we learned from Peter Brabeck just how successful the launch of Buitoni fresh pasta turned out to be. "Our recently introduced line of 'Fresh Buitoni' is now carried in the refrigerated section of all major retailers in the U.K. We have been able to convince our trade partners that there is more behind Buitoni than just the usual advertising. In spite of the economic crisis in the U.K., we have already gained a sales increase in double-digit figures. The Buitoni involvement strategy is an absolute success in the U.K. That's a tremendous accomplishment in today's tough competitive battle with both store brands and manufacturer brands."

The Not-So-New Frontier of Alternate Forms of Distribution

The ninth step in the MaxiMarketing continuum is Maximized Distribution—Adding New Channels. We have already seen in the personal computer industry how IBM, Compaq, Digital, and

Apple have all expanded their distribution by adding a direct-selling channel.

Nestlé is also studying alternate forms of distribution such as vending machines giving out hot pasta in offices, boutiques in shopping malls, street market stalls, home shopping (through the Club?), and even selling pasta through unconventional retail outlets such as gas stations. Of course, Nestlé knows that they will still need grocery and supermarket distribution. Through their new customer involvement initiatives they intend to sustain and increase the consumer demand needed to keep Buitoni on the supermarket shelves—successfully competing with lower-priced store-brand pastas—while expanding into new distribution channels.

Casa Buitoni Comes to Holland

While the United Kingdom has been chosen as the cutting-edge test market for the new Buitoni strategy, a glimpse of how Nestlé may extend the Dalla Casa Buitoni to other countries in the future is already being provided in The Netherlands.

There, the big food retailers publish their own well-read consumer information magazines and distribute them in the stores. When Buitoni was launched in Holland in 1992, Nestlé ran striking, double-duty advertising spreads for the brand in store magazines asking for a response. Tipped onto the right-hand page was a picture postcard with the trademark painting of the Casa and the handwritten words, "Invitation from Casa Buitoni." The copy alongside explained that Buitoni wanted to send the customer the little box of free "goodies" illustrated. "It will include a booklet of pasta recipes by Gualtiero Marchesi, owner of a three-star restaurant in Milan; an entry form good for a chance to win a free weekend in Milan; and a value coupon worth the cost of a trial purchase of Buitoni."

The fill-in portion of the card asks the right questions for starting a database of respondents. "How often do you eat pasta? Monthly? Semimonthly? Weekly? What brand? Would you like to be kept informed on the latest developments in our

Tuscany kitchen?" The reply postcard was addressed to Casa Buitoni in Italy.

Each respondent received an attractive Italian-designed cardboard box with the colorful Buitoni seal on the front. Inside, as promised, there was the recipe booklet, the contest entry, and the value coupons. In addition, there were information cards, and, a most unusual feature, two picture postcards you can address and mail to your friends.

These postcards are still another example of how this innovative campaign bursts the bounds of conventional promotion. It is a virtually cost-free way of involving respondents further and widening the circle of impact. Here, from one of the postcards, is the message a recipient can send to a friend:

> Since you are a cheeselover, this recipe will make your mouth water! It is a hot *Torchietti al Gorgonzola* from Tuscany.
>
> That means egg pasta with gorgonzola. Gorgonzola is one of the sweetest blue cheeses of all.
>
> When I prepare this, please come and eat it with me. Call me soon.

Just think how much this simple, inexpensive little postcard illustrates the power of the Involvement Marketing key to success. It gives the respondent an opportunity and an excuse to make a social contact with a friend, thanks to Buitoni. It interests the friend in Buitoni pasta. And if the friend accepts the invitation, this leads to getting together and further discussion of Buitoni. As the hostess and friend chat over the dinner table about the *Torchietti al Gorgonzola* they are eating, a favorable impression of the Buitoni brand is deepened in their minds—far more than just advertising might ever accomplish.

One final touch cries out to be added to this promotion to make it almost perfect. That would be to add a reply card which the hostess could give to her friend to mail, requesting his or her own Buitoni surprise package. Thus the circle of influence could keep widening and widening.

It is worth noting that the contents of the box could just as easily have been mailed in an envelope instead of an attractive carton, and it would have cost less. But the marketers of Buitoni pasta in Holland wisely realized that the extra expense of the box was worth it. It made the mailing package more desirable, more exciting to receive, and more memorable.

There are so many elements of the "Get Real" precept here. The reality of the Casa Buitoni. The reality of the Tuscany postage stamp. The reality of the prize of a free weekend in Milan. The reality of the three-star restaurant of Gualtiero Marchesi, author of the booklet of recipes. The reality of sending a postcard to a friend, and having the friend come to dine on a pasta dish made from a recipe in the booklet by Gualtiero Marchesi. The amount of real-world involvement is a far cry from the passive communication with consumers usually found in "make-believe" brand advertising.

All this fits in very well with Brabeck's new Buitoni strategy. "From the very first conception of how we wanted to present the product, we have taken into account the consumer's wishes and interests," he emphasized in talking with us. "The authentic Italian experience the consumer desires must exist in reality, not simply as a figment of the copywriter's imagination. We are conveying not only the art of Italian cooking but the culture, the wine, the ambiance—and everything must be conveyed with authenticity."

Since repositioning Buitoni in late 1992, Buitoni sales have increased not only in the United Kingdom and Holland but throughout Europe. And the brand has become a great success in Japan. It has been welcomed enthusiastically there, with a steady stream of Japanese retailers coming to visit the Casa Buitoni in Tuscany and leaving more enthusiastic than ever.

It's Early to Be Watching —But Not Too Early

The new Nestlé direction exemplified by the Buitoni initiative in the United Kingdom and in Holland is one of the few marketing programs in this book which is being reported too early for a final judgment on its effectiveness. But we feel that it is such an important experiment, by such a major marketer, that you deserve to know about it now. Watch for future developments in the United Kingdom, The Netherlands, and your own national market.

When the director of the world's largest branded food marketer says "advertising is out and credible communication is in" and "there is no mass consumer any more," then it pays to observe carefully the daring new direction he is taking for his company—how he is focusing the thinking of this giant organization on the relationship with the individual customer as the key to future success.

But one thing is certain. Nestlé in France and now in the United Kingdom has shown just how powerful a "Caring and Daring" strategy can be—even for a low-priced product selling through the feverishly competitive supermarket distribution channel.

Those branded-product companies that have limited direct-relationship marketing to targeted direct-mail promotions would do well to reconsider their shortsightedness. Looking after the consumer's interest in daring new ways, as you have seen, is much more than simply sending cents-off coupons to likely prospects in a database.

PART 3

MaxiMarketing Winners Selling a Service

9 Fidelity Investments: The Great Pyramid of Boston

What the Great Pyramid of Giza was to ancient Egypt of the third millennium B.C., Fidelity Investments is to the world of investment and money management today—truly one of the wonders of its time.

Of course, there is a world of difference between the two. One of the most important is that the Fidelity pyramid is upside down. The Great Pyramid of Giza pushes into the azure sky of Egypt as an enduring monument to the power and glory of the Pharaoh of 4700 years ago, King Cheops. But the way the Fidelity pyramid is constructed, the "base" of customers is actually on top. And everything beneath it is an extraordinary support structure tapering down to senior company management.

It is one of the most remarkable examples of customer cultivation, customer empowerment, and "Total Relationship Commitment" the business world has ever seen. Over the years, customers have flocked to take advantage of the unique brand of involvement found at Fidelity.

In this case study of an extraordinary MaxiMarketing winner, you will see the "tell, don't sell" key to success at work. And you will learn how Fidelity dared to start over and rethink the customer relationship at a time when they already stood head and shoulders above other marketers of mutual funds.

Fidelity Investments has grown from the $3 million plus in assets in the original Fidelity Fund in 1943 to over $200 billion in 1993. That means it has become *70,000 times larger*—surely a business growth triumph for the Guinness Book of Records. It *doubled* in size in just the first three years of the 1990s. In 1991, Fidelity posted record revenues of $1.5 billion and record profits of $89 million. (And since it is privately owned, these figures may be understated, according to *Business Week.*) Some 1400 phone representatives in four sites across the country handle an average of 80,000 calls a day from its 5 million customers, with another 170,000 calls getting an automated response.

Fidelity has become so mammoth, with so many features and services and products, that your first inclination may be to turn away in dismay. You might think it is *too* big and powerful to hold any meaningful lessons for your own marketing problems, which may be far more modest in size. But you would be making a mistake. There is plenty to be learned from how they got so big in the first place and even more to be learned from how they stay on top and keep on growing.

You might also think that Fidelity's problems and products are too different from those of your own business category. But many of the underlying principles they follow are applicable over a broad range of marketing situations.

There are so many ways Fidelity departs from conventional wisdom that it is hard to know where to begin. Here are a few that stood out for us in studying their operation:

1. Cast your bread upon the waters and worry about the "dough" later.
2. Make it easy for your customers to take their money somewhere else.
3. If you're not making any mistakes, you're not taking enough chances.

4. Don't bother your customers. Encourage them to bother you.
5. You can't truly empower your customers without first empowering your employees.

We'll see these principles at work as we look at where Fidelity stands today and how it got that way.

Although the original Fidelity Fund was organized in 1930, the present-day organization really got going in 1943, when a Boston attorney, Edward C. Johnson II, was brought in as president and owner. He began to create and add to a whole family of funds with different investment approaches and objectives.

By 1972, Fidelity had become over 1000 times bigger, having grown from $3.6 million in assets to $4.3 billion. That year, one of Edward Johnson's sons, Ned Johnson, succeeded his father as president. And Fidelity began an even more spectacular cycle of growth.

Ned Johnson cut his eyeteeth as a fund manager in his father's business, working alongside the legendary Gerald Tsai. They brought to the job of running the company a rare combination of qualities and attitudes just right for hurtling Fidelity into the future:

- Put the customer first.
- Constantly reinvent the business.
- To lick 'em, join 'em.
- To sell 'em, tell 'em.
- Create a financial product or service for every customer need (niche marketing).
- Dare the impossible.
- Stay on the cutting edge of technology in order to serve the customer better.

Putting the Customer First

Nowadays just about every self-respecting CEO, sales manager, and marketing director gives lip service to serving the customer.

But few have the courage to go so far as to put the customer's needs ahead of the company's own short-term profit goals.

For instance, if you as an investor decide to take some money out of a fund, it can still be a hassle involving writing a letter of request to the fund and having your signature guaranteed by your bank before you mail it. It can be justified as a protection against fraud. But it also serves the fund's interests by protecting it against impulsive spur-of-the-moment cash-ins.

In the 1970s, several mutual fund companies, notably Fidelity and Dreyfus, broke new ground in the way funds were sold. Previously, mutual funds were always stock funds sold through brokers, who were paid a sales commission or "load" levied on the purchaser.

Interest rates were skyrocketing, but bank yields were frozen, and checking accounts did not pay interest at all. So Fidelity and Dreyfus introduced a new kind of fund, the money-market fund, and started selling it directly to the public through direct-response advertising, with no sales charge added.

The new money-market funds were very successful. However—and this seems hard to believe today, when several thousand funds are bought and sold directly—many small investors were still hesitant to mail a substantial sum of money to a stranger instead of handing it across the desk to a friendly local investment broker.

Ned Johnson reasoned that if you made it easier for people to get the money *out,* they would be less hesitant to put it *in.* So he introduced a service which is taken for granted today in most money funds but was a breathtaking innovation at the time. You could make withdrawals from your Fidelity Daily Income Trust just by *writing a check!*

Reinventing the Business

Fidelity has stayed ahead of the crowd by always being in the forefront of new products and services reflecting new needs and opportunities.

In 1976, Fidelity launched the first open-end, no-load municipal bond fund.

In 1980 Fidelity began to build a nationwide chain of walk-in Investor Centers—retail stores, really—today numbering more than 70. So, they were able to satisfy those people who want to talk to someone face-to-face as well as by phone.

In 1981, Fidelity was the first to offer Select Portfolios, permitting investors to focus on an industry or market sector but still enjoy the advantage of diversification.

In 1986, they were the first to dare something which seemed almost impossible to accomplish at the time—*hourly* pricing of Fidelity Select Portfolio funds throughout the trading hours of the day. Ordinarily, the latest share price of a fund is set at 4 p.m., calculated by multiplying the various stock shares held by the closing prices of those stocks and dividing by the number of mutual fund shares outstanding. A typical fund has around 300 stocks in its portfolio. To make this calculation of fund value just once a day is tough. To do it *six* times a day was a nightmare. But they did it, and there are a number of Fidelity investors who love it.

Later in 1986, Fidelity became the first investment company to offer 24-hour service. We're talking about real live people on the phones, not just answering machines. Any time of the day or night, the investor could check his account, place a trade, and stay informed.

In the Wall Street crash of 1987, many investors panicked when they tried to call their mutual fund to sell or exchange and couldn't get through jammed-up phone lines. There is also the constant danger that fire, flood, or hurricane can down phone lines and make the phone center inaccessible. So, Fidelity acted to restore absolute confidence in the telephone connection. To ensure uninterrupted service and quick call-answering 24 hours a day, seven days a week, Fidelity now has four phone sites backing up each other—Boston, Dallas, Cincinnati, and Salt Lake City—staffed by 1400 representatives.

A master control desk in Boston automatically routes the call in split seconds over fiber-optic lines to the next available rep in any one of the four sites. The company invested $1 billion through 1989 and $150 million in 1990 alone (13 percent of revenue!) to develop this sophisticated system. Most calls are answered after no more than three rings (20 seconds). If you are an insomniac investor in New York or Miami, there are trained, knowledgeable Fidelity representatives standing by in Salt Lake City who will be happy to chat with you about your investment goals at 3 a.m.

Like volunteer firefighters, or regimental cooks who grabbed up rifles during the Battle of the Bulge, thousands of Fidelity employees are members of something called Corporate Reserves. They are registered with the National Association of Securities Dealers to talk to the public, and when the phone volume gets heavy, the Reserves are called out. Managers drop whatever they are doing and run to answer phones. They stand ready to protect the Fidelity reputation for reliability.

The company holds regular "fire drills" of the Corporate Reserves to make sure they will be in tip-top shape and ready to go when the next real emergency bell rings.

"It's very exciting," we were told. "It's a good way to get the whole corporation focused on customer service."

To help callers wend their way through the vast array of Fidelity products and services to obtain the information or assistance they need, Fidelity maintains over 20 toll-free numbers, surely a record for one company. Some use a combination of voice-mail and personal service, and others, such as price quotation lines and Touch-Tone Trader, are completely automated. There is even a dedicated toll-free line for the deaf and hearing impaired.

Licking 'em by Joining 'em

What if—horrible thought—people want to put their money into something other than a Fidelity fund? Like individual stocks, or even some other company's mutual funds?

Remember that part of Fidelity's secret of staying first is to put the customer's needs first. For example, in 1979, Fidelity became the first major financial institution to offer its own discount brokerage service, in competition with that upstart of the time, a young fellow named Charles Schwab.

In what must surely be a new form of "line extension," both their discount brokerage service and their Ultra Service Account (cash management account service) invite their customers to make buy, sell, and exchange selections not only from more than a hundred Fidelity funds but from over 1700 *competitor* funds offered by other companies as well!

How does Fidelity make money on that? On non-Fidelity load funds, they earn the normal sales commission. On non-Fidelity no-load funds, they levy a small transaction fee plus 0.8 to 0.08 percent of principal, depending on the amount. But many Fidelity investors are happy to pay this extra charge for the convenience of having all of their financial transactions conducted and reported by Fidelity.

Selling 'em by Telling 'em

In the go-go years of the 1960s, when mutual funds were stock funds sold through brokers hungry for the sales commission, many investors were talked into investments they later regretted. As prices tumbled toward the end of the decade, fund shareholders kept hanging on hoping that prices would at least recover enough to pay back their original investment plus the sales charge. When that failed to happen, many fund investors swore, "Never again!" Whether rationally or irrationally, they were often resentful of the brokers who they felt had led them down that garden path.

As a Fidelity fund manager during that period, Ned Johnson could not have been unaware of all this. As a result, when he assumed command of Fidelity in 1972, that experience may have been a strong influence on the laid-back, helpful, educational approach Fidelity follows today.

This is reflected by Fidelity's present approach to the customer in two ways: the low-pressure helpfulness of its telephone representatives, and the equally low-pressure and helpful air of its voluminous literature, enough to fill a shopping bag.

"We don't solicit people," we were told by Darla M. Hastings, a corporate communications spokesperson. "If they say they want it, we'll send the information out. But we don't do a lot of pro-active follow-up because we don't want to bother people...They will get information about new products, but they are not going to get hounded. We almost never do [outbound] telemarketing, like a lot of the brokerage houses.

"We don't want to sell them just anything," she continued. "That would be a disaster because either they are going to be in the wrong thing, or they are going to be unhappy in some other way, and then it's a problem. We have 5 million customers. We can't know them personally enough to give them great advice. What we try to do is provide lots and lots of educational help so they can make their own decisions."

A particularly impressive example of Fidelity's do-it-yourself approach to investment aid is the Fidelity FundMatch Workbook and Worksheet for people who want to achieve their own best diversification among stocks, bonds, and short-term instruments...You are led through a series of questions and calculations about your holdings, attitudes, and goals. You score yourself as you go along. Your final score tells you whether you should consider a Capital Preservation Portfolio, a Moderate Portfolio, or a Wealthbuilding Portfolio. Then an Action Plan gives you three choices:

1. Create your own portfolio of Fidelity funds—with assistance, if desired, by calling a Fidelity representative.
2. Choose one of three Fidelity Asset Manager Funds, based on your self-test score; each fund contains a different mix of stocks, bonds, and short-term instruments.
3. Consider Fidelity Portfolio Advisory Services if you would like someone to do the Fidelity fund selections and ongoing allocations for you. (Minimum investment for this option, $100,000. Any sales loads on Fidelity funds are weighted and an annual advisory fee of 0.25 to 1 percent is charged.)

How do you calculate your tax gains or losses from your investment in mutual funds? Naturally, Fidelity is right there at your elbow with a booklet on the subject. It doesn't do anything for Fidelity—except help create a pleased, loyal customer. Whatever you need to know, Fidelity has it for you.

Fishing for Business in Niches

It is hard to imagine a niche in the market that Fidelity has not reached out to satisfy.

Planning for your child's college expenses? The Fidelity College Savings Plan helps you estimate how much you will need and how much you should be putting aside monthly, explains the advantages of a custodial account, gives you a choice of four most suitable funds, and offers to automatically withdraw the right amount from your bank account and invest it in the fund of your choice.

Dreaming of owning your own home? It's another opportunity for Fidelity to do some more "telling" without "selling." And, indeed, they have prepared a folder of advice and encouragement, "Buying a Home: Putting the Dream Together." Of course, it does point out that the biggest stumbling block to home ownership is accumulating enough for the down payment. They explain that "most mutual fund companies offer a free service that automatically withdraws money from your bank account on a regular basis and invests this money in one or more funds, in this case accumulating assets for a down payment." Nine out of ten companies would have said, "*we* offer a free service." But this is Fidelity.

Are you a concerned parent who wants to teach your preteen kids to be savvy about money management? Fidelity first provided a learning guide with exercises for elementary schools, but teachers were so enthusiastic that Fidelity followed up with a revised version for home use.

Planning for retirement? A booklet and worksheet help you calculate how much you'll need and how much you need to save regularly to get there. And there's a special phone number for a Fidelity retirement specialist you can call if you wish.

Changing jobs or about to retire? You have some important decisions to make about the money you have accumulated in your employer's retirement plan. Fidelity's "Common Sense Guide to Taking Charge of Your Money" tells you just about everything you need to know. Of course, it includes the special phone number for talking to a retirement specialist.

Daring to Start Over Again —and Again

In 1990, when Darla Hastings was vice-president of customer relations, she commissioned a major piece of research. Here was a company that was the leader in its field, managing $100 billion of other people's money at the time. It would have been easy and tempting for them to rest on their laurels and rake in the profits. Instead, they said:

> Wait a minute. We've been looking at all the quarterly satisfaction surveys *based on our own expectations of what is important.* What if we went back to square one, pretended we were just getting into the business, and looked at everything again from the customer's point of view. How do our customers see us relative to our competition? And how can we really differentiate ourselves from where we have been going wrong as well as differentiating ourselves from the competition? And what would it cost to get in the game of doing everything right from the customer's point of view?

To get the answers, they sent out a mail survey that took 45 minutes to complete. They got a 44 percent response rate.

"What we learned was shocking," Hastings told us. "We were focused on telling customers how high-tech we are. We thought they wanted to know about our error-free handling of their accounts. But what we discovered was—they didn't want technology, they wanted people."

What Fidelity heard loud and clear was "deal with us as human beings. Stop treating us as account numbers." The company had been spending endless hours, talent, and money on creating a better monthly statement. But the research revealed that the customer couldn't care less about the fine points of the statement compared to the fine points of adding to their knowledge of the pros and cons of various types of investments.

What they heard from the market was, in effect: "You used to be OK, Fidelity, but now I need more. I've got a lot of choices and I like to shop around. I'm no longer a neophyte. I'm better informed and I expect you to move up a notch too. Give me better-informed reps—real communicators. I don't care if you make a mistake on my statement once in a while—I care about how you handle the mistakes you make." Fidelity also heard in their research that customers want to talk to reps who clearly enjoy and care about their jobs.

So they changed the company.

They completely redefined the role of the rep. Gave the representatives better training and the responsibility to make decisions and give answers rather than pass the buck to someone else. After daring to set a new course, the company's growth continued, at a record rate, right through the recession.

Today, Fidelity is not satisfied to simply provide customer satisfaction. They want it to be a pleasure to do business with them. "Not just satisfaction but a memorable experience is the goal." As a result, they have one of the highest customer referral rates. Some 30 percent of their business comes from customer referrals.

Something else makes customer satisfaction doubly important—literally. Many customers who are personal investors with Fidelity are also key decision makers in their business lives, in the management of pension funds and other institutional investments. For this reason, the high level of individual customer satisfaction undoubtedly plays an important part in the fact that nearly half of Fidelity's managed assets come from institutional investors.

Hastings recently told an industry conference, "We believe strongly that if we give people who do business with us what they want and give our employees a sense of empowerment to genuinely take care of the customers, then profit will take care of itself."

Power to the People—at Both Ends of the Line

These are the three most highly visible ways in which staff empowerment finds expression:

1. The work environment of the phone reps
2. The "electronic brain and memory" provided to make each phone rep fully knowledgeable
3. The permissive attitude toward mistakes made through trying to do better for the customer

When we visited Fidelity's "mother church" in Boston, we

expected to find management personnel ensconced in generously windowed outer offices with a sweeping view of Boston Harbor, and the phone reps jammed into typical little cubicles lit by overhead fluorescent tubes.

We were stunned to discover that things are done differently at Fidelity. It is the phone reps dealing with the customer every minute of the day and night who have the choice location—a bright, cheery area, two stories high, with a 100-foot window wall revealing a panoramic view of Boston Harbor. It is the managers who are occupying interior offices without a window.

Sitting in front of each phone rep is a computer loaded with Microsoft Windows and a mouse. It almost amounts to an add-on to the human brain, in the same way attaching an external drive adds on to a computer's memory capacity.

When a customer calls, the screen immediately displays that person's complete history: every piece of Fidelity literature the customer has requested; every Fidelity investment the customer has made; every question the customer asked in previous calls.

But that's just the beginning. Through pull-down menus, the phone rep becomes a kind of Superman or Superwoman of total knowledgeability and up-to-the-minute information. Here, as needed, is the feed from Dow Jones on what is happening in the market this minute...late-breaking news and historical information on any listed company the customer is interested in... announcements of economic data...and so on.

As a result, in nine cases out of ten, even the most rarified of queries can be answered right on the spot, instead of having to transfer the call to an expert or to research the answer and call back. "That new tax ruling on home office expenses? I have it right here—the rep says...."

When you think of the more than 190 Fidelity funds, the several thousand competing mutual funds, the many thousands of individual stocks and bonds and financial instruments, and the staggering range of questions from 80,000 customers or more on a given day, you can see how miraculous it is that the phone rep is able to discuss most of the questions almost instantly and in depth. What Fidelity has done is make the process so seamless and effortless that the rep is free to really listen to the customer on the phone while the information being accessed flows before him or her on the computer screen.

The corporate culture encourages risk taking and mistake risking at all levels of management. Darla Hastings told us, "Fidelity has no vested interest in the status quo. The company believes it must always stand ready to change direction. At every level of management, you must take risks in order to keep up with the momentum of the company, or you'll end up at the bottom of the heap." Fidelity doesn't penalize people for making mistakes, she told us, if those mistakes are the result of taking risks in attempting to serve the customer to the max.

Fidelity makes several thousand outbound callbacks per quarter to monitor customer satisfaction. A few years ago, the callbacks were handled by an outside research firm. But then Fidelity management realized that knowing what was working and what wasn't "was too important to leave to an outsider." Questions are open-ended. Customers can tell Fidelity callers anything they want. And Fidelity listens, and notes.

The Never-Ending Renewal Process

Act Two of Fidelity's 1991–1992 restructuring began on a cool day in October of 1991. Fifty top managers gathered at a Cape Cod resort to confront the hard reality that although Fidelity was still doing very well, the business was showing signs of leveling off.

Out of that meeting came a new company strategy: more customer guidance and an even wider range of products.

They still wouldn't "sell" a customer on a particular course of action. But they would train and equip the rep to do a better job of helping the customers help themselves.

"We're rewriting the rules for how financial services are marketed in the 1990s," President of Retail Marketing Roger Servison told *Business Week* soon after the company changed direction. And, in the following year, Fidelity would move further toward becoming a department store of financial services, offering everything from insurance policies and credit cards to financial books and magazines.

The process of self-examination never ends at Fidelity. Smugness has no place in their corporate culture. For all the complexity of this vast and enormously successful venture, in the end it is the ability to listen to the customer and put the customer's interest first that drives their success.

Fidelity is a MaxiMarketing winner that does it all in a consistent way—responding to what the customer is saying each and every day, daring enough to go back to square one and start over, being involved in customer *and employee* empowerment.

What you will be pleased to know is that every one of these keys to success can be used successfully by almost any company, each in its own way.

The Ever-Expanding Bottom Line

Constantly innovating, breaking rules, doing what people say can't be done has made it possible for Fidelity to become a mammoth organization that retains a personal relationship with each of its millions of customers. They were the first mutual fund company to hit $100 billion in assets and then went right ahead to top $200 billion. In good times and tough times, they remain the largest privately held financial services company in the world.

When challenged by critics who say Fidelity can't provide full service without raising prices, the company's CEO responds, "Undiluted bull." Fidelity is the No. 1 example of an Information-Age service company that has put huge investments into technology to "free people from the nonproductive tasks so they can use their brains." By investing in technology *and people,* there seems to be no limit to their growth.

10
Ryder Turns the Business Around

In our research for this book, a clear pattern began to emerge. The recession at the beginning of the 1990s made consumers acutely price-conscious. But the smartest companies serving them realized that newly empowered consumers were asking for something more than the best price: they also were demanding the best *value* and the best *service* as well, all at the same time. The consumer was asking for "gain without pain."

This is the story of how a company in move-it-yourself truck rental got the message and turned their business around—*going from double-digit losses to double-digit profits in the first year of the turnaround.*

Ryder is the world's largest truck-leasing firm, with 166,000 trucks and over $5 billion in revenue. But in the approximately $1 billion field of truck rental by consumers and small merchants, Ryder was running second in 1991. The field had always been operations-oriented, with discounts as the usual method of stimulating business. The leader was U-Haul, the generic name that most people thought of when they thought about doing their own moving. For three years in a row, from 1989 through 1991, both Ryder and the industry experienced a double-digit decline. Bad news was the order of the day.

Faced with this gloomy prospect, management with lesser vision might have issued stern orders to ride out the recession and hang on until better times. How? By cutting prices; downsizing the staff; and reducing operating costs, equipment investment, and promotional expenses to the bone, of course.

But in a textbook model of corporate boldness, CEO Tony Burns and Ryder's board of directors decided to steer in the opposite direction.

They decided to put consumer truck rental into a separate division—Ryder Consumer Rentals, shift from a product-oriented to a marketing-oriented approach, bring in a marketing director with a brand-building background, and set their sights on becoming No. 1 in sales.

(*Note*: Those terms "product-oriented" and "marketing-oriented" should not be misinterpreted. They do *not* mean product excellence versus advertising excellence. Rather, they mean that the *product*-oriented provider of consumer goods or service says to the public, "We'll give you what *we* want and do what works best for us," the *marketing*-oriented provider communicates to the public, "We'll give you what *you* need and want.")

The marketing director recruited for the challenging Ryder assignment was one of the stars at Procter & Gamble, the proving ground for so many marketers who have gone on to great achievements at other companies. In this case, it was C. Mack, who had turned P&G's Pert Plus from No. 13 in the shampoo category to No. 1, with annual sales shooting up from $40 million to $180 million.

One month after the new consumer division of Ryder was announced in May of 1991, with Jerry Riordan as division president, Mack was brought on board as director of marketing and marketing services.

Ryder Consumer Truck Rental then embarked on an ambitious program of building the brand and building the customer relationship. It involved an extraordinary complex of components that began with listening to the customer and putting the customer's interests first. This meant committing to significant investment at a time when business was poor. But Ryder gambled that the popularity of self-moving was not a short-lived expedient but was here to stay, for the following reasons:

- Even when the economy began to bounce back, the $1000 or more a person might save by renting a truck instead of hiring a commercial moving van was no trifling sum.
- Corporations have become more cost-conscious, and are encouraging transferred employees to move themselves.
- Self-moving gives people more control over their precious possessions. For many people, 90 percent of what they own is on that truck. By moving themselves, what they own never leaves their sight.

The first advertising campaigns of the new consumer division were, by Mack's own appraisal, "ineffective." Says Mack today, "Our message to consumers was almost a message du jour, sad to say but true. For three months, we would be on a transaction strategy. Three months later, we'd be on a price strategy. And so on."

The television advertising featured TV actor and comedian Steve Landesburg. But research showed that consumers didn't believe someone like that would be moving himself.

Mack decided to develop a long-term strategy for positioning and building the brand, using a new cutting-edge approach to brand marketing called "strategic platform research."

At the heart of this search for a caring strategy, says Mack, "we wanted our platform to be based on consumer needs, not hatched in a corporate office. The idea was that the consumer would lead us in our decision making and sales would follow."

Climbing the Research Ladder

Market research is a billion-dollar business, and much of that billion dollars is wasted on foolish, useless, misleading investigations. Far too much time and money are spent on measuring "retention" and "recall" of an advertising message, even though—as shown only too often—these factors may have little or nothing to do with marketing effectiveness or sales results.

But Ryder used research as the powerful marketing tool it can be, when used the right way. First, they went about searching out what prospective customers wanted most from a truck rental company. Then, they devised product and service features to satisfy the most important expressed needs. Finally, they ran test advertising that incorporated these findings and did audience research to see how the advertising affected the buying intentions of prospective customers.

All this involved what they call a "laddering process": working their way up from the general human benefit to specific benefits to consumer-approved features that deliver those benefits and advertising that successfully communicates them.

Ryder started with 30 things people said they wanted from a truck rental company: safety, low price, high-quality truck, and so on. Then, in focus groups, they learned which of these 30 things were considered most important. From this broad-based approach, they were able to narrow the benefits down to five considerations. Finally, through additional focus groups and quantitative testing—surveying an adequate cross-section of prospects—they narrowed the focus down to one key benefit: *convenience.*

One expression of the convenience factor would be ease of loading the truck, and features to make that possible would include truck redesign for easier loading. Another meaning of convenience is getting in and out of the rental center as quickly as possible, with a minimum of hassle. Achieving that would call for overhauling the whole reservation and delivery system.

This meant, as is so often the case, that for the advertising message to be improved, the product and service had to be improved first.

The Product Is the Message—and So Is the Service

Service companies that deal in tangibles really have two products: the product itself, and the service wrapped around the product. When you hire a window-washing service, you don't care what kind of buckets and sponges they use to clean your windows as long as the window-washer is neat, quiet, quick, courteous, reasonably priced, and gets your windows clean. But when you go to a fast-food place like McDonald's, you demand both a good burger *and* fast service.

So Ryder had the dual challenge of (1) making it as convenient as possible to rent and use a truck by offering the right *service,* and (2) making it as convenient as possible to do the actual moving by offering the right *products* in the form of trucks and moving aids. But it is not enough merely to *claim* product or service superiority. Says the Eliza Doolittle in all of us, "Show me!" Or as Ring Lardner advised young writers, "Don't just say, 'The old lady growled.' Bring her in and let her growl!"

"When you look at what a marketing department should do," Mack told us, "producing good ads, creating good promotion, is probably just the beginning. What we were seeking to do was to understand the customer's needs and wants, and then *refocus our entire operation around meeting those needs and wants.* [Italics ours.] That was the magic of what we did here."

Compared to conventional company practice, that is a radical statement of the marketing director's responsibility. Too often his or her job is to grab the ball (the product or service handed down by operations or management) and run with it. But if marketing, as we believe, is everything a company *says and does* that favorably (or unfavorably) impresses prospects and customers, then the marketing director needs to have a voice in determining what the company will *say and do.*

Ryder quickly set about making their claim of convenience more than just a claim.

Rolling the Dice: Rolling Out New Trucks

In 1992, Ryder's consumer division replaced nearly one-third of its entire truck fleet with new vehicles. They replaced older trucks with 8500 nice, new, shiny trucks.

These vehicles were not only newer. They were also more convenient and customer-friendly. They were lower to the ground, making them easier to load. They had larger, more expensive rear-view mirrors, making them easier and safer to drive. The roof of each vehicle was translucent, allowing more light to come into the interior and making it easier to see what you are doing as you pack.

Then there was what we might call the singular "Dial-a-Truck phone number." The single phone number to contact for a company with hundreds of local dealers has been pioneered in many fields. It requires operational overhaul to achieve, but the first company in a category to advertise such a number scores a significant advantage. (In Canada, Pizza Pizza made their central phone number, 967-11-11, the best-known number in Toronto. Having just one number to call helped them build a $100 billion business, the Canadian equivalent of a $1 billion company in the United States, before they ran into some unrelated problems.)

As an essential part of its new strategic positioning, Ryder developed its own central telephone staff and mnemonic 800 number, 1-800-GO-RYDER to provide real convenience for the person who wants to reach them. Previously, a customer would call or visit one of the approximately 5000 independent Ryder dealers and ask, "Do you have such-and-such a truck available for rent?" In response, the dealer might look out his window at his available inventory of trucks and say, "No, sorry." The number of trucks he would have on loan from Ryder would rise and fall depending on the current demand, and sometimes the demand would unexpectedly exceed the inventory, causing a disappointed or lost customer.

To get things right, Ryder management rolled the dice again. They decided to invest $25 million in "RyderFIRST (sm)," a computerized reservation system that called for installing a computer in every single Ryder dealership. It was the largest distributed PC network in the country.

Now, when a call comes in from a customer who asks to reserve a certain size and type of truck, the trained phone operator is able to help the customer, knowledgeably and courteously, decide what size and type of truck to reserve; to promise (usually) that the desired vehicle will be available; to direct the customer to the nearest dealer; to alert the dealer via computer that the customer is coming; and, by computerized inventory control, to make sure that the dealer will have the right truck ready and waiting.

Also, there is the opportunity to maximize a second revenue

stream derived from the sale of moving supplies: boxes, bubble wrap, tape, rope, mattress and sofa covers, and so on.

The phone operator can discuss these needs with the customer, and then make sure that the dealer will have on hand the supplies that the customer wants.

Let a Smile Be Your Umbrella—But Wear a Raincoat, Too

To deal directly with the public, Ryder established and trained 200 phone operators. Ryder calls them, more accurately, "agents." Agents answering 1-800-GO-RYDER calls must first go through two weeks of training. They must acquire a firm understanding of the size of trucks, features on the trucks, how they compare to competition, the pricing, what packing supplies the customer will need, and so on.

In addition, there is a second group of phone personnel, based in Ryder's Miami headquarters, made up of service representatives who are especially trained and skilled in troubleshooting. Explains Mack, "They are really trained so that no matter what the issue is with the customer, they are empowered to fix it. It comes back to convenience. We don't want that customer to have to call us more than once to make a reservation. And if anything ever does go wrong (and we do everything we can to minimize that), we don't want them to have to call us more than once before we have remedied the situation."

In other words, these operators are really the customer's ombudsman, ready to step in and do what has to be done to make the customer happy. One Ryder television commercial shows an operator answering a call for help by giving road directions to a customer who has gotten lost while trying to drive the Ryder truck from the old home to the new one.

How the Marketing Became the Message

Finally, after making or blueprinting the product and service improvements needed to fulfill the promise of convenience, it was time to reach for the top rung of the ladder: advertising to successfully communicate all this to the public. Mack worked painstakingly with his advertising agency, Ogilvy & Mather ("they've done a great job with all of this," he says) to develop a long-range strategy for building the brand, with the central theme being (as you would expect) the promise of convenience and the new features designed to fulfill that promise. And, of course, 1-800-GO-RYDER was made an important element in all of the double-duty advertising.

When they did consumer research on the new advertising, they were startled to find that exposure to it resulted in *doubling* the "intention to buy" of prospective customers, an unusually high score. But that wasn't all. In true MaxiMarketing fashion, while gaining awareness, the invitation to call the Ryder phone number was generating the names of "hot" prospects. By this time, Ryder had totally transformed itself into the model of a MaxiMarketing winner—customer-focused, information-driven, ready to do whatever is necessary to please the consumer.

"Yes, But Where's the Money?"

As the new marketing director, Mack was faced with a problem only too familiar to brand managers. Brand building takes time, but top management wants sales results right away.

This is the trap that product managers fall into all too often. To meet sales quotas, they juice up sales with discounting promotions, which then tend to weaken the brand and cut the margin available for brand advertising. Mack was determined to avoid that trap.

Fortunately, while the new convenience-theme commercials were building up a favorable brand image over the long haul, the toll-free number, 1-800-GO-RYDER, was producing immediate sales results. The new campaign was launched on April 20, 1992, and the calls started right away. By October, the number of calls had risen to 15,000 a week.

Because peak season for moving is June through September, that is when Ryder advertises. The advertising stopped in September, but the calls continued. Not only because of the carry-over effect of the advertising, but also because Ryder was displaying the phone number on every piece of collateral sent out or distributed to customers and was featuring it in their Yellow Pages advertising.

The following spring, six months after the television advertising stopped, Ryder was *still* getting 15,000 calls a week, and forwarding the phone reservations to the new computer terminals installed in their 5000 dealerships.

We Care about You—and You—and You

The smartest advertisers are learning to appeal to different niches in their market with copy variations in their advertising that gets a response from the individual targeted. Ryder is one of them.

There are many subgroups in the move-it-yourself market. For instance, there are people who aren't moving to a new home at all but need to bring home a new cash-and-carry refrigerator or a just-inherited sofa. There are those people making only local moves, who are just moving across the street or across town and can make several trips with a light vehicle. Long-distance movers, who need a real van for all their household possessions. The households of military personnel who are frequently transferred to a new post. Small merchants who may need additional delivery vehicles during a holiday rush.

To each of these niches, Ryder direct-response advertising reaches out with a separate message, but always with the same fundamental appeal of convenience.

Eliminating the Anxiety

There is another consideration that ranks high with movers—peace of mind. Under the best of circumstances, moving is an extremely stressful experience.

For this reason, Ryder has expanded caring about its customers to include everything they can think of to make self-moving as calm, pleasant, and hassle-free as possible. This includes everything we've already seen: one easy-to-remember number for phone reservations, the vehicle and supplies you need ready and waiting for you, trucks that are easier to load and easier to drive.

But they don't stop there. For instance, moving is especially destructive of peace of mind for kids. It means being torn away from friends in school and the neighborhood, and the familiar surroundings of home and bedroom. It means having to plunge into the unknown, make new friends, build a new nest.

Ryder went to Kidvidz, producers of award-winning special-interest videos for children, and asked them to create a video to help kids and parents survive the jolt of moving. With believable kids and situations, "Let's Get a Move On!" explores common anxieties, and counters them with credible and reassuring depictions of saying goodbye, moving day, and making new friends in the new neighborhood.

Ryder sells the video to parents for little more than actual cost, a hefty discount off its retail price. They have received favorable feedback from grateful parents who are enthusiastic about how helpful the video was in relieving a child's anxiety about moving.

There is an even more dramatic example of how Ryder pursues the "tell, don't sell" key to success. They offer a free 21-page step-by-step guide to do-it-yourself moving, "The Mover's Advantage." It provides what size truck and roughly which and how many packing supplies you will need for your size of household; a list of things to do beforehand (pick up laundry, return library books, close bank accounts, etc.); a household possessions inventory worksheet; a day-by-day move-planner calendar; how to pack up; how to load and drive the truck; and what to do about your pets. The booklet is so thorough and sensible that it must be a delight to people who are naturally well-organized and a godsend to those who are not.

Goodbye El-Cheapo—Hello Domino

For five years prior to the new strategy, the industry had been suffering from oversupply. In the old days, to fight for market share and stimulate sluggish business, Ryder would match the competition and run special promotions offering 10 percent, 20 percent, or even 30 percent off.

The trouble with that approach, of course, is that if you're not careful you can promote yourself right out of business. Or become like the apocryphal business that was supposed to have boasted, "We lose on every sale, but make it up in volume."

Ryder determined to dig themselves out of that hole and avoid it in the future by being helpful and not trying to compete on price and price promotions. Instead, Mack told *Brandweek,* "Our plan has been to create a position that's sufficiently attractive to justify a higher—though still reasonable—price. We do this by adding value: through convenience, reputation, promotions, and last but not least, image."

The promotions they do undertake are designed to add value in a way that fits the demographics or needs of their customers. For instance, when you wearily pull up in front of your new home with your Ryder truck, the last thing in the world you feel like doing is digging out pots and pans and canned goods and trying to rustle up something to eat. So one of Ryder's promotions offered customers a coupon good for a free Domino's Pizza on arrival at their new home. Mack said it was the most successful promotion the company had run in six years. It reinforced the image of Ryder thoughtfully taking care of the customer. And because it gave Domino's first crack at a new customer in town. Supplying the pizzas probably cost Ryder little or nothing.

The next promotion offered a free NCAA college jacket of your choice with every truck rental. Like the Domino's pizza gift, this offer reflected an awareness of matching demographics. Typical self-movers have the same demographic profile as Domino's Pizza customers and college basketball fans.

Ryder evaluates and considers repeating promotions in a way that many other companies would do well to emulate. They set financial objectives for each promotion beforehand. If it reaches or exceeds its goals, it goes up for reconsideration the following year.

This may sound elementary, but we never cease to be amazed at how many advertisers never repeat a premium promotion, no matter how successful it may have been.

Easy Ryder All the Way

Just turning the pages of the catalog of sales aids and take-ones offered to dealers provides a mind-boggling glimpse of what is involved in constructing a TRC (Total Relationship Commitment) Marketing system in this category. One finds:

- "The Mover's Advantage," the guide to moving given to every prospect and customer (published in Spanish as well as English)
- A protection-plan brochure, explaining the value of purchasing Ryder's insurance covering damage to the truck
- A military moving guide
- A towing equipment brochure, describing the advantages of towing a vehicle using Ryder's towing equipment
- Supplies and accessories brochure, to help customers determine what quantities of moving supplies and what types of accessories they will need
- A corporate discount brochure and poster
- Towing instructions, using the Ryder tow dolly and car carrier
- Educational how-to-move posters which also promote Ryder equipment, supplies, and accessories
- Truck comparison chart, comparing Ryder trucks with those of the competition
- Customer satisfaction survey card, designed as a hang-tag for the truck steering wheel and saying in big bold letters: "This truck has been checked and is ready for you...Is everything OK?"

Another catalog covers just about everything that hits the consumer's eye outside and inside and helps create an instant impression that this is a smart, orderly, clean, helpful facility—a good place to do business. Signage. Banners. Literature racks. Road maps. Moving supplies, and neat pegboards and racks for displaying them. Ryder-logo apparel for sales personnel. ("When customers enter your dealership, it should not only be readily apparent where they should go to be serviced, it should also be obvious who will serve them.")

These catalogs make it as easy for a dealer to order supplies as it is to order a pair of boots from L.L. Bean. Nothing has been overlooked. No stone is left unturned in Ryder's caring approach to every detail. But because Ryder is working through 5000 independent dealers, there is obviously a limit to how far the company can go in forcing dealers to do everything the right way.

For this reason, Ryder uses the carrot, not the stick. Formerly, a dealer would receive a visit from a member of Ryder's field organization about four times a year. Today, it's more like once a month. The field rep is the go-between who encourages, aids, and monitors full implementation of the marketing strategy at the dealer level. In addition, there are local dealer councils, national dealer councils, and a national dealer convention where Ryder can talk with dealers—not *to* them, but *with* them—about how everybody can work together to serve the customer better.

As Mack puts it, "A quality chain goes from our headquarters to our field organization to the dealer base and then to our customer base." In less than two years, a total program incorporating many of the steps of MaxiMarketing—and often going beyond anything any company had ever done previously—was developed, was installed, and became an instant success.

What made all this possible?

"I think the biggest help," Mack told us, "is to have a chairman and CEO [Tony Burns] and a division president [Jerry Riordan] who really believe in the business and who are not afraid to take risks. Quite frankly, as smart as the plan may have been, it never would have been sold and implemented without the support of both of them. And they have been not only supportive, but have gone a step further to be advocates, and that has really made a tremendous difference."

Together with their brilliant marketing director, executive management at the highest level has shown that total commitment to really caring about the customer, really listening to the customer, and taking risks to reshape the company in a way that really helps the customer can not only build a profitable brand in the long run, it can pay off in the short run too.

A household move to a new home is ordinarily not undertaken on the spur of the moment. It is preceded by weeks or even months of worrying and planning.

If Ryder could use direct-response advertising to identify those future movers well in advance by inviting them to call early, and then expose them by mail to the full range of Ryder moving advantages, aids, and options, it would surely result in signing up more wavering prospects. This could be important not only for those who are considering U-Haul, but also those who are considering hiring professional movers instead of doing it themselves. It could be done in a way which would strengthen the Ryder brand, not weaken it.

Ryder is a MaxiMarketing winner that has set its sights on becoming a totally customer-involved operation and its management pursues that goal consistently and creatively.

They have demonstrated the ability to turn around the company in a down market while the competition still doesn't understand that Ryder is playing by a new set of rules. They dared to go back to square one and rethink what is needed to be a winner today. With so much accomplished in such a short time, there are unlimited possibilities for moving in new directions and to new heights as the economy picks up.

11 Beginning Again at Canada's North American Life

One of the fascinating questions we had to deal with in writing this book was whether it is possible for a huge, ponderous, bureaucratic conglomerate to undergo a fundamental change and transform itself into a truly caring and daring marketer.

Many of the most impressive winners we studied were either privately owned companies, like Fidelity Investments and LEGO Brand toys, or public companies that are still personally run by the founder, like Dell Computer, or like Harley-Davidson, which is still headed by Vaughn Beals, Jr., the man who led the leveraged buyout and the reinvention of the company that followed.

How can an established public company—with its traditions and mindsets and customary ways of doing business—compete with these nimble, unfettered entrepreneurs?

Good news: It can be done! It *is* being done.

Sometimes it is accomplished by a new-thinking marketer establishing a beachhead in the company and then gaining steadily wider acceptance within it by proving that the new marketing really pays, as Richard Shaw is doing at Seagram.

Sometimes it is the result of a top officer of the company having the vision and the perspective to see that radical new approaches are essential for long-range survival, as has been the case with Peter Brabeck at Nestlé.

In any case, the basic requirement is the courage or the willingness of top management to challenge conventional wisdom. The issue was framed succinctly in a thinkpiece in *Brandweek* by Peter J. Flatow, president of a consultancy called CoKnowledge:

> What did Microsoft, Intel, and Ford do that General Motors and IBM didn't? What did Gillette find out in the nick of time? Regardless of size or category dominance, if you don't reinvent your franchise, someone else will.
>
> Reinventing your franchise requires foresight. It requires the courage to challenge conventional wisdom. It means having the confidence to think outside the comfort zone. It taps all of the company's resources to leverage its assets and skills.

North American Sharpens Its Focus

North American Life Assurance Company of Toronto is one of Canada's largest financial services companies, with over $15 billion in assets under management. The company was built by selling policies through a large commissioned field force of agents, supported by awareness advertising. But increasingly, in recent years, this method of distribution has become less efficient. It was costing more than it was bringing in. Management realized it had to reinvent its way of doing business without rocking the boat and losing what it already had.

They began by looking for the market segments where they might find the most success. Instead of trying to be everything to everybody, and not doing much extraordinarily well, they would focus on just a few market segments in which they could meet and surpass customer expectations. And since 62 percent of a traditional agent's time was wastefully spent in prospecting, they would use external databases to market directly to the target and generate highly qualified leads for highly trained representatives.

A research committee determined that a very promising, underserviced market segment was women 30 to 44—owners, executives, managers, professionals, childless or with children up to 9 years old, university-educated, dual-income, with average household income over $70,000. Competitors were already closing in on this market—one of them had opened a Women's Financial Center in the downtown Toronto financial area and recruited a number of representatives to deal exclusively with these prospects.

Focus groups of typical prospects were held. They uncovered some of the common concerns of women in this category, such as what their position in life would be if their spouses should die or become disabled; what would happen to them if they got a divorce; how they would manage their retirement.

What Women Wanted

Women in the focus groups said that:

- Women were less likely than men to open a mailing.
- "Insurance agent" had unfavorable connotations.
- The representatives should be salaried, not commissioned, so they wouldn't push too hard to make the sale. A low-pressure approach was vital.
- The knowledge and expertise of the reps would be very important.
- It wouldn't matter if the rep was a man or a woman.
- Telemarketing would be the kiss of death. "And please don't call us at work!"

Next, how could North American learn to serve this specific market in a radically different way without snarling up their established way of doing business?

Skunkworking Toward Success

To find the answer, and to protect the process from the idea-killers waiting in every organization to shoot down any new approach, North American turned to the model made famous by Peters and Waterman in their classic management guide, *In Search of Excellence*—the "skunk works."

As Peters and Waterman reminded the world, the idea was the brainchild of Clarence L. "Kelly" Johnson, who organized the first such unit in 1943 to design, build, and test the first U.S. tactical jet fighter in record time. A small handpicked group of zealots is given separate space, a separate budget, and a free hand, with no organization charts, no red tape, no layers of management approval, as little paperwork as possible. "Just go do it."

At Lockheed, thanks to the skunk works, they were able to design, build, and fly their plane 143 days after the project was started. Since then, Peters and Waterman pointed out, a number of companies have used this approach to unleash entrepreneurial dynamics outside the bureaucracy of a large organization.

Following this model, in the spring of 1991, two North American executives, David Hales and John McEachen, were told to cancel their committee meetings, empty their desks, and find office space in another building away from the North American tower.

They were given a mandate to *build a new, profitable, targeted sales and service company that could create unique relationships with its customers* (on a first-year start-up budget, which eventually added up to $2.8 million).

They moved into a 150-square-foot office containing only two desks and two telephones. They started setting up what soon would become a wholly owned North American subsidiary, FNA Financial—devoted to selling not just insurance but a wide range of personal and business financial products. And they began looking for key people from outside the industry who could bring fresh ideas to the enterprise. They went to a direct-marketing conference and found a savvy, experienced, talented direct marketing manager, Ben McLean.

It was a daring move by North American, a classic example of daring to begin again. (The board of directors of the new company included the president of North American Life and his senior executives, thus providing both support and some measure of control by the parent company.)

To get their new subsidiary off to a flying start, Hales and McEachen had already prepared—and in the new company's first week, in early January of 1992, started sending out to 90,000 women—a traditional direct-mail sales letter promoting retirement savings plans. Four full-time telemarketers had been hired to handle the anticipated flood of response.

The mailing bombed. It netted a total of 90 sales.

This was the challenge that greeted Ben McLean when he walked in the door that same month to report for duty as the fledgling company's associate for creative and marketing direction. Of course, the good part was that, from that low point, he had nowhere to go but up.

He brought with him solid experience as a copywriter at JWT and ad manager at Avco Financial Services. "They offered all the empowerment and hands-on marketing I was enjoying at Avco Financial, plus a chance to help blow the doors of the industry," he says.

He would be given a chance to play three roles: to develop the marketing strategies; to model customer profiles from within external databases; and to actually create, produce, and direct the lead-generation and customer relationship-building programs for the various media.

It Really Works

What McLean was able to accomplish in a very short time is especially gratifying to us as authors because of the verification he offers that the ideas in our books played a part.

"There are about 20 stick-on notes peeking out of the underlined and highlighted pages of my autographed copy of *The Great Marketing Turnaround,*" he writes. "I had pulled out the book to see just how many MaxiMarketing ideas we've implemented in the successful launch of FNA Financial just 18 months ago...We're test-marketing database-marketing techniques in one segment in one urban center with a budget of just under $1 million. But we've been able to test and launch an integrated marketing effort that is making us formidable competitors to the largest, richest institutions in our selected block faces" (the smallest unit of Canadian postal districts).

The urban area chosen to develop a database-marketing model for the rest of Canada was Toronto. The first job was to define, with utmost precision, and identify the best target prospects buried somewhere in the external databases. McLean wrote to us, "The key for me was on page 307 of *The Great Marketing Turnaround: 'Being able to send a relevant, motivating and promotional message to precisely those people who are most ready, willing, and able to respond can be counted on to produce astonishing short-term results while setting the stage for a profitable long-term relationship.'*"

To lay the groundwork for this, McLean worked with some of the most innovative experts at StatsCan, R. L. Polk, and leading list owners. He was also able to consult an unusual Canadian resource, Canada Post, the postal system, which extends itself much further than most of the world's postal systems in advising direct marketers and helping them succeed.

The Quest for Maximized LTV. McLean and his task force decided to look for the greatest Lifetime Customer Value within their target segment. They narrowed their market down to dual-income-household women five to ten years younger than the age at which they would be of interest to other financial competitors. This meant FNA would focus its efforts on a smaller percentage of the market segment with a greater profit potential over the long run. FNA would start building a relationship with these women early, and thus be in a good position for cross-sell opportunities even after their assets became large enough to interest many of FNA's competitors.

Defining the Target. The composite portrait of the woman they decided to look for was:

- She is a dual-income-household career woman, university-educated, aged 30 to 44 years, probably married to a slightly older professional.

- Both husband and wife are approaching their peak earning years.
- They have at least five years of equity in their home, which means they have at least some disposable income.
- They have kids from 0 to 9, so they have a good reason for seeking financial protection.
- She is just a few years away from considering an investment broker, and is just beginning to realize that she needs the benefits of a professional financial plan.
- She is often disappointed with the knowledge and expertise of the banks and trusts in helping her manage her money, but at the same time is anxious to avoid undue risk.

Hitting the Target. Mail in Canada is first sorted by "FSA" (Forward Sortation Area, the first three digits of the postal code number)—then by a smaller unit, the "block face"—and finally by the "postal walk," a letter-carrier route involving 50 pounds of mail or 400 homes covering a number of block faces. FNA was able to use the first four characteristics of its target woman to score all the postal walks according to how high a concentration of likely prospects they contained.

These rankings were achieved by a computer search of *Taxfiler,* a database compiled by the government which identifies financial and demographic characteristics of households in each postal walk as revealed by the latest income tax returns. Using FNA's set of customer assumptions, Statistics Canada's Small Area Administrative Data Division, a government department, was able to manipulate this data further for a modest fee and grade each postal walk from A+ to D– as to the likelihood of the residents fitting the target profile.

A "kill file" was used to screen out all existing North American accounts, to avoid incurring the anger of existing North American agents by seeming to compete for their customers.

Now McLean had the hot postal walks. To get the largest universe of names and addresses, he went to Info-Direct, a division of the telephone company, who could supply up to 74 percent of the phone numbers that were listed for households in each postal walk and available for telemarketing. "We were supplied with diskettes we could load directly into our computers for on-screen telemarketing with the ability to capture response, add data, send faxes, trigger mailings, and set appointments with financial advisors," he explained to us.

McLean had used the current state-of-the-art technology to zero in on his target market. Now he was ready to have the hot prospects self-select themselves by responding to his letter or phone calls.

The New Math at Work

In his first summer (1992), McLean tested personalized sales letters, followed up by phone calls, to women in the selected postal walks versus cold phone calls alone. The mailings and follow-up calls produced an 8 percent response. The cold calls alone brought a 7 percent response. "This meant," says McLean, "that it was costing us 155 percent more for mailing costs to get 1 percent more responses," and that it would be more profitable to abandon the direct mail.

Got that? Time out for an exercise in the New Math using our own hypothetical numbers, not their actual ones. If their mailings cost $500 per thousand and produced 10 percent more responses than phone calls alone, that would mean 10 additional responses at a cost per additional response of $50. Let's say the phone calls alone cost $2.25 each to make or $2250 per thousand. A 7 percent response meant 70 respondents, at a cost per response of $32 ($2250 divided by 70). Thus the $50 cost per order resulting from mail plus phone would be 155 percent more than the $32 cost per order from phone alone.

Building Brand Awareness, Selectively

One of the things FNA learned from this test was that although focus groups can provide invaluable overall guidance, some of the things panel members tell a marketer can be dead wrong, and must be tested by that most scientific of all testing methods, measured direct response. The focus groups had said that telemarketing would be "the kiss of death"—remember?

The other thing they learned is that financial direct mail is not highly regarded or warmly welcomed by busy working women. Canada Post research has found that women give financial sales letters the same "significantly unwelcome" ranking as contest mailings, real estate flyers, and book and record club offers.

Did that mean that nothing could be done to provide a favorable impression of FNA in a woman prospect's mind before she receives a phone call from an FNA representative? Not at all. Some readers of our two previous books have gotten the idea that we look down on awareness advertising. They are wrong. We would never be so foolish as to deny that building up a favorable impression of your product or service in the minds of your prospects and customers has an important place in your marketing program, as long as it can be done in a cost-effective way.

What we have pointed out is simply that too much brand-awareness advertising is allowed to become silly and ineffective because of the difficulty of measuring its effect precisely, and is wasteful because millions of dollars are spent exposing the advertising to people who are not and never will be prospects.

Buying a Big Image in Small Areas. Says McLean, "We simply don't have the dollars to get share of mind across the city, much less maintain it against the banks, trusts, and other well-established financial companies. We're new, unknown, and asking to handle people's hard-earned life savings. *But in selected FSAs, and on individual postal walks, we can afford to build the name recognition and awareness it takes to be accepted and have our telephone calls well received.*"

This is a proven technique used by regional marketers against national competitors. It's like being a coffee company that's too small to compete nationally in the face of the giant ad budgets of the major brands. By spending all of its ad money in, let's say, just the state of Oregon, the local marketer can outgun the major brands there and become the best-known and most favorably viewed coffee brand in the mind of the consumer of that state.

Now FNA Financial has taken this strategy a step further. It set out to become "famous" only in selected neighborhoods and city blocks of Toronto, with concentration in just those areas.

Pinpointed Outserts Precede Calls. In December of 1992, after analyzing the results of the test of telemarketing with and without direct-mail support he had done that summer, McLean ran 250,000 full-color inserts in two financial newspapers and polybag outserts (separate brochures delivered with the publication) in the Toronto edition of *Chatelaine,* a women's magazine. This served the purpose, he told us, of making "the media, key influencers, and early adapters" aware of the new company.

He followed this by dropping another 260,000 inserts into community newspapers in the most promising FSAs. Then, they started making 5000 telemarketing calls a week to the most promising postal walks within those FSAs. There is a striking similarity to a military campaign in which the air force or the artillery (the inserts) first softens up the target, and then the tanks and infantry (the phone calls) move in to complete the conquest.

The campaign was so successful that, after the first two weeks, FNA had to suspend its in-house telemarketing operation. It was no longer needed. The campaign had doubled appointments, and the financial advisors were overbooked.

This multimedia technique is still being refined. In the next wave, McLean planned to polybag his ad insert with *Images* magazine, to be given just to women who have made purchases of upscale cosmetics at Shoppers Drug Mart stores serving his "hot postal walks." He was also scheduling backlit mall posters in selected upscale malls in the target areas, with a rotation schedule to match the telemarketing effort. This MaxiMarketing winner provides a model of how even the smallest company can compete effectively in mini-markets.

"You Are in Control"

A key component in the swift success of the company has been the recruiting and the training of the financial advisors who would genuinely help prospects and not just try to sell them.

Women in the focus research panels had said that they didn't like "insurance agents"; they would like the representatives who approached them to be salaried, not commissioned*—remember?

So, the FNA advertising literature carefully points out, "Our financial advisors are salaried, and they take the time to listen to your needs and concerns. *You are in control.* [Italics ours.] We will give you the facts you need to make the best decisions and organize your finances the way you want."

Note the theme of customer empowerment in this. It is a striking example of sensitivity to the new consumers, wary of being sold a bill of goods, demanding to be in control, asking for the information they need to make their own decision.

FNA's financial advisors are recruited and trained to fit the market segment they will be serving. Over 40 percent are women. All are made aware of the importance of avoiding sexist language and approaches. They go through a five-week "boot camp" training run by FORUM Corporation of Boston. Selling-skills training starts with Rule No. 1: "focus on the customer." Focus on the customer's problems and needs, not your own goals and needs.

Old Wine in New Bottles

The basic principles and discoveries about what makes people feel like responding to an advertising offer or invitation are timeless. It is the challenge of each new generation of marketers to find new, appropriate, contemporary ways to harness these timeless discoveries.

We were amused and fascinated to note in an FNA Financial reply form a technique that can be traced back to successful response advertising of well over half a century ago. And that is to let your respondents tell you, in the printed reply form, both their problem and your solution.

For instance, there was the classic ad for Charles Atlas, the

*They have since learned, according to customer satisfaction surveys, that what is most important to the customer is the knowledge and expertise of the financial advisor and "low pressure," not the method by which the advisor is compensated. One more example of unreliable research findings.

home course in bodybuilding, headed "Give me your measure and I'll make you a new man." (There were no female bodybuilders in those days.) In the reply coupon, the respondent wrote in his present body dimensions and asked Charles Atlas for free information on how to achieve dramatic improvement. It is an effective way of reminding the reader quickly of the reasons for responding.

It may seem like a far cry from that to the dignified, tasteful, low-key advertising literature of FNA Financial. But take a second look and note how the wording of their reply form accomplishes the same purpose as the Charles Atlas reply form.

> YES. These issues are important to me if FNA Financial is going to help my family with financial planning:
>
> - ❑ No pressure
> - ❑ Salaried financial advisors
> - ❑ Convenient. We will meet at your office or your home at the time that's best for you
> - ❑ Customer in control
> - ❑ Support from specialists within FNA and the North American Life group of companies
> - ❑ Full range of RRSP, savings, investment, and security products

Passing Out Pieces of the Action

In *The Great Marketing Turnaround,* 1 of the 10 trends away from mass advertising that we cited was the movement toward active consumer participation in advertiser-sponsored events. There are millions of consumers, we wrote, "who are saying if you, the advertiser, want us to hear you above the deafening roar of today's hawking, give us a piece of the action."

FNA Financial's basic telemarketing campaign is surrounded and reinforced by a brilliant mix of advertising and newsmaking events and activities designed to increase awareness and build relationships through networking and participation.

They Sponsor Local Fund-Raisers in a Unique Way. FNA Financial was the official sponsor of Women Who Make a Difference 1993 Awards, along with the Hudson Bay Company and Toronto Life Fashion. They sponsored the Lifetime Achievement Award at the 1993 Woman Entrepreneur of the Year Awards. They sponsored the Mother's Day Breakfast for a service called The Kids Help Phone, a number that kids can call if they are having problems with child abuse.*

But, as McLean points out, that's routine. For generations, advertisers have been sponsoring and donating to worthy causes and organizations for whatever ephemeral good will and publicity value it yields.

What makes FNA's sponsorship activity different is that they use these occasions not to try to "sell" the attendees—which would be inappropriate and distasteful—but rather to actively build acceptance and credibility among the guests, almost all of whom fit the prime prospect profile, and to provide a benefit for their customers.

Most companies who buy tables at a fund-raising lunch or dinner for a worthy cause will then hand out the tickets to corporate execs as a "perk." But not FNA. Instead, *they give the tickets to the company's financial advisors and their customers.* Then the breakfast, luncheon, or dinner becomes a customer networking opportunity. Business cards are exchanged across the table. New business alliances and personal friendships are formed—and FNA is the catalyst.

"We know that our first customers are early adapters and key influencers," says McLean, "so every effort we make to go beyond the usual level of customer relationships is clearly reciprocated. That is why we are eagerly expanding our efforts to get customers to our sponsored events."

*At last report, FNA had also signed up as a sponsor of an extremely innovative fund-raising proposal, a Duck Race for The Kids Help Phone. If all went well, 100,000 bar-coded yellow plastic ducks would be released into a river with thousands of cheering families lining the banks. Donors would earn sponsorship of one of the ducks by making a contribution. After about an hour, the ducks that cross the finish line first would earn the winning sponsors donated prizes like trips and gift certificates. The event was expected to raise $350,000. And FNA was thinking of providing a hospitality tent for customers and their families.

They Have Taken Over Prime Sponsorship of "The Women's Small Business Directory." They were planning to invite customers to the launch of the ninth edition. It lists women and their areas of expertise and encourages networking.

They Have Established a Fax Information Service. Women who are small-business owners can ask to be put on the broadcast fax list and receive timely opinions from experts within the North American Group of Companies on events or new legislation that affects small business.

They Have Prepared over 20 Fact Sheets for Customers. Topics range from "Cottages and Taxes" to the "Financial Aspects of Marriage Breakdown." They are making a complete list available to their customers. Then a customer who is interested in a particular Fact Sheet can obtain a copy by phoning in a request. This triggers a follow-up response by a customer-service person and provides an opportunity for cross-selling.

They Run Free Workplace Seminars and Do Informative Radio Advertising. They focus on controversial topics that competitors are too timid to touch, such as marital breakdown, elder care, and financing children's higher education. From 50 to 100 percent of those who attend such seminars sign up for a private appointment with a financial advisor.

You Can't Fake It

We see in these activities a pattern of genuine caring about issues that are important to business and professional women, not just an advertising or public-relations gimmick. It is strongly reminiscent of the way in which Puget Sound Bank went about winning the trust of environmentalists.

Karen Fraser, publisher of *Women Like Me,* a small-business and networking directory, says she is constantly approached by companies wanting to reach women. But when she asks them if they have a budget, the answer is invariably no.

She was pleasantly surprised and impressed by the serious

commitment of FNA Financial, and agreed to having FNA information sent to her mailing list with her personal endorsement enclosed. In it she wrote:

> A company can change its advertising almost overnight to attempt to appeal to women. It takes a far more serious commitment to change your distribution system, the way you train and reward your marketing people, and how to use existing financial products in ways that really meet women's needs.
>
> North American Life has made that commitment through a fully owned subsidiary called FNA Financial.
>
> They started several years ago with a task force and research that told them what women did and didn't like about financial institutions.
>
> Then to create a new corporate culture and distribution system, they hired outside the industry and launched a new corporation miles away from the head office.
>
> ...This is much more than lip service. It's the kind of serious commitment that deserves support and your feedback.

An example of this commitment in action, and its consequences, was provided by a highly favorable story in *Financial Times of Canada* which wrote:

"One FNA client, Judy Huyer, a senior manager at Unitel Communcations Inc., is a chartered accountant and knows well how much financial-planning services can cost. That's why she says she was so impressed that the financial plan provided by her FNA advisor was not only free, but comprehensive. She liked the fact that she wasn't given the hard sell on FNA products, and was actually steered away from them in some cases. Since the service is so good, Huyer says, she'd be willing in the future to stick with FNA even if a competitor had a slightly lower price."

If you were a Toronto business or professional woman, wouldn't *you* welcome a call from FNA after reading this? And as a marketer, you can see how powerfully this demonstrates the difference between attempting to change public perception by merely changing your claims...and profoundly changing public perception by changing the *reality* of the way you deal with the public?

Maximized Media

We have already touched on such creative use of media by McLean as the polybag inserts and mall posters confined to the target neighborhoods. McLean reports that publications have been eager to cooperate because the recession has made them hungry for revenue. "The willingness to provide split runs and regional buys, or polybag advertising in certain selected areas, has increased." (There is a startling reference buried in that statement. "Split-run" testing, in which two or more coded test ads are given equal exposure in alternate copies of the same issue, has long been the secret weapon of mail-order advertisers. But the new breed of relationship marketers been slow to discover and use this powerful tool.)

Another big step forward in creating a bond with the target market is scheduled for the future. The focus groups had indicated, and direct-mail tests had confirmed, that women in the target audience were not very receptive to direct mail. But magazines are a much more welcome vehicle. So FNA was planning to launch its own 48-page glossy magazine designed for them by a top magazine publisher, *Financial Strategies for Women,* with articles by freelance writers. Although it was conceived as a prospecting piece to get through to women who ignore financial direct mail, FNA was also going to make sure that its existing customers received the first advance copies.

This is a striking example of what we called, in *MaxiMarketing,* "the educational model" for interaction with a prospect-customer database. Giving their prospects something of value, an informational magazine, enables them to break through the media clutter with the product messages.

The Payback from Feedback

One of the biggest mistakes a cost-conscious company can make is to think that customer satisfaction surveys cost money. They don't cost. They pay, in more ways than one.

FNA sends a customer satisfaction survey to every new customer, and follows it up with a phone call to increase the response. They use the results of this customer feedback immediately in their marketing and their training programs.

For instance, it was from the customer satisfaction survey that FNA learned that knowledge and expertise are the most wanted qualifications in a financial advisor, "low-pressure approach" was second, and "salaried" was only No. 6. Soon FNA was reflecting these preferences in lead-generation and event-promotion materials.

The high customer satisfaction is used as a selling tool. The ad inserts report the high degree of customer satisfaction and back this up with customer testimonials and photographs. And FNA invites prospects to phone for a copy of the survey results, which indicated a satisfaction rating among the first customers of 95 to 97 percent good to excellent.

FNA Financial Arrives

At last report, FNA Financial had 20 trained financial advisors, soon to grow to 40.

A part-time in-house telemarketing staff of 16 people was making 5000 calls per week, working four evenings a week, and getting a 9-percent response.

It is a state-of-the-art operation, with call numbers fed to the telemarketers by computer and call results punched in and fed to the financial advisors electronically as well. Within a year, they expect to reach 250,000 households, estimated to be 73 percent of the identified universe of prospects. And they are doing it at a cost of $23 per acquired lead, compared to $103 per acquired lead paid an outside telemarketer for leads that were not as strong.

Within three months, FNA's rookie financial advisors were outselling competitors whose reps had years of experience, and they plan to double that record within a year. At the one-year mark, the advisors were outperforming three-year veterans of the traditional agent system, and making more sales per households than their parent company, North American Life. Using the Toronto experience as a prototype, FNA is about to start expanding the operation to other cities in Canada.

One of the remarkable aspects of this success is the swiftness with which it was achieved, barely more than a year after FNA opened its doors. It is a striking example of what can be accomplished by moving boldly and knowledgeably, by showing prospects and customers you really care about what is important to them, and by finding creative ways to give them what they are asking for.

It is also a dramatic example of the power of the new Individualized Marketing when properly done. At the end of *MaxiMarketing,* we provided checklists of questions to ask yourself so that readers could audit their own companies or job performance. Writes McLean, "As I look over the MaxiMarketing Audit, I can answer yes to every item...[Using these principles] we've been able to test and launch an integrated marketing effort that is making us formidable competitors to the largest, richest institutions reaching our selected block faces."

While FNA is currently marketing to professional women, the methods used can be transferred to any target group in the future. "What we are trying to do," Hales told Canada's *Direct Marketing News,* "is see if we can find ways and means of bringing more discipline, efficiency, and therefore profitability to distribution of financial service products. What we learn from this will be applied to the overall distribution of our [North American's] products." In other words, they are looking at FNA Financial as the answer to breathing new life into all of the North American Life empire.

12

Amil Group: The Master MaxiMarketer of Brazil

On July 4 of every year in the United States, Macy's department store presents New York City with the gift of a spectacular fireworks display over the East River.

In the summer of 1993, as we were nearing completion of this book, skyrockets once again soared up and burst open, shooting a dazzling spray of color in every direction over the night sky.

The electrifying pyrotechnics provided an apt metaphor for our next case history—the story of Amil Assistencia Medica, now the second largest health plan provider in Brazil and that country's fastest growing company.

Like the fireworks lighting up New York's skyline, Amil too rocketed straight up out of nowhere to brighten the horizon of the biggest economy in Latin America. (As in most metaphors, this one too has its limits; unlike a bursting skyrocket, Amil is in no danger of burning out.)

Despite the troubled, inflation-battered business environment of Brazil, Amil has been growing at an astonishing, compounded average growth rate of 45 percent a year for the past 10 years. Revenues for the Amil Group will climb to over $300 million in the current fiscal year in an economy less than one-tenth the size of the

American GNP—the equivalent of a $3-billion business in the United States.

The early instinctive use of MaxiMarketing principles by the founder of Amil, Dr. Edson de Godoy Bueno, predates the publication of our book by that name in 1986. Yet Dr. Bueno acknowledges that "in the last ten years the role of the MaxiMarketing approach has been central to our accelerated growth. Since the beginning of my career as a business man, I was working the MaxiMarketing way without knowing it. It was pure intuition and feeling. But I was always aiming for direct contact with the customer, knowing them by name and address, and getting extremely involved with them as human beings."

In 1990, one of the authors of this book, Stan Rapp, following a talk he gave at an Amil-sponsored event, was asked by Dr. Bueno to provide marketing counsel on an ongoing basis. It was a marriage of like-minded businesspeople. Before long, the entire Amil management team had consciously embraced MaxiMarketing as a core corporate strategy.

The Broken-Down Little Hospital Where It All Began

Amil had its modest beginnings over 20 years ago. Young Edson de Godoy Bueno had gone from shining shoes on the streets of São Paulo to working his way through medical school. In 1971, he was just completing his training. He was very poor and had no money—but somewhere within him was the brain and soul of an entrepreneur destined to leave his mark on how business is done and won—not only in Brazil but elsewhere as well.

Young Dr. Bueno became aware of a broken-down 35-bed hospital, Casa de Saude Sao José in Duque de Caxias, an impoverished city of 600,000 near Rio de Janeiro. Some 90 percent of the hospital's beds were occupied by obstetrics patients.

The hospital was teetering on the edge of bankruptcy. Actually, it was more of a modified house than a true hospital facility. It had just three patients coming in for weekly prenatal care. There was no pediatrician on duty, just one who paid a daily morning visit. Many invoices, including large ones, never got sent out. The payroll was four months behind. There was no centralized purchasing—anyone on the staff could buy whatever they thought was needed. It was about as sorry a launching pad for a great enterprise as one could imagine.

But when you come from poverty as Dr. Bueno had, you are accustomed to acquiring and working with broken things. So with youthful audacity, he asked the owner to *give* him the hospital.

Because a quirk in the Brazilian legal system made that a more attractive option than declaring bankruptcy, the owner agreed. "Everyone thought I was crazy," Dr. Bueno recalls today. "But I knew the problem was bad management. I knew that in such a poor city, in which all of the hospitals were adapted houses and their medical service was right out of the nineteenth century, whoever offered the smallest differential of improvement would have the city in his hands."

Dr. Bueno began looking for a small differential.

The Hospital's First Extra-Value Proposition

Most of the patients who came to the hospital were extremely poor, from households earning an average of $60 a month. Just buying a Coca-Cola would be an unimaginable indulgence.

So Dr. Bueno decided to offer pregnant mothers—and the children they brought with them if they already had any—a free Coke each time the client came to the hospital for a prenatal exam.

In the world's developed economies, this treat would have been merely a nice little extra, like the dentist giving your child a free lollypop. But to the struggling people of Duque de Caxias, it meant something far more. It meant they were being treated as human beings—that somebody cared about them, no matter how poor they were.

It was Dr. Bueno's early experience with one of the keys to business success described in Chapter 2: offering "gain without pain." And, it would prove to be only the first of many extra-value propositions developed in the following years.

Since the cost of each visit to the hospital was paid by the government, the expense of providing Cokes had to come out of the allocated coverage. It amounted to 6 percent of the government payments—no small consideration. But Dr. Bueno was convinced that the resulting increase in the number of patients would more than make up for the smaller margin per patient. He was right.

Another extra-value benefit he provided was free transportation. The hospital had a van which was only used in the afternoon for institutional needs. Dr. Bueno decided to make the van available during the morning hours to give the mother and her newborn baby a free return ride home. This quickly became a much-appreciated demonstration of caring for the mother and provided an important benefit at the same time for the women of Duque de Caxias.

Often, patients had been staying at the hospital longer than necessary simply because they had no money for the bus ticket to go back home. After the van service began, space available in the hospital doubled because the beds were occupied only half as long.

Information-Age Marketing Ahead of Its Time

Next, Dr. Bueno managed to obtain the use of the rooms of the local trade association for the purpose of conducting free seminars and courses for pregnant women. Women who attended got basic knowledge about preventive health care and much more. They were offered something to eat. They could enter a sweepstakes or drawing in which they might win such things as diapers, high chairs, and cribs. And, of course, there was no charge for any of this.

You can imagine how much the seminars meant to the poorly educated women of the area and how much they appreciated the hospital that was offering so much to them.

Soon it all began to pay off. At the beginning, there were only 70 baby deliveries per month. Within one year, the number had risen to 140 per month. Salaries now were paid on time. Purchasing was centralized. A staff pediatrician was on duty in the nursery night and day. As the hospital's income grew, Dr. Bueno once again displayed his natural genius for building a business by ploughing all of his first year's profits back into local advertising.

The Brain Trust Is Formed

In 1973, he needed to hire another doctor, and interviewed Dr. Jorge Ferreira de Rocha for the position. The managerial talent and sensitivity of the young doctor were most impressive. Dr. Bueno felt he had found someone with whom he could share his dream of building a great enterprise.

He offered Dr. Ferreira de Rocha a staff position at a salary of 6000 Brazilian cruzeiros a month.

"I'll need 8000," said Dr. Ferreira de Rocha.

For a moment, Dr. Bueno recalls, he was disappointed, thinking, "This guy is only interested in money, not in sharing my dreams."

But then Dr. Ferreira de Rocha explained. "I'll keep 2000 for myself, and use the other 6000 to bring on board three other doctors with whom I am now working at my present hospital."

It was then that Dr. Bueno knew he had found the man he was seeking. Dr. Ferreira de Rocha's visionary and managerial qualities matched his own. A powerful combination was formed.

Two of the other three doctors brought on board, Dr. Paulo Marcos Senra Souza and Dr. Carlos Oswald Monteiro also brought very special talents to the little company. Together, the four young doctors created a management team which proved to be unstoppable.

By the fifth year, the number of births at their hospital had climbed to 640 per month, a 900 percent gain, and the successful medical entrepreneurs looked for new worlds to conquer.

Dr. Bueno bought a general hospital and decided to transform it into a children's hospital. The space needed for four children's beds was no greater than the amount of space previously occupied by just one adult bed. Result: the revenue increased fourfold while the fixed overhead costs remained the same.

By the end of the 1970s, they had added a third hospital in Duque de Caxias, this one for adults, and a fourth in another city. Each of these hospitals became known in Brazil as a model for advanced technology and innovation. The children's hospital, for instance, came to be recognized as having the best intensive-care unit for children in the entire country.

Amil Is Born

One day, the four doctors were sitting around the kitchen table chatting. One of them was reading a newspaper, and noted that Golden Cross, the leading health insurance company, had increased tenfold in size.

Suddenly, they got excited about starting their own health insurance plan. They would have a lot in their favor. They were doctors. They had a management style that worked. They were more experienced at running hospitals than Golden Cross.

Of course, there was a downside, too. They were "hillbillies" from outside the big city and knew little about life in Rio de Janeiro and São Paulo. They knew nothing about about how to sell or administer a health insurance plan. And there were many well-established companies already in the field.

But, being young, idealistic, and confident in their ability to achieve whatever they set their sights on, in 1979, they launched Amil Assistencia Medica International—or simply AMIL in its abbreviated form. Dr. Bueno and his three close associates were determined that someday, somehow, Amil would become the biggest and best health plan in Brazil. Following this "think big" strategy, they ploughed every penny of profit earned in Amil's early years back into advertising, just as they had done with the first hospital venture in Duque de Caxias. Soon after launching Amil, they stumbled upon one of the secrets of their success.

The Best-Remembered Phone Number in Brazil

Two years after Amil began, Golden Cross was still 140 times bigger than the neophyte company. Dr. Bueno knew that perception often becomes reality—how a company is perceived in the marketplace can be as important as how big they really are. To be taken seriously, Amil had to be perceived as a major player in the health care field. But what could they do with little capital and a tiny share of market?

The answer was an unusual television advertising strategy. What Amil did was to combine the power of direct response with the image-building power of brand-awareness commercials. Then, as the business grew, they established a dominant presence in prime-time programming.

They poured advertising dollars into expensively produced TV spots and always included the phone number to generate a steady flow of leads for the sales force. It was the kind of double-duty advertising that makes every dollar work twice as hard. And they also found a way to turn their phone number into the best-remembered number in Brazil.

Because Brazilian phones do not have any alphabetical letters on the push buttons or dials, as phones do in America, it is not possible to substitute an easily remembered word or two such as "Dial 1-800-COLLECT" for MCI's collect-call service. But what was impossible for other advertisers in Brazil, soon became possible for Amil. Since "mil" means "one thousand" in Portuguese, a phone number was obtained for Rio de Janeiro, and later for São Paulo, ending with "1000." The next step was to substitute "MIL" for "1000" and repeat over and over again in their São Paulo advertising, "CALL AMIL: 221-1000."

One night when Stan Rapp was dining with Dr. Bueno in Rio, the Amil founder offered to prove that the Amil phone number had become "the best-known number in Brazil." Dr. Bueno called over a waiter and said, "Quick, tell me the first phone number that comes to mind." The waiter replied instantly, "221-1000." "You see," laughed Dr. Bueno, "he knows our number even better than that of his own mother."

The number 221-1000 is so well remembered that some of the calls received each day are from Golden Cross customers who dial the Amil top-of-mind phone number by mistake. How's that for recall!

4000 Percent Growth in a Decade

By 1982, Amil was producing annual operating revenue of over $5 million. By 1990, it shot up to $165 million. By 1992, it had reached $229 million, 40 times bigger in just a decade. This spectacular growth brings to mind the "bursting skyrocket" metaphor mentioned earlier—a proliferation of unique services and "Caring and Daring" initiatives lighting up the life of residents of the Rio de Janeiro and São Paulo districts of Brazil.

The total architecture of the Amil Group—its hospitals, dental plan, clinics, laboratories, doctors, service offices—is too detailed and complex to be fully described here. But we can take a look at a number of activities that demonstrate the keys to success identified in our studies of outstanding MaxiMarketing winners.

Here are some of the "fireworks" that spark Amil's continued growth and innovative managerial style.

The Amil Emergency Call-In Service. The service operates around the clock and includes a doctor always on duty for consultation if first aid is required or if a more serious emergency arises.

If, in the doctor's view, the patient's condition calls for immediate admission to a hospital, arrangements are made by Amil with the best available facility. The doctor on the line tells the caller, "Go there at once," and then reassuringly, "a doctor will be expecting you and waiting for you when you arrive."

It's one of the many real-life demonstrations of how Amil goes beyond the expected to send the message, "We take care of you."

The Amil Rescue Plan. One of Amil's most unusual and daring points of difference had its origin in a visit Dr. Ferreira de Rocha paid to an old friend, a farmer outside of Itabuna in the state of Bahia.

His friend was a wealthy man, living on a beautiful farm far from the big cities. But he was not completely happy because he worried about the possibility of a medical emergency. He might not be able to get to a good hospital quickly enough, even though he could afford to buy the entire hospital. There were long distances to travel, and the possibility of serious traffic jams along the way. He shared his concerns about what might happen in case of a sudden stroke or a heart attack.

Out of this experience, an idea was born in Dr. Ferreira de Rocha's mind. When the new concept was first proposed to the management team at Amil, they could not believe he was really serious about it. It was like a thousandfold multiplication of the little extra touch of caring provided 20 years earlier by that first little hospital in Duque de Caxias, when they provided a van to transport new mothers and their babies home from the hospital. This time Amil would provide a helicopter to swoop out of the sky and transport a stricken person to the emergency room of an intensive-care facility located at a considerable distance from the scene of the rescue.

When they fully understood what Dr Ferreira de Rocha had in mind, his colleagues began to warm up to the daring idea. The Amil Rescue Plan would require a $5 million investment for equipment and infrastructure and there was no way to know beforehand how the public would respond. But it represented a dramatic way to demonstrate Amil's commitment to putting the customer's interest first and to making a critical difference in the lives of those who sign up with Amil. The decision was made to proceed.

Within a few months time, the first helicopters were ready to take to the air and a fleet of shining new "total-care" ambulances were ready to carry out the plan on the ground. These were not just colorfully painted helicopters and ambulances but fully equipped mobile surgery and intensive care units with specialized medical crews, capable of very fast response including application of lifesaving technology en route to the hospital.

Announcement of the new Amil Health Rescue Plan was a major advertising and public relations event. The entire multimedia campaign was expertly put together by Clemente Nobrega, Amil's marketing director and general manager of Promarket, the company's in-house ad agency.

The offer was kept simple. Anyone could sign up, even if they belonged to another health plan. The price was only $2 per month for Amil customers and $5 per month if you were unfortunate enough to be a member of a different health plan

The direct-response TV commercial for the Rescue Plan opens with a fascinating shot of the blue and orange helicopter filling the screen as it comes in for a landing to reenact a rescue mission. At the close, in São Paulo the "221-1000" phone number flashes on the screen. When the first commercials appeared, the switchboard at the telemarketing center was jammed by the biggest response in Amil's history. Within a few months, a hundred thousand people enrolled in the Amil Health Rescue Plan—with 20 percent of the business coming from people who were customers of the competition.

It is difficult to imagine an advertising concept an ad agency might dream up that could better convey Amil's positioning as a provider of superior health coverage than the stark reality of the Amil helicopter ready at a moment's notice to fly to the rescue of a subscriber.

Once more—by actual deeds—Amil was adding credibility to what they were saying in their sign-off line, "We take care of you."

The Amil Children's Club. In 1992, Amil launched Clube do Amilzihno. Parents were invited through advertising inserts to enroll their children in a club and receive free gifts for the kids delivered to the home and a free, fun-to-read children's magazine teaching good health habits. Copies of the magazine could be picked up at the Amil Service Centers located throughout Rio de Janeiro and São Paulo.

Amilzihno Club membership was available for a six-month free trial to families already enrolled in an Amil health plan as well as to Golden Cross and other plan members. Amil sent follow-up questionnaires to determine the families that belonged to each plan and the families that had no plan. The survey also included questions about the health status of each child in the family.

At the end of the trial enrollment period, families who qualified were offered a special health plan covering the child's medical expenses and all the parents were invited to continue picking up copies of the Amilzihno magazine at the service centers.

The Amilzihno Club works three ways for Amil:

First, it makes friends with a new generation of youngsters who in 10 to 15 years will be approaching formation of their own families and the time when they will be buying their own health insurance.

Second, by reaching out to all the children of Brazil, it opens the door to contact with families who are insured by a competitor's plan while reinforcing the relationship with their own plan members.

Third, by adding child-specific health information to the database, they are in a position to offer the best possible rates to Amil health plan families who want supplemental coverage and for conquest marketing aimed at the competition.

The University of California Wellness Letter. At the suggestion of their marketing consultant, Amil acquired the rights to publish a Portuguese edition of *The University of California Wellness Letter.* This is one of the largest-circulation consumer newsletters in the United States, reaching nearly 1 million subscribers.

For a company dedicated to beneficial involvement with its customers, this acquisition was a natural. The publication supports Amil's MaxiMarketing strategy in multiple ways. All enrollees in the Amil Individual Plan receive free issues of the newsletter periodically. Just as important, the newsletter is used as a "door opener" in seeking to win over enrollees from other health plans. Amil's marketing director, Clemente Nobrega, tested this approach by offering a three-month trial to members of other health plans in a blockbuster magazine insert. "Because you belong to another health plan doesn't mean that you can't catch up on the latest direction in the world of medicine and health. Amil is now offering you, as a member of another plan, the same opportunity that Amil members already enjoy," the copy proclaimed.

There was a reply form asking for respondent's name, date of birth, profession, and current health plan membership. A tipped-in envelope made response easy and private. More than 3 percent of the magazine's readers responded, an extremely high pull by U.S. standards. Nobrega is convinced that fine-tuning the ad approach can raise the response level even higher in the future.

Once the request is received, a series of letters begins the process of converting the newsletter trial subscriber to an Amil health plan. The first follow-up mailing offers a forthright explanation of why Amil is being so good to the reader:

> Why is Amil making this offer?
>
> Because we want you to know more about Amil. And we also want to get to know you better.
>
> We would like to explain how we have become the leader in our sector. A good example of how this happened is precisely this pioneer initiative of introducing in Brazil the world's widest-read and most-respected publication on medicine and health.
>
> And that's not all:
>
> It's no secret that clearing up doubts regarding health improvement contributes to cutting medical expenses. This is a vitally important matter throughout the world, one that Amil is also very much concerned with.

With the third and final issue of the free subscription, the respondent receives another gift—a free computer analysis of his or her health condition and suggestions for daily self-care routines based on the analysis. To provide the personal information needed for the recommendation, the prospect is asked to fill out a questionnaire designed by PMS, a software company that provides computer-based health analysis in many countries. The relationship continues through additional contacts until either the switch to Amil is completed or the prospect is put on hold for follow-up again at a future date.

You can see at a glance how this innovative approach demonstrates the "stop wasting money on nonprospects" key to success. Instead of the usual frontal attack on everyone in the marketplace, the promotion singles out just those people in another health plan who are willing to carry on a dialogue with Amil. Nobrega then can afford to send customized direct mail to these hot prospects and get cost effective enrollments.

New Worlds to Conquer: The Story of EAT

As the decade of the eighties was drawing to a close, senior management at Amil realized it was time to broaden the operation and move into new ventures. If they were going to provide new opportunities for their talented staff and meet the ambitious goals set for themselves, something more than the Amil Health Plan was needed. They were ready for their first attempt at diversification.

For some time, Brazil has struggled with an extremely volatile economy and at times something close to bushel-basket inflation. In such an environment, even workers who have jobs can have real concern about finding an affordable restaurant for lunch or being sure of putting enough food on the family dinner table.

In 1976, to address this common problem, the Brazilian government launched a restaurant meal-voucher program. As a valued fringe benefit, any business could issue meal vouchers to its employees with the government paying 48 percent of the cost, the employer 32 percent, and the employees a maximum of 20 percent. To get the program started, the government granted exclusive rights for two years to a French multinational firm called "Ticket." Then, the market was thrown open to competitors.

With its favored status, Ticket gained a commanding lead which it has retained despite competition from four other major companies. In Brazil, Ticket has become as synonymous with company-issued meal tickets as "Jell-O" is with gelatin dessert. Today, the Ticket enterprise still has 51 percent of the market of some 60,000 companies participating in the government plan.

Amil decided to enter the food voucher business by establishing a new company called EAT, the acronym for its full name in Portuguese, which is the "Brazilian Workers Nourishment Corporation." An important advantage enjoyed by EAT was that, as part of the Amil Group, they could write to Amil's corporate health plan customers and promise "the quality, commitment, reliability, experience, and affordability that you have come to expect from any Amil service."

Prior to launching the company in 1990, the newly appointed general manager of EAT, Dr. Paulo Marcos Souza, at a meeting in New York declared: "I will make EAT a MaxiMarketing company from day one and we will drive the competition crazy." Dr. Souza proceeded to develop a sales strategy emphasizing multichannel distribution, response mechanisms in all communications, database information accumulation, telemarketing, and double-duty advertising. It was a vigorous marketing program designed to consciously apply the principles of MaxiMarketing to winning food voucher and food basket business for the new company.

Here were some of the highlights:

- EAT was introduced to the business community at a special event before the introductory campaign in mass media. They sponsored a dinner which drew 1000 personnel executives during the 13th annual meeting of Brazil's Association of Human Resources Executives. Dinner invitations had to be confirmed by telephone, providing an opportunity to feed the database with valuable additional information about the responding companies.
- All communications, whether aimed at employers or employees, always called for a response, using a phone number ending in 1000, to obtain information for the database and to permit additional education and involvement with the prospects.
- Feedback was obtained by including an additional ticket in each computer-personalized book of EAT-checks, to be returned by the user with an indication of what restaurants he or she would like to see included in the plan.
- Personal relationships with contact points within the client companies were strengthened by sending greeting cards on birthdays, at Christmas-time, for Secretary's Day, and so on.
- Key executives in targeted companies were invited to attend free management seminars by noted speakers from abroad: Brad Gale on "Profit Impact of Marketing Strategy," Leonard Fuld on "Monitoring Competition," Peter Drucker on "The New Realities," Gifford Pinchot on "Intrapreneuring." To encourage the executives who replied to the invitations to provide additional information, an oversized bar of chocolate with the logo EAT was promised to every respondent who answered a few questions.
- The EAT booth at the Exhibition of Human Resources featured a computer loaded with a program that gave nutritional

advice. To use the program, human resources managers were required to provide information about their companies.

- EAT sponsored a new entertainment theater called "Imperator" designed for audiences perhaps best described as the business and cultural elite of Brazil—the pacesetters and "early adopters" whose opinions and attitudes have a strong influence over the rest of society. The theater presented shows headlined by famous stars, and Dr. Souza invited corporate prospects to see the show from a special private table. Nearly 100,000 corporate influencers attended these shows over a three-month period.

The list is just a sampling of the inventive, multifaceted marketing programs initiated by Dr. Souza to break through the clutter of the marketplace and create a community of interest with the employer, employee, and restaurant constituencies of EAT. As a result of these and other activities, despite an economy shrinking as much as 6 percent a year, EAT has grown within just three years into a $90 million enterprise.

Farmashop: The Drugstore Comes to Brazil

There are 45,000 pharmacies in Brazil: either small, old-fashioned establishments or impersonal units of a large chain. Amil has just begun to develop its own chain of "Farmashops," which will combine a clean, courteous, well-stocked, well-run pharmacy with—for the first time in Brazil—the modern American drugstore. They will be selling a wide assortment of toiletries and variety merchandise in addition to prescriptions. In the first year, the plan calls for opening Farmashops in 15 locations.

Dr. Monteiro, the member of the management team most involved in new ventures, believes the Farmashop project can grow into a business that will rival the Amil Health Plan itself in size. "The first reaction to the new concept has been very good," he reports. "One of the ideas we are looking at will transform the Farmashops into places where people can get health counseling and educational advice."

We have been told by Dr. Monteiro that the MaxiMarketing approach will be the basis of his strategy. Customer names will be captured; the frequency, recency, and monetary value of transactions will be monitored; and there will be a total commitment to building a close relationship with shoppers. Before long, if past Amil experience is any indication, drugstore retailers in the United States will have a lot to learn from Brazil's Farmashops.

Daring new initiatives are on the drawing board, but Dr. Monteiro would rather not get into specifics at this time and let the competition know what is coming.

A True Information-Age Customer-Focused Company

If ever it could be truly said that a company is information-driven, it is Amil. Dr. Bueno has had a lifelong obsession with learning and teaching as the key to success in his business and personal life. He now spends 90 percent of his time in learning, teaching, and motivational activities. Up to two months out of every year is devoted to taking courses, attending seminars, and visiting other companies. In the mid-1980s he took two grueling courses at Harvard Business School, one in owners' program management and the other in strategic marketing management.

This same attitude is promulgated throughout the ranks of the company. "The only way to increase the wealth of a nation is to train and develop people," Dr. Bueno told us. Every three months, all employees are expected to read a leading management book and discuss ways to apply its ideas to their own operations.

The apex of this teaching and learning protocol is the Amil School of Business Administration, ABA—surely the only company institution of its kind in the world. As described admiringly in the Tom Peters newsletter, *On Achieving Excellence:*

> Each of the company's 12 directors teaches an average of 100 hours of classes per semester in Amil's own MBA program...This 14-month course was designed in-house for future Amil executives. "ABA is comparable to the best MBA programs in Brazil—better in the opinion of many who have attended both ABA and outside programs," says Paul

> Dinsmore, an international management consultant who has worked with Bueno. "There's now a demand from outsiders to attend Amil's courses."
>
> Although senior managers constitute most of the faculty, top-performing employees, regardless of rank, also teach. "Our goal is to stimulate everyone in the company to become teachers," reports Marketing Director Clemente Nobrega.
>
> ABA offers 216 courses spanning economics and strategic planning to personal leadership and time management. Classes are held one day a week, with heavy homework assignments. Yet competition for enrollment is fierce. Each year, 150 employees apply for 60 spots.

Dr. Bueno believes that this emphasis on self-improvement creates a rich atmosphere of mental stimulation and idea generation. It inevitably leads to an explosion of new product features, marketing benefits, and symbiotic ventures. "Those who learn to impart information to each other are then far better prepared to impart information to the public and to use information as a marketing tool."

Do you remember the early days back in 1971—those free courses for pregnant women clients of Casa de Saude São José, the little broken-down 35-bed hospital in Duque de Caxias? Dr. Bueno's belief in the value of information was present right from the start.

It was also part of the early success of EAT, when Dr. Souza invited personnel managers of prospect companies to attend lectures by marketing experts from abroad. And it is an important part of what Dr. Monteiro has in mind for the future expansion of the Farmashop venture.

Mastery of Information-Age Marketing, putting telling ahead of selling, is the key to success that foreshadows continued spectacular growth for the Amil Group in the remaining years of this decade.

Over a 10-year period, from 1982 to 1992, while the Brazilian economy grew only 2 percent and the health-care sector grew only 10 percent, Amil enjoyed an average annual growth rate of 45 percent. Now, the senior executives at Amil talk confidently of becoming a billion-dollar company by the end of this decade.

When you look at their amazing record of learning, serving, caring, and daring, it doesn't seem at all hard to believe.

13

Puget Sound Bank: Marching to a Different Drummer

As we said earlier, marketing in the postindustrial era is no longer just what you say to the public about your product or service. It is everything you do.

In the timeless musical comedy, *My Fair Lady,* one of the unforgettable moments comes when an enraged Eliza Doolittle sings furiously, "Don't talk of love! Show me! Show me now!"

Sophisticated consumers weary of advertising claims are saying that to advertisers today. "Don't just say you care about quality and service and helpfulness and all that easy talk. Show me!"

One marketer who has done that with conspicuous success is Puget Sound Bank (now part of Key Bank) in the state of Washington. It has won awards, reams of favorable publicity, intense devotion from customers, and a substantial increase in market share. All because it had a marketing director who dared to see the challenge of differentiating the bank from all of its competitors in an entirely new way; and a bank chairman who came to realize he deserved his full support.

Life in the Seattle-Tacoma area, on the western side of the state, revolves around Puget Sound. People swim in it, sail on it, fish in it, and even commute to work on it from outlying residential islands. It offers 2000 miles of beautiful coastline.

Unfortunately, a rapidly growing population living and working and driving and playing in the area has also threatened to turn the Sound into a sinkhole of pollution. Understandably there has been increasing public concern over that issue. In the mid-1980s, a series of articles in *The Seattle Times* sounded a warning about the declining quality of the waters of Puget Sound and the reasons for it.

By sincerely sharing in this concern, and doing something about it, Puget Sound Bank has won an enviable position in the community.

In 1987, after 100 years as the dominant bank in Tacoma and surrounding Pierce County, next door to Seattle, Puget Sound Bank had grown to $4.5 billion in assets. This made it substantial, but not huge on a comparative scale. It was facing incoming competition from large, aggressive, well-funded out-of-state banks.

Don Piercy, the bank's marketing director, was charged with the responsibility of protecting the bank's 35 percent share of market in Pierce County. In addition, the bank wanted to expand in Seattle (King's County), where it held only 2 percent of market and had only eight branches. The challenge was to differentiate itself from other banks, since the products and services of all the banks were similar. To do it purely through massive image advertising would be prohibitively expensive.

As so often happens, the breakthrough came not in a single blinding vision but through an evolutionary process. The process was guided by genuine caring and driven by genuine daring.

It all began with a copywriter at the bank's advertising agency staring out the window and trying to think of a big idea for a new ad campaign for the bank.

Fortunately, his window happened to look out on a nice view of the Sound. "That's it!" he said to himself. "The Sound! We'll tie the bank in with the Sound!" The idea he came up with was actually a very modest one. The bank would publish a calendar with scenes of Puget Sound, sell it, and do some good things for the Sound with the money. For various reasons, the calendar was not very successful. For one thing, it came too late in the year. For another, people were accustomed to getting calendars free from banks, not having to pay for them.

But out of that modest beginning grew a bigger idea. In 1987, Piercy persuaded the bank to launch something called Puget Sound Fund, to be financed by customer transactions. The plan was announced by a poster-sized newspaper ad with the headline superimposed on a beautiful photograph of a ferryboat peacefully making its way across the Sound at sunset.

> **Introducing a machine that will help clean up Puget Sound**
>
> Every time you use one of our Quickbank machines, we'll deposit a little money into Puget Sound.
>
> Puget Sound is one thing we all have in common. We sail on it. Fish in it. And watch magnificent sunsets over it. But it's not as clean as it used to be. So the people at Puget Sound Bank think it's time to do something about it.
>
> Now every time you use any of our over 80 Quickbank machines, we'll make a contribution toward Puget Sound Fund. This money will fund projects to clean up the Sound and let people know what each of us can do to help.
>
> Puget Sound has been home for Puget Sound Bank for over 90 years. And like all good citizens we feel a responsibility to give something back to the communities where we live.
>
> We encourage you to get involved, too. And a good place to start is by opening an account with us. You'll get to use Quickbank as often as you want. Unlike a lot of bank machines, it won't cost you a cent extra to use and at the same time you'll be making a Sound investment.

The ad was greeted warily, and was actually ridiculed by a local professor of marketing who said it presented too pretty a picture of the Sound. The public has grown suspicious of "green marketing," which latches onto environmental concerns as just another promotional gimmick of the year.

Results of a highly revealing global research study released by Research International and reported by *Advertising Age* in the spring of 1993 indicated that consumers around the world are concerned about the environment, but they are often confused by the glut of information on how to deal with the problem. The report commented "feeding into the overload, most evident in highly developed countries, are marketers that have jumped on the environmental bandwagon, sometimes with specious, ill-defined claims of environmental 'friendliness.'"

Simon Chadwick, chairman of the research firm, said that consumers are "looking for clarity of information that can lead people to make decisions. And they're looking for evidence of social and ethical behavior on the part of manufacturers. 'Is this manufacturer being honest as well as clear?'" Companies that try to exploit interest in the environment without contributing to it themselves will be quickly recognized by increasingly savvy citizens, according to Chadwick.

But to Piercy, Puget Sound Fund was not just another gimmick. He saw in it the foundation of a long-range commitment that could transform the bank's position in the marketplace.

To make sure that happened, he took an important step.

Any other bank considering such a promotion might have decided simply to delegate to a staff accountant the job of tracking the share of transactions owed by the bank to the fund, and of parceling out the accumulated money to environmental groups in the area.

But Piercy realized that operating the fund would present some delicate problems as well as a promising opportunity. The fund would have to walk a tightrope between opposing environmental forces, such as those who wanted to preserve the wetlands and those who felt that private property rights came first. It would have to steer clear of acting like Puget Sound environmental police, and pointing the finger of shame at polluters who might turn out to be corporate customers of the bank. It would need to avoid controversial environmental groups whose militant demonstrations and stands stirred up public anger as well as public support. (Even an innocent suggestion in a brochure, later on, that readers contact World Wildlife Fund for more information drew a complaint from a hunter that the bank was antihunting.)

Piercy realized that he would need a real professional to help guide the Fund through this minefield. So he recruited a talented, knowledgeable social activist, David Parent, to come in and serve as administrator of the fund. As a result, the fund began to take on a life of its own as a serious, ongoing corporate commitment. Its focus would be on a credible program of providing and supporting environmental education and appreciation.

Defining the New Direction

At the time, charting this new course was nervier than it may seem today. No matter how the fund was described, it still meant carving substantial money out of bank revenue that would otherwise go to conventional image advertising, and using it for a purpose of unproven value. Says Piercy: "It was very lonely in the beginning." It required what is seen again and again in the marketing success stories examined in this book—a daring leap of faith.

During the first year of Puget Sound Fund, Piercy told us, they took small steps. They cultivated and established credibility with local environmental organizations. "We earned their respect—by being very sincere and upfront about what we were doing."

The chairman of the bank, W. W. Philip, was a quiet man who was busy with other matters. But Philip had grown up in the area. The health of the area environment was important to him. After a while, he began to realize how important the Fund could be, not only to the Bank but also to the Puget Sound community, and started giving it his full support.

He told Piercy, "We really want it [the Fund] to go out and accomplish something." (As a later annual report put it, they didn't want to earn the kind of damning with faint praise that Theodore Roosevelt bestowed on his political rival, William Howard Taft, when he said of Taft, "He means well feebly.")

In 1988, the Fund raised $96,000, and donated most of it to local groups. In 1989, the figure rose to $118,000. By 1990, it had soared to $300,000. In 1991, the Fund took in $396,550 and donated $320,000 of it to a total of 52 local institutions and activities devoted to nature and the environment.

By this time, the scope of the Fund's support had broadened far beyond the original announced objective of merely cleaning up the waters of Puget Sound. The annual report of the Fund listed such contributions for environmental education as $500 to Discovery Elementary School, $1351 to Wild Olympic Salmon, $500 to the United Citizens Betterment Organization, and so on.

You can imagine the widening circle of good will this sensitive support of local groups created. Parent became more than just an administrator of the Fund. He was also a sort of goodwill ambassador from the bank to local environmental and nature groups. In a letter of thanks to the bank, The Clover Creek Council, an organization devoted to "Living in Harmony with Nature," wrote appreciatively, "Mr. David Parent, Puget Sound Fund Administrator, even helped plant trees with us last year."

Administrative, operational, and professional services for the Fund in 1991 were kept down to a lean $33,074. Soon the bank was investing more than money in the environment. They started investing themselves as well.

Employees Hit the Beach. In 1988, the Fund began to sponsor an annual Puget Sound Bank Employee Beach Cleanup Day. One day a year, on a volunteer basis, bank employees and their families are encouraged to go out and pick up trash strewn on the beaches. The first year, around 700 volunteers showed up. By 1991, it was up to 2800 people, mostly bank employees and their families but including 200 from supportive local groups. Bank branches also invite their customers to join them, and it was not unusual to see some of the bank's best customers out on the beach working shoulder to shoulder with bank employees. In 1991, the clean-up volunteers collected and disposed of 17.5 tons of trash and marine debris from 55 beaches up and down the Sound.

As you can imagine, the favorable publicity that has resulted has been enormous. TV stations and newspapers have covered the event, and newspaper editorials have praised the bank for its devotion to the environment. Piercy estimates it would have cost three to five times as much money to have achieved that much favorable awareness through advertising alone.

The Beach Clean-Up Day has been an employee morale-booster as well. Bank employees began to look forward to the annual event as a family outing and block party, complete with picnic hamper (followed by careful clean-up, of course), and have taken great pride in being employed by a bank engaged in such a worthwhile and highly praised endeavor.

Keeping Oil from Troubled Waters. In 1990, another important Fund initiative was born when Parent happened to read something about the pollution problem arising from dumping of used motor oil. Used oil is a deadly polluter. One pint of oil can form a slick covering an acre of water and threatening the entire food chain. One gallon of oil can ruin one million gallons of drinking water.

In Washington State, more than 4 million gallons of used oil was being improperly disposed of (dumped into sewers, poured on the ground, etc.), and 2 million gallons of it was finding its way into Puget Sound.

Parent had a simple idea that turned out to be not so simple.

"Okay, we can do something about that," he told himself. "We'll just give out free oil collection tubs at all our bank branches, and our customers can take their used motor oil to their nearest service station and turn it in for collection." He teamed up the Fund with Washington Citizens for Recycling (WCFR) to develop a used-oil collection project.

But local service stations refused to cooperate because of liability issues. If the oil had been contaminated with brake fluid, then the collection tank had toxic waste that could cost up to $500 to be cleaned out.

So Parent and WCFR went to Schucks Auto Works, a large auto parts retailer in the area, who agreed to install large collection tanks outside their stores. Later, another chain, Al's Auto Supply, installed collection tanks *inside* all 39 of their statewide outlets, where the clerks would actually sniff the oil and ask, "Is this oil?" before dumping it into the collection tank.

Within three years, this collection system has been responsible for collecting 400,000 gallons of used oil. But collecting the used oil was only half the problem. What to do with it was the other half.

Oil, which is as old as dinosaur bones, never wears out. It just gets dirty. But it can be re-refined and used again, and this saves energy. It takes just one gallon of used oil to make 2.5 quarts of refined motor oil. In order to produce the same amount from scratch takes 41 gallons of virgin crude oil and much more energy.

Motorists who wished could purchase re-refined motor oil for their cars, but there wasn't a big demand for it. Altogether, Washington State was collecting 19 million gallons of oil but re-refining only 1 million gallons of it. Fifteen million gallons was being sold to ships, releasing dangerous chemicals such as lead, chromium, and arsenic into the atmosphere.

So Parent decided that the Fund should also work to "close the loop" of recycling and encourage new markets for re-refined oil.

It so happened that in Tacoma, where the bank was headquartered, there was a small company named Lilyblad that was producing a re-refined oil product called "Eco-Green." The Fund began working with Lilyblad to help them sell their product. It launched a public education campaign to encourage not only oil collection but also use of re-refined oil. It enlisted the help of a Seattle radio station which ran public service announcements almost every hour. It sponsored an entire exhibition tent devoted to recycling at the Western Washington State Fair, one of the largest in the country, and made educational materials available to the 1.4 million fairgoers.

In 1992, the Fund produced a seven-minute educational video, "Oil and Water Don't Mix," featuring television star John Ratzenberger from *Cheers* and the voices of Public Radio's *Car Talk* hosts Tom and Ray Magliozzi. The video explained the problem of used motor oil and urged Washington residents to turn in their discarded motor oil for recycling and to purchase re-refined oil for their cars.

The video cost $30,000 to produce—"a giant decision," Piercy told us, "a huge amount of money" for their little fund. But it was enthusiastically received. In Thurston County, it became required viewing for high school kids taking the drivers' education course. Gray's Harbor County started showing it to its employees and staff. Many other government agencies followed suit.

It is important to note that the video makes no mention of the bank or the Fund except for a credit line at the end. An important part of the success of the entire campaign has been the way educational materials produced or sponsored by the Fund have gained widespread acceptance by modestly downplaying the bank's role.

To set an example in the use of recycled oil, the bank became one of the first businesses in the state to change its corporate fleet of more than 20 vehicles to exclusive use of re-refined motor oil. They were joined by Baby Diaper Service, the City of Seattle, the City of Olympia, the Port of Bellingham, two local universities, and many others.

Bank Branch Lobbies Serve as Media. Over a period of five years, the Fund published or cosponsored an impressive number and variety of environmental education materials. These included the *Puget Sound Book,* a 54-page booklet on how to live on Puget Sound and have the least environmental impact; *Soundwatch,* an environmental guide for boaters; *Wonders of Puget Sound,* a four-page activities newspaper for children distributed to 120,000 people through the branches; and *Preserving Washington Wetlands,* a guide to The Nature Conservancy's Preserves in the state, 20,000 copies of which the Fund gave away to customers, environmental groups, government agencies, and so on.

In *MaxiMarketing,* we pointed out that there is "an embarrassment of riches" in new media, and urged looking at new ways to "break out of the box" of the traditional channels provided by the Big Five: magazines, newspapers, radio, television, and direct mail.

One untraditional channel is in-store "take-one's," and Puget Sound Bank has made full use of this way to communicate. Says Parent, "When we are producing environmental materials, we always put those in branches and sometimes advertise their availability in branches. Or we'll just put them out on display tables where people can pick them up. I can put out 2000 of an item and it's gone in a couple of days. Some of the pickup is teachers getting copies for their classes. They certainly look to the branch now as a source for environmental material."

The Big Payoff. Overall, the program has resulted in the kind of broad familiarity and favorable reaction by the public that could make a strong public relations director weep for joy.

One typical letter from a delighted area resident said, "I am switching my bank accounts to Puget Sound Bank because of the fund that you have which contributes to the cleanup of Puget Sound. I am glad to be putting my money into a bank which supports protection of our local environment, as I do. Thank you for making this commitment."

Wrote a board member of Citizens to Save Puget Sound, "Our group will do all it can to promote business for Puget Sound Bank, and to pass the word that PSB cares about its people and environment. You are doing an admirable job to promote cooperation to make our communities better places to live."

From the acting director of an institute for environmental studies: "I have been impressed with how sensitive Puget Sound Bank has been to organizations that are trying to focus on some of Puget Sound's problems and solutions...so impressed, as a matter of fact, that I have moved a bank account of an organization that I now head to your bank."

In a 1991 survey which tracked unaided recognition of local institutions, more people were aware of Puget Sound Fund than Greenpeace, which came in a distant second.

But what about the proverbial bottom line? Did the bank really do well by doing good? Well, for one thing, the bank's ATM withdrawals went from $4.7 million in 1988 to $7.3 million in 1992. The bank can't say precisely how much of this was due to public desire to support the Fund, but that was obviously an extremely important factor.

Piercy told us that 10 to 15 percent of the bank's total business over five-and-a-half years was considered incremental business attributable to the Fund. That would mean, in a bank with $3.5 to $4 billion in deposits, roughly $350 million to $450 million in incremental deposit growth. Not a bad return from a little more than $1 million of bank revenue turned over to the Fund. And the bank's share of market more than doubled in Seattle.

There is another benefit harder to measure, and that is the strong customer loyalty engendered by such a program, and the amount of business the bank may have kept despite rising competition. In other words, even if the bank had only managed to keep from shrinking, that might actually have been a success.

Another New Direction

As we wrote this, that customer loyalty was being put to the test by a merger of Puget Sound Bank into the larger Key Bank chain, announced in January of 1993, and the changeover of all the branches to the Key Bank name. Piercy believed the loyalty and goodwill built up by the bank would aid in the successful transition to its new persona.

"What I am sensing as I talk to people in the branch system and bank customers," he told us, "is that people who come to you because of the best rates are often the first ones to leave when the bank down the street offers a better rate. The people that came to us because of our environmental commitment have a greater sense of loyalty to us, and I think they are the ones who are staying with us through this conversion process."

For its part, Key Bank has vowed to continue Puget Sound's environmental commitment. And it has expanded it to include support for environmental projects all over the state through transformation of Puget Sound Fund into a new entity, The Washington Waters Fund.

Half a century ago, bankers were viewed by the public as cold-hearted skinflints who foreclosed on loans and mortgages and took away the debtors' homes and cars. Since then, as banking chains have grown larger and competition has become fiercer, banks have hired ad agencies to repaint their images in the public mind as warm, friendly, eager to serve, almost downright cuddly. But too often the image created has failed to match the reality.

Puget Sound Bank blazed a trail in marketing by demonstrating that creative commitment to responsible corporate citizenship can pay off bigger in the long run than any number of superficial or fawning image campaigns. Puget Sound Bank dared to march to a different drummer and make caring for the customer synonymous with caring for the quality of life in the community the bank serves. It's another dramatic example of what a truly "Caring and Daring" corporate culture can accomplish.

14
How MCI Used Corporate Jujitsu to Trip AT&T

We have a good friend who has always been especially dedicated to world peace, to the extent that he even disapproves of the use of military metaphors.

We share his love of peace. But the history of warfare is so interwoven in our culture and thinking, sometimes comparisons with military situations and strategies are so apt they are almost unavoidable. In marketing, Trout and Ries found the comparison so useful they wrote an entire book on the subject, *Marketing Warfare.*

In looking at the major offensive that the outgunned long-distance phone service provider MCI unleashed against the mighty AT&T in the spring of 1990, an almost inevitable comparison with blitzkrieg or lightning warfare springs to mind.

In blitzkrieg, used so skillfully by Hitler in his conquest of Europe and then used against him with equally devastating effect by armored division commanders like the American general George Patton, you find a weak spot in the enemy line, punch a hole in it with a ferocious concentration of armored vehicles, and pour your forces through the hole with lightning rapidity.

As you will see, MCI executed a maneuver like this just when it seemed as if the early gains of the challenger had come to a halt and a standoff with little movement in market share was likely in the immediate future for either MCI or AT&T.

When we met with Gerald Taylor, MCI's president for consumer markets, and Tim Price, at that time senior vice-president for sales and marketing (now president of MCI's business services division), they explained to us how a number of forces had converged in the spring of 1990 to give birth to what may well be the most successful conquest marketing campaign of all time.

- Technological developments had created a new capability to generate a discount in the monthly bill when one MCI customer called another.
- Calling people up to persuade them to switch to MCI as their phone-service provider was just barely meeting an acceptable cost of acquiring new customers.
- The phone lines were near capacity during the daytime, but there was open time in the evening and nighttime hours, and evening-time phone calls were very profitable.
- Job changes, divorces, and other factors in the 1980s had increased U.S. population mobility even more, creating a market of people who were emotionally close but geographically scattered to the four winds.
- AT&T's recent counterattack commercials had bluntly told customers that, to fend off competitor enticements, "make them put it in writing." The tough tone of these commercials may have been effective, but it had put a dent in the warm image AT&T had built up in the 1980s with their effective "Reach Out and Touch Someone" message.
- At the same time, AT&T's "Reach Out and Touch Someone" had done MCI and Sprint a favor by greatly increasing discretionary calling and taking the guilt out of running up a big phone bill.

- MCI focus research kept pointing to a fact which was obvious but the significance of which had never been fully taken in: most personal calls, including long-distance calls, are made to the same people over and over again.

Pondering these factors, Jerry Taylor looked for a way to use what he thinks of as a corporate version of jujitsu—defined in the dictionary as "using the strength and weight of an adversary to disable him" (or her, we would hasten to add today).

AT&T had well over 60 percent of the $65 billion long-distance calling market compared to MCI's 14 percent. How could that "strength and weight" of AT&T be used against them?

Suddenly, he realized that since AT&T had about four times as many customers, a generally available discount would hurt them four times as much. That is, for AT&T to hold old customers and reach out for new ones through a users' discount, they would have to give up some of the income they were already enjoying from the largest part of the market. So AT&T would be very reluctant to match an MCI continuity reward program.

But anybody can compete and lose by starting a no-strings price war, as we saw in the computer price war involving Dell, IBM, and Compaq.

Jerry Taylor felt there should be at least a few strings attached to his new plan, so customers would value it more.

And he saw a way to take the high road of warm feeling that he felt AT&T had strayed away from.

MCI would introduce a program called Friends & Family. Customers would be invited to form a "calling circle" by giving MCI the names and phone numbers of up to 12 people (later increased to 20) they call the most. Then calls to and from any of those names who also were or became MCI customers would enjoy a 20 percent discount.

It was a once-in-a-lifetime Big Idea, and they decided to put all of their resources behind it in blitzkrieg fashion. The entire advertising budget of $50 million was committed to it, and a year later this was doubled. Worried that AT&T might get wind of the plan before it was launched and move to block it, they hurriedly launched a teaser campaign of 30-second television commercials even before all the preparations had been completed. Each of these teasers looked in on a celebrity such as George Burns, Tammy Wynette, Jackie Mason, or Zsa Zsa Gabor musing humorously over whom they were going to include on their "list." Then a voice-over asked, "Why is [name of celebrity] making a list and giving it to MCI? Find out March 18."

Then after the program was launched and explained to the public, the television campaign switched to statements of approval and enthusiasm by real customers. The commercials created by MCI's agency, Mesner Vetere Berger Carey Schmetterer, were among the best we have seen in a long time—vivid, credible vignettes of the American people almost good enough to be included in a documentary on nonprofit public television. And marching across the bottom of the screen the invitation to call the MCI 800 number to join Friends & Family.

Here is an excerpt from just one spot that both advances and pays tribute to the credibility and likability of the campaign. A woman customer says earnestly:

> I think one of the things I like most about the MCI mentality, if you will, is that they do seem to be devising creative ways to help their customers. I don't think it's motivated just by being competitive with AT&T and Sprint, but they really are concerned about their customers and they really do want them to realize savings.

What we are glimpsing here is a benefit that goes beyond cold-blooded calculation of savings on long-distance calls. We talked in our discussion of Key 5—"Bringing People Together"—about the hunger today for a sense of community. And we showed how this is appealed to by local chapters and regional rallies attended by owners of Harley-Davidson motorcycles and other MaxiMarketing winners identified and described in this book.

The people in your personal phonebook, the ones that you call the most, make up one of the most important communities in your life—for many people, the *only* community—and it is the telephone that holds it together.

By listing these people with MCI as your "calling circle," you give that little community a formal existence. And the TV commercials that bring other warm, funny, likable MCI customers into your living room to talk about the joys of Friends & Family somehow, on a purely emotional level, make you feel almost as if *they* are part of your calling circle too. You become part of a great nationwide family of MCI customers.

If the campaign went only this far—you give us the names, we give all of you a discount on your long-distance calls when you call each other—it would have gone down in marketing history merely as an interesting discount promotion.

But remember, Taylor attached a few strings to the Friends & Family Plan. One of them was that to enjoy the 20 percent discount, *both* parties on the line must be MCI customers. Later, this would be used *against* MCI by Sprint, which started offering an automatic 20 percent discount on calls to people you call the most with *no* strings attached. But in the opening phase of the campaign, it provided MCI with enormous leverage.

Customers not only provided referrals, which anyone in personal selling will tell you are priceless sales leads, but were motivated and encouraged to call these referrals themselves and urge them to join the fun. This, then, became a "pincer" attack: MCI telemarketers approaching the AT&T market from one flank and MCI customers approaching it from the other urging friends and family members to switch from AT&T to MCI.

Something else worth noting about this breakthrough campaign is that it is super database marketing, and would not have been possible without the advanced computer capability needed for the complex tracking, record keeping, and customized communication. This may seem obvious. But it is certainly worth mentioning, because in the preceding decade the term "database marketing" was too often bandied about to describe little more than a mailing list of prospects or customers stored in and printed out by the computer.

Thanks to the computer, MCI could send customers a Calling Circle Status Report. First, it listed the new members of your circle who have also signed up. ("You could be saving 20 percent. Why not give them a call?")

But then, more important, it listed the names and numbers of your "nominees" who had not yet been converted to MCI. "To save 20 percent on calls to each of the nominees below, help us encourage them to join MCI and our circle. They can join quickly and easily by calling the toll-free number."

There is one more piece in the picture of how MCI became such a big winner so quickly. It recognized its need for direct marketing expertise, and retained a skilled direct marketing agency, Devon Direct, to maximize the direct-mail effectiveness of the Friends & Family campaign.

Reportedly, the direct-mail budget soon rose to $50 million a year, matching the measured media budget in size and importance. The execution of the Friends & Family strategy is a demonstration of the power of Integrated Direct Marketing Communications.

Direct marketing turns an advertised *product* ("This is what we have to offer") into a *proposition* ("If you'll do this for us, then we'll do this for you"). The proposition can be as simple as, "If you'll send us the price, we'll deliver the product or service." But skillful direct marketers can find ways to embellish the proposition in order to stimulate response and increase customer value.

For this reason, a year after Friends & Family was up and running, the 5 million phone users who had enrolled received a large blockbuster mailing in a 9 × 12 envelope announcing, "You're a very special friends and family member. Wait till you see what we're doing for you in '92!"

Inside was an impressive full-color, eight-page, 11 × 17 circular that conveyed the excitement surrounding the successful formation of Friends & Family and announced a fistful of new benefits "to celebrate Friends & Family's first birthday."

- *Double savings in May.* Forty percent off instead of 20 percent, on all calls between calling circle members that month. "Think of how affordable this extra 40 percent in savings makes a long chatty catch-up call to Dad or Grandma...your wonderful next-door neighbor who moved away, a child at school, your fiancé or college friends. Think of saving 40 percent on Mother's Day. Now's the time to nominate everyone you call who isn't already in your circle. Call your Friends & Family benefits advisor 24 hours a day toll free at 1-800-999-6242."
- *Circle size increased to 20.* "Many members have suggested that they have more Friends and Family than we could accommodate with the limit of 12 families in their circle, so we have expanded your opportunity to save."

- *Call your nominees with the good news...free.* "We will give you a 5-minute free call to every person you nominate. Here's how. When you give us your nominations, by mail or phone, we will automatically credit your account with a 5-minute free evening call, so you can call your nominees and tell them how MCI's Friends & Family program works. Let them know you want them to join your circle so you both can save 20 percent on every call to each other, and tell them about our fabulous 40 percent savings birthday celebration during May. Many more of your nominations will be happy to join when they hear from you personally. Be sure to give them our toll-free hotline number."
- *Free cards for every traveler in your family.* The card "enables you to call anyone in America, from any phone in America, and to call over 225 foreign countries and locations and to call the U.S. from over 60 foreign locations....But that's not all. Your new Card comes with *speed dialing* to make calling your circle and your own home faster and simpler. Every time you use the card, a friendly voice will remind you of what to do to complete the call...(It also) comes with advanced features so you can get the *latest weather, stock quotes, sports scores...even horoscopes...*You can even *leave messages* for people whose lines were busy or who weren't there when you called. And one of the friendliest features is the capability of placing a *conference call* to several together."
- *Your own toll-free 800 number.* Then friends and family can call you toll free, just like they do to companies with an 800 number. As a member of Friends & Family, you pay only $5 a month for this service and then only 20 cents a minute instead of the regular price of 25 cents—with double savings in May.
- *A way to save 20–40 percent when calling your home or circle from overseas.* "If you travel abroad or are taking a vacation this summer, call your Friends & Family benefits advisor and request the free MCA Call USA Information Package."
- *Include one special overseas friend or family member in your calling circle.* Then "every call you make to them saves you an extra 20 percent, and 40 percent during May." (Obviously this can be only one-way, since a friend in Sri Lanka can't join Friends & Family.

We have taken the trouble to spell out all of the benefits featured in this impressive direct-mail piece because we want you to see how different direct marketing advertising can be from image advertising. While image advertising, especially on television, usually has time or space to make one salient sales point, direct marketing *takes* time and space to make point after point, and to pile on benefit after benefit, in order to complete the sale. MCI has done this superbly.

The capstone of the campaign came in the spring of 1993, when MCI created an air of excitement about the approach and then the arrival of a grand total of 10 million members of Friends & Family.

Did the campaign move the needle? MCI gained four share points. In the hotly contested $65-billion market for long-distance calls, that adds up to $1.2 billion in additional revenue.

Feeling the heat, AT&T finally responded with full-page newspaper ads proclaiming: "We want you back." And in the mail they bombarded the MCI converts with checks worth up to $100 (based on the size of your phone bill) to return to AT&T.

A year after our conversation with the man who originated the Friends & Family concept, Jerry Taylor, and two years after the launch of the program, we spoke with Cari Sanborn, director of Friends & Family marketing. This was her update:

- Membership is expected to grow to 11 million by the end of 1993.
- 65 percent of MCI customers are now enrolled in Friends & Family.
- MCI estimates that at least 5 million members switched from AT&T.
- Friends & Family members speak on the phone longer than the average user, spend more, and are more loyal.
- Heavy users within Friends & Family are now automatically enrolled in "Customer First" for additional perks.

Sanborn spoke about the MCI risk-taking corporate culture, the drive to "never stand still" in constantly looking for better ways to benefit the Friends & Family Calling Circle members. Sounds like as good a definition of what makes a "Caring and Daring" company as we've heard in any of our talks with the MaxiMarketing winners.

PART 4

MaxiMarketing Winners in Retailing

15
NBO Dares to Start Over

Some day, business analysts may look back on the recession that began at the end of the 1980s and continued into the 1990s as The Great Awakener. The economy slowed down just at the time when rapidly changing information technology and changing consumer attitudes were making the marketing world a very different place from what it had been.

It was known that companies live or die by their ability to gain and hold a comparative advantage, but suddenly what was always relied upon to provide that edge over the competition went out of kilter.

Consumers who had gotten accustomed to quality and service during the 1980s became price-conscious and bargain-hungry. Only they demanded it all—they wanted lean prices without giving up the quality and service.

Computer-controlled robots on the factory floor and computer-controlled information processing at the retail checkout counter were shaking up previous assumptions about how quickly and how intelligently managers could respond to changing consumer likes and dislikes.

In this new environment, victory had to be redefined. To have the courage and the flexibility to change with the changing times, to defend a powerful market position against all comers, to see trouble ahead and reverse direction in time to begin a new cycle of growth—now that is a victory worth celebrating and saluting.

NBO (National Brands Outlet) is such a marketer.

It is a $100 million chain of 36 stores selling menswear in the Greater New York metropolitan area and Washington, D.C. It is privately owned by a Canadian company, Dylex Ltd., which seems to give its American management team free rein to respond to the realities of the new economy.

NBO sells 200,000 men's suits a year. (That is the rough equivalent of outfitting every single adult male in a city of a million people.)

Their goal has been to bounce back from a scary 35 percent profit falloff in 1989 by rethinking the way they do business. Within three years' time, despite the recession, they were well on their way to realizing their objective. They broke new ground at eight of the nine checkpoints in the MaxiMarketing continuum and have earned a well-deserved place for the company in the MaxiMarketing winners circle.

We often wonder why so many specialty-store retailers are so slow to grasp the opportunities presented by the telecomputing marketing revolution. They come face to face with their customers every day: men and women who by the very act of walking into a sporting goods store, an electronics store, a clothing store, or any other retail outlet are looking for assistance in making a wise buying decision. Yet most retailers let that priceless opportunity to register a name, make a friend, or start a lifelong, profitable relationship slip away day after day.

If you are in retailing management, there's a lot to learn from NBO's "Caring and Daring" initiative in making the NBO shopping experience responsive to their customers. And if you are the marketer of a product or service, you can force-fit their retail experience to your own situation. You can ask yourself, how might I adapt what is happening here to solve a problem faced by my company?

Now let's turn the spotlight on NBO—a store management that does things differently from its competitors.

They *zig* when the competition *zags.*

They go *in* where the competition wants to be *out.*

They invest for the *future* when times are tough in the *present.*

They tell the *truth,* while some others deceive with *half-truths.*

NBO avoided accumulation of debt at a time when the department stores were building mountains of it. And, as you will see, probably no other retailer in America knows as much about the identity and buying behavior of such a large percentage of their individual customers—and does something about it to increase sales and profits.

NBO's Plain-Pipe-Racks Heritage

They began in 1971 as BFO—"Buyers Factory Outlet"—an off-price chain. They would buy from the manufacturer, at greatly reduced prices, large quantities of clearance and closeout merchandise. They went after everything, from low-end clothing to famous-brands and even designer garments when they could get them, and sold them all for much less than the usual retail price. It is a practice as American as apple pie. At NBO, as the company was later named, this catch-as-catch-can selection was sold in a no-frills environment, what used to be called "from plain pipe racks." There was minimal sales help and little or no tailoring service.

One problem with this way of doing business is that you are constantly at the mercy of whatever happens to be available as closeouts or clearance merchandise at any given moment. It's difficult to maintain an every day good selection of clothing in all sizes. Customers may find a great buy, but they may also turn away in disappointment because they can't find what they want or need at that moment.

Another problem was that some of the snootiest brand names refused to sell closeouts to such discounters as NBO. They were afraid that the hard-sell bargain atmosphere of off-price stores would hurt their image and that permitting the advertising of deep discounts would undermine their regular prices.

Still, NBO thrived as a discounter and, by 1987, had annual sales of $86 million.

Gathering Storm Clouds

A year or two later as the economic downturn began to take hold, there was a sharp change in the competitive environment. Department stores that had always set the high-margin prices for NBO to knock down suddenly changed their strategy. They began to slug it out with the off-price stores. As the recession made everyone increasingly price-conscious, the department stores battled for revenues and market share with a constant bombardment of sales proclaiming "Up to 50 percent off!" on brand-name menswear.

NBO's difficulties were illustrated by a typical customer, quoted in an *Adweek's Marketing Week* company profile. He was a suburban shopper who had purchased his suits at the NBO store in Paramus, New Jersey, for years. "There's really no reason why I need to make a special trip to NBO any more. Macy's runs sales practically every day. And I like their jeans and other casual clothes better, so I can shop for both at the same time."

NBO faced heightened competition on other fronts as well. Some well-known apparel brands like Harvé Benard and Phillips Van Heusen were increasingly bypassing off-price stores and selling leftover merchandise through their own outlet stores. And, formidable popular-priced competitors, such as JC Penney and Sears, were adding more brand-name goods in their stores.

As if that wasn't enough trouble for a chain getting 60 percent of its business from selling business suits to men, there was also bad news in a dramatic lifestyle change taking place across America. It was the shift toward more casual dress for "white-collar" workers in the office.

An example of what was happening could be seen at the Pittsburgh headquarters of the Aluminum Company of America, surely a bastion of the style-setting business establishment. During a two-week United Way drive at their offices, Alcoa allowed employees who contributed to come to the office in casual dress. This proved to be so popular, the company decided to make casual dress an everyday option!

At some divisions of American Express, as part of the attempt to create a more relaxed corporate culture, Friday was proclaimed to be casual-dress day at the office. A more laid-back style on the job translates into fewer suits in the executive's closet at home.

With these pressures mounting, the economy weakening, and earnings taking a nosedive, NBO Chairman Gene Kosack decided it was time to take a good, hard look at his operation and his situation.

"The rules of the game have changed," he declared to a *Wall Street Journal* reporter in the spring of 1990. "We can't just win on a price war because when a department store goes on sale, they have a lot more advantages than us." He followed this up with a frank, blunt assessment in the garment industry's *Daily News Record*, "We made a terrible mistake promoting price alone last year. Off-price is not as hot as it used to be. The niche we had has been eroded by the Campeau, Hooker, and Macy's stores."

Kosack Turns the World Topsy-Turvy

Early in 1990, as a result of these pressures, NBO took a daring gamble. Kosack announced he was going to restructure the company radically. They would continue to follow the Unique Selling Proposition (USP) that had served them so well—the message that NBO was the place "where you will always find designer menswear at 30 to 60 percent less than the department stores." To this, they would add what we have termed an Extra-Value Proposition (EVP)—an innovative new customer pleasing policy that went far beyond anything you might expect from an off-price retailer.

- Just as any department store or specialty store does, they would move away from being a largely closeout operation and start buying regular in-season menswear—designer suits, quality private label goods, and other apparel—at the best wholesale prices they could find. (Thanks to the recession, makers of designer apparel who had snubbed NBO in the past became more cooperative. Says Kosack, "Let's just say that a lot of people we chased for a long time finally became accessible.")

- They would still feature significantly lower prices than the competition for the exact same goods.
- They would invest in upgrading the physical store environment to make shopping at NBO more inviting and satisfying.
- They would combine the lowest price with attempting to provide an exceptional level of personal attention often found lacking at even the upper-tier of men's clothing retailers.
- And, before long, they would begin to identify hundreds of thousands of prospects and customers by name and to reach out to them as individuals.

NBO decided to play against the competition by a set of rules of their own making and then methodically went about winning the game.

"Gain without Pain" Appears Again

As Jim Frayne, the current marketing vice-president, explained it to us, "We are not going to make the customer suffer" in order to save himself some money. (Another example of the "gain without pain" strategy we saw at other MaxiMarketing winners.) "They don't have to jump through any hoops. They are going to find sales and service to be very good. They are going to find the tailoring to be the equal of if not better than department and specialty stores."

Now, wait a minute! How could NBO maintain a satisfactory profit margin on the same merchandise the competition was buying on the same wholesale market and yet afford to offer improved service and ambiance? It sounds like some kind of magic trick.

First of all, explains Kosack, "We buy like any other retailer, we just don't pay the same price. Why? Because we don't ask for markdown money or return privileges. We don't ask for fall goods in July—we'll take them in October. We don't advertise their name in the public media. And we pay our bills on time."

But to pull off the trick of NBO's successful turnaround, even more magic was needed. Actually, they needed four things: a magician's wand, a tall silk hat, a piece of black cloth, and a rabbit to pull out of the hat. They found them: store location, customer identification, customer cultivation, and image changeover.

The Magician's Wand: Selecting the "Wrong" Locations

By this time, just about everybody knows the three fabled secrets of retailing success: *location! location! location!* Today, that usually means for specialty stores, getting a location in a shopping mall or some other high-traffic location, snuggling up as close as possible to JC Penney or Macy's or Nordstrom. That way you get lots of impromptu "walk-in" store traffic.

Whoever heard of a strategy that calls for just the opposite: moving into a less traveled, less desirable area? That is exactly what NBO has done. Sometimes, they do it just when their competitors are moving out. And for a very good reason. In the words of a popular song, "Somethin's gotta give."

Even with sharp wholesale buying, you still can't afford to whack deep cuts in the prices of name brands *and* offer superior customer hand-holding *and* pay the rent in a posh shopping mall on a marble-floored emporium with a crystal chandelier. For this reason, NBO has adopted what they call a "destination location" strategy. In a nutshell, that means you have to make the store your destination before you leave home to go shopping. You can't just drop in on impulse because you happen to be over at Macy's next door.

The NBO store may or may not be near a shopping center, but in any case, it is usually far enough away from mall traffic to benefit from much lower rent. NBO actually has moved into residential neighborhoods of Brooklyn and Queens just when some of the big department stores were not doing well or fleeing from those areas. "That," Frayne pointed out to us, "makes NBO a company that is particularly sensitive to marketing and promotion."

Without a powerful magnet to "make the people come," Kosack's dream of a new NBO would quickly wither away. To steer interested customers to the nearest "destination location," NBO widely advertises and publicizes its store-locator 800 number, 1-800-688-EASY. When a prospect calls, the cheery recorded operator's voice sings out,

> "Good afternoon! Thank you for calling NBO's fashion hotline, where you will always find designer menswear at 30 to 60 percent less than the department stores. For sale information, press 1. To locate the NBO store nearest you, press 2" [and then enter your zip code numbers as directed].

Note that this simple message does triple duty:

1. It informs the caller of the nearest store location.
2. It delivers the Unique Selling Proposition, loud and clear.
3. It promotes selected sale items of the day. (The announcement compares the sale price with the higher regular NBO price and the still-higher department store price.)

The Tall Silk Hat: Identifying Each Customer

If you live in an area served by Fox Television, you are surely familiar with the 10 p.m. station-break announcement which has entered the language by now: "It's 10 p.m. Do you know where your children are?" We have a question that we think should be ringing in the ears of every marketer every night: "It's 199- (fill in current year). Do you know who your customers are?"

Of course, for a service company like a hotel or motel chain, a car rental service, a cruise line or an investment house, it would be almost impossible *not* to know. The customer has to "sign up" and supply a certain amount of personal data in order to have a relationship with you.

Department stores have the names of customers carrying the store's own charge-account card but these are a distinct minority of the people visiting the store. Little or nothing is known about the customers using cash or other charge cards.

On the other hand, if you are manufacturing and selling a low-price, low-usage consumable or disposable product, it just may not be economic or productive to build a database of end-users.

What is most surprising is that thousands of other marketers, particularly in retailing, *haven't the faintest idea who their individual customers are.* These companies are in an ideal position to acquire customer data in their daily face-to-face contact, and pay a heavy price for their continuing ignorance.

How NBO Created an Instant Database. NBO took the first steps down the path toward building a unique program for identifying, profiling, and cultivating individual customers back in 1989. This early experience later developed into one of the most impressive examples of one-to-one marketing by a retailer we have seen anywhere.

In 1992, Pete Hoke, the visionary publisher of *Direct Marketing* magazine, interviewed Claude Johnson, NBO's executive vice-president. Johnson explained how NBO had first found their way into database marketing as an aftermath of a sweepstakes promotion they ran in the spring of 1989, offering customers a chance to win a BMW. To enter, the customer had to deposit an entry form with name and address. Some 250,000 entries came pouring in. NBO realized there was value in knowing who had entered the sweepstakes, but without relevant additional data about each individual, all they had was a list of names and not a database.

Next, they thought about doing something that few retailers had ever done before. Why not take the information from major credit card transactions at the store and merge it with the sweepstakes-entry information?

There was one small problem. The financial department had records of every credit card purchase recorded by card number, not by name and address. NBO then turned to an outside service company to match the credit card input with the sweepstakes-entry names and addresses, and the first NBO database was born. It also may have been the first time any retail chain improvised an instant database, using transaction information from other than their own credit card transactions.

The first NBO mailing went out to a list of 242,000 customers in November of 1989, at a cost of $69,000. It was a two-page flyer with coded discount coupons attached. When a customer made a purchase, the redeemed coupon along with the sales receipt was sent by the store manager to the central NBO office. The individual sales could then be traced back to the customer record in the database.

The $69,000 mailing generated $1.4 million in sales.

With numbers like that, Kosack decided to go back into the mail right away. Thirty days after the first mailing, the same flyer was dropped again—this time, at a cost of $76,000. The second mailing generated another $2.4 million in sales—a 3000 percent return on the investment!

Today, the company spends $60,000 to $120,000 per month mailing to names in its customer database of 660,000. Rather than merely saying: "All this advertising produced all these sales, we think!" now NBO management was able to say: "This particular advertising produced exactly this many dollars of sales from precisely these customers." The era of advertising accountability urged and predicted in *MaxiMarketing* had arrived for NBO.

The NBO Paradox: Retail Direct Marketing. After hitting the jackpot the first time out, NBO became and remains a deeply committed direct marketer with a mailing going to the database at least once a month, in order to bring customers into NBO's "destination locations." The usual NBO mailing is a private-sale circular with dated and coded savings coupons facing outward alongside the customer's name and address. The offer can't be overlooked.

Each savings coupon displays the sale item, the sale price, the higher NBO regular price, and the even higher price "elsewhere." For instance, in one circular we looked at, one of the coupons reads:

PIERRE CARDIN* BLAZER
On Sale Now
$119
NBO regular price: $139
Elsewhere: $250

Directly below the coupon is the customer's imprinted ID number, and a sign-off line, "Coupon must be presented at time of purchase, expires (date)."

The measurement capability built into this system is particularly noteworthy. As Frayne pointed out to us, "The critical questions you can answer by carefully looking at the results are, what product and price point to choose to put into future mailers; what works and what doesn't work for each segment of the database. The bigger the numbers you have going out, the more times you mail, the more accurate you become."

The system makes it possible for a retailer to make the important measurement mail-order catalog merchants live by—RFM, the *recency* of response, *frequency* of purchase, and *monetary value* of each individual customer name. If a customer stays on the list too long without coming into the store to buy or without buying very much, then it may be economically advisable to drop his name from the file or mail less frequently to him.

Don't for a moment think that this monthly NBO mailing is just another retail "private sale" circular with a coded store redemption coupon thrown in. There is a major additional element that makes the direct mail budget do double duty. More than half the piece is devoted to copy that builds the NBO brand image and the relationship with the customer: "It's NBO's private $99 sale. Only customers on our mailing list can get great-looking suits for $99....This offer is limited to our customers....

*The unspoken understanding NBO has with makers of designer apparel that NBO will not mention the designer name in advertising apparently does not apply to direct mail sent to their own customers, presumably because of its private nature. Thus, their circulars are richly studded with such famous names as Nino Cerruti, Christian Dior, Perry Ellis, and Pierre Cardin.

Current season, quality garments you'll be proud to wear. And, don't worry, you won't have to search through closeouts to find them....As for tailoring, we don't employ hacks. Our work is prompt and perfect....If you're not satisfied with your purchase (which is highly unlikely), you won't have to put up with a nonexistent refund policy."

Not exactly what you'd expect to hear from your everyday men's clothing discounter.

The ID Number You Can Never Forget. Purchases made when a customer comes shopping *without* the coded coupons from a mailing are tied to the database record by the sales clerk asking for the customer's ID number. But how can the customer be expected to remember his ID? That's easy—it's the same as his phone number.

New names are steadily added to the database at the rate of about 10,000 a month. This is done by continuing to identify new customers from their use of a major credit card and by training and motivating sales clerks to ask a new customer for his name and address at the time of purchase "so we can let you know in advance about our sales and offers." In the 1992 Johnson interview, the database was said to consist of 650,000 customer names and profiles. When we talked to Jim Frayne six months later, he told us that it had "grown significantly since then."

The customer file is constantly being refined and enhanced as well as expanded. A valuable resource is the additional information obtained by matching the names against the demographic data available from Donnelley Marketing's public database.

As a result, NBO not only knows the customer's last date of purchase, amount of current purchase, amount of purchase by year, maximum purchase each year, and, of course, which store location the customer patronizes, but also the typical customer's likely age, income range, education level, length of residence, probability of having a child under 18 living at home, and more. One benefit of this detailed customer record, Johnson pointed out, is that it helps NBO to select the best local advertising media, differentiate the appeal, and stock the right inventory for the various kinds of customers living around each of the different store locations.

Before each mailing, store managers are sent a sample of the piece and told what to anticipate in sales results. Afterwards, the actual results are provided to the store managers, so that they can see which customers bought what, how much, and when. "In general," according to Johnson, with NBO's high-powered individualized marketing "direct mail now can generate 50 percent of a day's receipts."

One way that the marketing team has found to do cost-efficient mailings that reach out beyond the database (while attracting new names for it at the same time) is to do cooperative mailings with major credit card companies. For instance, NBO selects 30,000 Amex cardholders who made a store purchase with an American Express credit card. To these names, Amex adds another 70,000 names of cardholders living in the NBO trading areas who fit the NBO customer profile. Amex then pays part of the cost of the mailing.

The usual customer transaction averages about $92. But when respondents to one of these Amex cooperative mailings comes in to shop, their average transaction jumps up to $233, according to Johnson. By also promoting to "clones" of their customers found among nearby Amex cardholders, NBO gets magical results every time.

The Magician's Cloth: NBO's Image Makeover

The old, outdated image many people had of NBO, says Frayne, was "that we didn't have any sales people, that we didn't have tailoring, that we were a warehouse, rack-type company, and that you had to struggle through the odds and ends to get a good deal." To counteract this image, Frayne oversees a carefully planned marketing program that combines price appeals with an upgraded image of quality stores catering to the customer. The measured media advertising budget, at last report said to be around $1 million, is judiciously divided among television, radio, and newspaper ads. (In addition, our guess is that the company spends another several million on direct mail.)

At a time when the ability of advertising to build a brand is coming under attack as losing its effectiveness, NBO is proving—as we found in our examination of winners like Ryder and LEGO—that brand-building advertising can play an important role when it is double-duty advertising or is teamed up with the other tools in the MaxiMarketing toolbox.

NBO's recent 30-second TV spots, actually shot in the company's Scarsdale, New York, store, focus on real NBO customers. The CEO, Gene Kosack, in a typical spot appears as the company spokesperson and poses the question: "Do real men hate to shop?" Immediately followed by: "Don't ask me, ask my customers." After we hear from a customer, Kosack talks about NBO's values, adding convincingly at the end, "You can't go wrong."

Kosack believes that by featuring personable, real-life shoppers in the TV ads, he'll make new customers feel comfortable about NBO. Everything about the advertising on TV, radio, and in newspapers reflects the warm and open relationship that takes place after a sale is made. The "whole-brain" creativity of the advertising is a vital link in the MaxiMarketing chain of events used to fuel NBO's turnaround.

The image change at NBO has been supported by a program of redesigning and renovating the stores themselves to give an "upgraded but not upscaled" appearance. A design firm was hired to create a new look for both existing stores and new stores: neutral colors, tile floors, wide aisles, bright lighting, photo posters of the "NBO Man," and a wall display with interchangeable slots for displaying brand names found in the store.

"We wanted a design that made it easier for our customers to shop, but not so glitzy and glamorous as to chase our target audience away," explained Kosack. Traffic flow was improved to increase unit sales by encouraging shopping in more than one department. Kosack said that in the newly redesigned Scarsdale store, sales went up 30 percent after the changeover.

And to hit home that "the new NBO" is not just suits, "when walking into a new or remodeled NBO store, customers are greeted with a sea of brightly colored sports shirts, slacks, and activewear," says Kosack.

Another innovative component in NBO's image-rebuilding drive, we learned from Jim Frayne, is their Dress for Success Seminar program. The director of the seminars puts on meetings for corporations and institutions, such as the Prudential sales office or the local Rotary Club. It is part fashion show, part do's and don'ts of dressing properly, and part sales promotion—members of the audience are given sales coupons to redeem, and many become NBO customers.

As you have seen with so many of our MaxiMarketing winners, direct involvement with prospects in an unexpected setting and the staging of events that benefit the consumer often play an important role in the new marketing.

The Rabbit in the Magician's Hat: Customer Care

"The best customer of all is the one you already have," Frayne told us. "Many companies forget about that best customer and take him for granted. We don't! Every customer is hard won, particularly in today's environment, and we want to make sure that we don't forget them."

The company's *caring* attitude is reflected in a host of impressive and often *daring* ways. At the time of the announced company overhaul, Kosack began a retraining program for sales personnel. "Before, our salespeople were basically traffic cops directing shoppers to the 40 regulars," he said. "We must provide our customers with more, whether that involves greeting them by name or spending an hour with them." To carry out this mission, private dressing rooms were installed, an almost unheard-of amenity in off-price stores.

Probably the most exceptional service feature at NBO is an on-premises tailoring shop for alterations, at each store. Alterations are done not by seamstresses, but by master tailors with decades of experience. And they personally do the fitting on the customer of the garment they will be altering. This is in striking contrast both to warehouse stores, which may offer no alteration service at all, and department stores where too often the person who does the fitting is not the one who does the alterations, which often are sent out to be done elsewhere.

"What you see in a lot of large stores," Frayne told us, "is virtually a factory type of situation for alterations. NBO gave a lot of thought to that. Should we send all of our tailoring to one location [as many other stores do] and try to save money? Or should we save our customers from aggravation by assuring them top-notch tailoring? We made the right choice. We wanted the tailors themselves to be the ones that fit the garment. So at NBO the suit doesn't go to another location. It stays right in the store (they have their own little shop right there). Any adjustment in the alteration can be done right away. And it gets done right the first time almost all the time."

Men love it. So much so that NBO started letting customers bring in garments for alteration that were purchased elsewhere! NBO now does hundreds of thousands of dollars worth of business in alterations that way.

There is a charge for the tailoring when you buy a suit at NBO. As Frayne explained it to us, "When you see free alterations advertised, you wouldn't have to think about that too long to realize that nothing's free, and the cost is mixed in with the price. With our customers, everything is in the open. You see the price for the suit, and you see the price for the alteration.

"In some places, when the sales person has sold a suit that is not the right silhouette for the customer, the tailor is called over to fit him into it. If the suit needs a lot of work, what does he care? It's the tailor's job to get the guy fitted and get him out of the store. So the suit gets marked up so much, it's really destroyed.

"We tell our tailors, if it requires too much alteration, call the salesman over and say this is the wrong suit for this person. Tell the customer he can't buy the suit because it will never fit right."

It certainly sounds as if NBO has put someone "in charge of loving the customer," as we have been advocating for years.

Pulling the Next Rabbit Out of the Hat

Maintaining sales of $100 million is quite a feat in NBO's limited regional marketing area when you're in the middle of a recession and many of your competitors are in desperate straits. If NBO's regional sales total were projected across the entire U.S.

population, it would be the rough equivalent of achieving well over $1 billion in sales nationally.

Since adopting their new turnaround strategy, NBO has maintained a strong marketing position by mastering the art of identifying, contacting, motivating, converting, and cultivating the men who are potentially their best customers.

When asked how all of these efforts were paying off, Marketing Vice-President Jim Frayne told us: "The average amount of the sales transaction continues to rise and the average number of units per sale also is going up. We've seen steady improvement over the past two years. This tells us not only that we are reaching our marketing goals, but more important, that customer confidence is improving. It is a key marker for us. You can have a great database program to bring them into the stores. But if they don't have a positive experience when they get there, you've wasted a lot of money."

Gene Kosack and his forward-looking team have shown what can be done when a deteriorating situation is tackled head-on with a "Caring and Daring" corporate approach. They have boldly pursued a company vision that recognizes how much the world has changed.

NBO's management is winning the game by having the guts to change the No. 1 retailing rule from "location! location! location!" to "names! names! names!" Considering the power and sophistication of the database-driven marketing program they have developed and are still refining, our guess is that this is just the beginning of the NBO turnaround story.

16

Zellers Makes the Marketing the Message

It's a jungle out there. The larger retailers get, the fiercer the competition between them becomes.

Today the struggle for customers between such hard-hitting discounters as Wal-Mart and Kmart is like a free-for-all brawl among dragons. In just a slightly more refined contest, such elegant department stores as Neiman-Marcus, Saks Fifth Avenue, Nordstrom, and Bloomingdale's are slugging it out with equal retailing ferocity.

In courting shoppers, there are three basic enticements. These 3 *D*s of retailer seductiveness are *deference, dollars,* and *dreams.*

"Deference" is the word we have chosen for every shopper's desire to be recognized, well-served, and appreciated. In the United States, Nordstrom has become legendary for the lengths to which they will go to please a customer and has been rewarded with legendary success.

The potency of the second enticement, "Dollars," is obvious. The power of dollar savings offered through everyday low prices, seasonal sales, value coupons, and special promotions has always been with us and undoubtedly always will be. It has become more important than ever in the price-conscious, competition-crowded 1990s.

The third appeal, offering "Dreams" instead of dollars, has a long, impressive history, and seems to come and go in popularity. It raises a profound marketing question, "Do customers prefer to be rewarded with dollar savings and rebates, or with gifts they can dream about long before they actually earn them with their purchases?" Keeping these three enticements in mind puts some perspective on the story of our next MaxiMarketing winner—Zellers.

In this chapter we will present the incredible story of this discount chain that totally dominates the retail scene in Canada. Zellers has taken the "3 Ds" of retailer seductiveness to new heights. They make their marketing innovations the message in their advertising, and have penetrated a staggering 63 percent of Canadian households with their Club Z reward program.

Dreams Instead of Dollars

Possibly the earliest great success in "dream merchandising" was S & H green stamps, born in Jackson, Mississippi, in 1896. The concept hit its peak in 1969, when 75,000 U.S. stores were offering green stamps as rewards for purchase. Many of our readers undoubtedly have childhood memories of licking sheets of S & H stamps and pasting them into little brown albums. Your mother or grandmother dreamed of accumulating enough stamps to be exchanged for a new set of dishes or silverware.

This is essentially the system adapted by the airlines in their frequent-flyer programs, pioneered by American Airlines in 1981. But instead of giving away tableware or coffee-table books, they were able to give away a product that cost them virtually nothing yet was one of the most desirable gifts of all to most people—empty airline seats.

Of course, with the advent of the computer age, the messy stamp book was replaced with automated mileage reports in statements mailed periodically to the home. Marketers now are able to keep a detailed record of the purchases earning the points and other vital information in a database.

Since the heyday of S & H green stamps, supermarkets have tended toward cash discount rewards, given to shoppers who join their customers' club and present their membership card at the checkout register. Department stores on the whole have been curiously slow about setting up any reward system at all, perhaps out of a complacency born of the days when they were almost the only game in town. And superstore discount merchants use customer clubs chiefly as a form of discounting and may provide additional discounting through rebates.

On the continent of North America, two conspicuous exceptions stand out. Two famous retailers have returned to offering the dream instead of, or in addition to, the dollar as an enticement to customers—while not neglecting the importance of proper deference to the customer's needs and wishes. One of the two appeals to the upper-middle class, the other to the masses. But both of them find exciting ways to put old wine in new bottles. One is Zellers, the rapidly growing discount chain in Canada. The other is Neiman-Marcus, the fabled Dallas-based department store. There is much to be learned from both of these MaxiMarketing winners.

Zellers' Zoom

In 1931, Walter P. Zeller founded a Canadian variety store which he called Zeller's (somewhere along the way, the apostrophe before the "s" was dropped). He added stylish women's and children's clothing and shoes to the usual variety-store merchandise, giving his stores a noticeable difference. His company grew nicely, and by 1952, had 52 stores. After being acquired several times, the chain has been owned outright since 1981 by Hudson's Bay Company, Canada's oldest company, founded in 1670 by King Charles II of England. With the acquisition, Zellers became the cash cow of Hudson's Bay's impressive retail empire.

By 1991, Zellers had 266 stores blanketing most of Canada, and celebrated its sixtieth anniversary with an impressive leap in sales to $2.3 billion, 8 percent more than the previous year, and a 12 percent gain in operating profits to over $200 million despite a flat retaining scene in Canada. This rose again to $2.8 billion in sales the following year, totaling 22 percent of all Canadian department store sales.

The management said they expected to increase sales to $4 billion by 1995, and to become Canada's largest department store chain in terms of market share, with 360 stores blanketing Canada. Since most of this growth will have to come at the expense of competitors, a map in the executive boardroom pinpoints the location of every Zellers, Canadian Tire, Kmart, and Woolco store in Canada. Company executives feel that growth is critically important because volume drives down expenses and makes possible the lowest possible prices essential to their successful Unique Selling Proposition.

Putting It All Together

Sales began to skyrocket in 1986, when the company took a number of important steps marking an overall change in direction. In a moment of bold vision, they determined to become such a powerful force in discount retailing that a giant like Wal-Mart might think twice before marching up into Canada to do battle with them.

- They adopted a new slogan, "The lowest price is the law," and promoted it so heavily with aggressive TV advertising that it now has the highest recall of any advertising slogan in Canada.
- They backed up the slogan with a flat-out no-quibbling lowest-price guarantee. If a customer brings in a Canadian ad containing a lower price for a product sold by Zellers, they will beat that price, no questions asked. If you buy at Zellers and then find a lower price within 30 days, Zellers will refund the difference.
- They targeted millions of customers in their database with circulars now distributed weekly to households across Canada.
- They developed a new no-frills, no-carpeting, easy-to-shop environment, with wide aisles for shopping baskets and fast check-out lines. Shoppers can zip in, grab what they're looking for, and zip out again with minimum hassle.

And—here comes the *daring* part—somehow, despite their already narrow markups, they also managed to offer customers the benefits of earning gift merchandise through a new frequent-buyer program, Club Z. (The Canadian and French pronunications happily are all the same: "zed." As a result, it is pronounced "Club Zed" in both of Canada's prevailing languages.)

Club points earned by purchases (100 points per dollar of purchase) represent an additional discount on top of the already-lowest prices anywhere—a truly formidable competitive advantage. Gift merchandise in the Club Z rewards catalog can then be obtained either by points alone or by a smaller number of points accompanied by cash.

Since the gift items in the Club Z catalog are all upscale articles not carried in Zellers stores, it is hard to place a dollar value on them and therefore hard to say precisely how much of an additional discount they represent. But a significant clue is provided in the catalog by an offer to exchange earned points for certificates usable as cash in the stores.

One dollar of purchases earns club members 100 points. Thus, $1000 in purchases would earn 100,000 points. These are redeemable for $50 in certificates. Since $50 is 5 percent of $1000, this suggests strongly that the retail value of the gifts earned by purchases amounts to an additional discount of 5 percent (although, obviously, it costs Zellers much less than that to acquire the gift merchandise in large wholesale lots and many of the points are never redeemed).

Most of the gift offerings consist of merchandise not found at Zellers. Club Z rewards its frequent buyers with dream items they would love to get but may feel they cannot afford to buy.

The Club Z Extravaganza

Publication of the 156-page Club Z catalog is big news when it is distributed each year in Canada. A heavyweight TV advertising campaign makes certain everyone knows what has been added and what great values are now offered free for points. As far as we know, this is the only major prime-time ongoing TV advertising campaign for a frequent-buyer program anywhere in the world.

Garnet Kinch, vice-president for sales and advertising says,

"It is merchandise our customers would not have the disposable income or the ability to buy over the years. With Club Z, they can get it for free. And that's very, very important for a lot of people—to get something extra. We look to fulfill the dreams of our customers with Club Z."

The rewards, depicted in full color photographs in the club's catalog, range from Giorgio perfume to Pierre Cardin watches to Samsung and JVC color televisions, as well as 30 pages of toys. Available rewards even include cruises to glamorous destinations like Acapulco and Waikiki offered by Zellers' own 19 in-store travel agencies. (The three pages describing these travel rewards serve a dual function, because they also provide free advertising for Zellers' travel agencies and the cruises they sell.)

Zellers had made a determined effort to hold the line on prices and point values in the catalog, Kinch told us. "We have to put ourselves in the shoes of the customer who's saving points. We can't destroy their good faith. So in the last three years, we have not allowed a single price to go up in the catalog. In fact, because there was a recession, about 80 items in the catalog went down in price. We negotiated harder and better with suppliers and did other things in order to cut costs."

Club members don't have to save up any little green stamps or do any home bookkeeping to keep track of how many points are in their account. Every time they make a purchase, their membership card is scanned by the computer and their total accumulation of points is printed out for them on their cash-register receipt.

The point system enables Zellers to turn up the heat at will on selected items and to generate additional sales excitement by featuring not only the sale price of that item but also double Club Z points earned with that purchase.

Club Z Targets Niche Markets

Bonus club points can be earned by applying for a Zellers credit card, by joining the Zellers auto club, or, through partnership promotions, by expenditures with Midas Muffler, Imperial Oil, Discount Car Rentals, Travelodge, or specific grocery items.

Here are some of the subsets of special benefits to niche markets within the customer base:

Members who have accumulated 500,000 points get a VIP "Gold Card" entitling them to special offers and discounts and free courier delivery of certain Club Z rewards.

Senior citizens get an "Advantage 60" card entitling them to a 15 percent discount when shopping on the first Monday of every month, and a 10 percent discount at Zellers Restaurant any time. *Over half of all the senior citizens in Canada carry an Advantage 60 card!*

Kids have not been forgotten, either. They can join Zeddy's Cub Club (its mascot, a teddy bear named Zeddy) and receive their own Cub Club Card. They get a free coloring book, admission to special free kids' movies, and free milk and cookies when they visit a Zellers Restaurant with Mom and Dad. And Zeddy sends them a birthday card every year.

Members of an organization can get a special "Community Card," which pools the points of all of the group's members in order to earn free gifts and services to benefit their community programs.

Charity-minded Club Z members can arrange to have the cash equivalent of their points donated to the Club's Horizon Foundation, which has donated over $211,000 to children's hospitals and other children-related charities.

Membership in Club Z has grown rapidly, and today is up to over 7 million—a staggering 63 percent or more of all the households in Canada! Around 75 to 80 percent of Zellers shoppers have become members of the club. Zellers mails out 7 million circulars *a week* to draw club shoppers into the stores. The size of the membership is a testament to the popularity and power of the idea. We have never seen anything come close to the market penetration of Zellers' database-driven relationship marketing program.

It seems unlikely that if Zellers had decided merely to provide another 2 or 3 percent in cash rebates to frequent buyers instead of the Club merchandise, it could have had the same appeal and sales impact as Club Z. And yet, astonishingly enough, few retailers in North America have taken a cue from Zellers' success and their unique approach to Extra-Value Marketing.

What makes the Zellers program stand out is that the rewards program is not simply an appendage to what they are selling, it is an integral *part* of it. You go to Zellers not just for discounts, but for discounts *and points.* And new Club gift merchandise and reduced-points offers are just as big advertising and shopping news as offers on the store merchandise itself.

Zellers has made the marketing the message it sends to the marketplace. "Club Z makes shopping at Zellers a rewarding experience everyday," proclaims the advertising.

Everything works together to deliver a rock-solid customer proposition: Quality + Lowest Price + Club Z = Can't-Be-Beat Value.

And Can't-Be-Beat Success.

What almost every marketer in the world still doesn't realize is the power of putting together all of the keys to success followed by the MaxiMarketing winners in combination with the new marketing technologies of the new economy. The result can be the kind of explosive growth and the startling turnarounds you have seen in the pages of this book.

17

Neiman-Marcus: Very Far Out Front, Very Early

In the United States, the elegant department store chain of Neiman-Marcus has gotten a clear head start among quality retailers with its two-tier rewards program for customers.

Neiman-Marcus began with the "InCircle," launched in July of 1984, the first "recognition" program in department store history, designed to recognize and reward the store's best customers. It was open only to people who spend at least $3000 a year at Neiman-Marcus.

This was followed, in February of 1991, with the announcement of "NM Plus" for customers who weren't spending enough to qualify for InCircle. By paying a $50 a year membership fee, NM Plus members could get most of the same benefits. And if, later on, their total purchases for the year reached the $3000 requirement, their $50 would be refunded.

The InCircle was the brainchild of Bernie Feiwus, now president and CEO of the Neiman-Marcus Mail-Order Division, and Billy Payton, who is now manager of both InCircle and NM Plus. Back in 1980, both men were working in the credit department. At that time, the only charge card that Neiman-Marcus accepted was their own proprietary store card. About 75 or 80 percent of the customers charged their purchases to their account. So, thanks to computerized charge-customer records, it was easy enough to spot who the store's best customers were.

Feiwus started printing out, and circulating internally, lists of customers who were spending at least $1000 a year and those who were spending over $3000.

Everyone agreed it was very useful information. But when Feiwus wrote a memo proposing that these good customers receive some kind of special recognition, he received a call from the top boss at the time, who told him in no uncertain terms, "As far as I'm concerned, there will never be separate classes at Neiman-Marcus."

Feiwus filed the idea—but he didn't forget about it. As Neiman-Marcus moved into the 1980s, they were opening new stores around the country and running into increasingly stiff competition in the upscale-department-store field. Feiwus felt something should be done to show the best customers at these new stores that Neiman-Marcus recognized them and appreciated their patronage.

After a change in top management, he tried again—and this time won management approval for the launching of InCircle. Most, but not all, of the store's top management was behind the idea. In the complacent retailing world of 1984, there was not yet the same keen appreciation of the importance of customer-coddling as there is today. For this reason, a few NM executives looked on the program as an unnecessary expense. Some of the resistance was said to have come from those in charge of the advertising budget, because that's where most of the start-up investment money had to be obtained. (As we have observed too many times, this frequently happens in companies where someone tries to start a long-range relationship marketing program.)

To start off the program with a bang and make sure it got attention, the store delivered to the $3000-plus charter members of InCircle, via United Parcel Service, a gift basket of gourmet foods, with a card from Richard Marcus, the Neiman-Marcus chairman at the time. The card thanked recipients for their past patronage, welcomed them to membership in InCircle, and said that details of the benefits would follow.

The response was tremendous, say Feiwus and Payton. "We didn't get little thank-you notes," they told the editors of *Colloquy,* a highly regarded marketing newsletter. "We got two- and three-page handwritten letters from customers telling us how much they appreciated our recognition. When you're a store like NM, the expectation level of any customer is very high before they shop with us, and the ability to exceed the expectations, which is always key, is more difficult for us than it is for a store that doesn't emphasize service at the level that we do. As we hoped, this was a demonstrative way for us to *exceed our customers' expectations.*" (Italics ours.)

Neiman-Marcus had developed the program in total secrecy because they were "absolutely paranoid" about competitors getting wind of it and beating them to the punch. They even created leaked disinformation to throw the competition off the trail. They wouldn't talk to the press about it, and when they did, they would say bad things about it.

They couldn't believe that they were the only major department store group that was taking the trouble to find out who their best customers were and strengthening those customers' loyalty through a rewards program.

As it turned out, they needn't have worried. A Saks executive admitted to the editors of *Colloquy* that they lost some business as a result of the InCircle program. Nonetheless, it took Saks *eight years* to respond by launching the next upscale-department-store customer club, Saks First, in 1992. And even then, to Feiwus and Payton, Saks seemed so cautious that "it appears as if they're easing into a program, so, up to this point, we've essentially considered it to be a nonevent."

However, with the steely nerves of riverboat gamblers, they are prepared to counter a bolder move by the competition if and when it comes. As they put it, they believe that one of the secrets of a successful program is "to not play all of your cards on day one. This way, when your competition reacts, you have something to throw back at them. *I can assure you, we certainly haven't played all of our cards.*" (Italics ours.)

Perhaps one reason Neiman-Marcus did not consider the Saks program a threat when it appeared was that Saks First offered nice "perks" but no exceptional rewards. Thus Saks First members received such benefits as priority alterations, coat checking and check-cashing privileges in the store, a fashion newsletter, early notice on sales, and a personal store contact. But there were no points earned and no incentive to buy more.

As we have seen so often, the competitive latecomer offers a pale imitation of the original because they lack the passionate belief in the idea of the innovator. The copycat version never makes the impact of the daring original.

Meanwhile members of the Neiman-Marcus InCircle were receiving such nice perks as a toll-free hotline, special offers, a members' newsletter, gift wrapping on purchases over $25. They were also awarded 100 points for each dollar of purchase, and these points could be redeemed for really exciting, valuable, glamorous rewards such as Waterford crystal, sterling silver pieces, trips to the Summer Oylmpics in Barcelona or the Kentucky Derby, and so on.

Furthermore, unlike the Zellers plan, accumulation of InCircle points ends December 31 of each year and must be redeemed by March 31 of the following year. (The first Frequent Flyer program, American Airlines AAdvantage, also did not permit carryover of mileage points to the next year until competition from other airlines forced them to change the rule.) So InCircle members, as they approach each qualifying level of annual purchase, have an incentive to buy more from the store in order to go over the top and earn their choice of rewards at that level.

In 1991, Neiman-Marcus launched their second-tier program, NM Plus, by granting a number of free charter memberships. They reached down into the database for customers spending more than $1000 a year but less than the InCircle memberships' $3000. After the launch, other NM customers could join NM Plus by paying a $50 membership fee, refundable upon reaching InCircle status.

Benefits of membership in NM Plus included a free one-year subscription to *Harper's Bazaar* or *Connoisseur* magazine, a $50 certificate good on any American Airlines coach fare of $250 or more within the continental United States, and a Parfums Givenchy fragrance. (Note the partnership deals at work here, good for both partners.) But most important, NM Plus members could earn and redeem InCircle points as well.

"But aren't these programs too extensive?" doubting Thomases may scoff. As Feiwus and Payton put it, "Our competitors look at the program and think, 'Oh my God, this is going to cost NM a fortune.' They never took the time to understand the intricacies of our program, not well enough to see the benefits of customer recognition that lead to increased customer purchases and loyalty."

Feiwus and Payton have been as secretive about the dollar success of the program as they were about the details of the plans at launch time. This reticence makes it difficult for us to point to this as a dramatic case of breakthrough marketing. But they are willing to admit that the growth of membership is *six times* greater than they expected, And, they say, "we continue to be committed to both programs."

They also have very little to say publicly about the extensive mining of the database information that is now standard procedure at Neiman-Marcus. You can be sure that they are customizing their offers and their messages to specific individuals and segments at the high end at least as well as Zellers and NBO do it at the lower end of the market.

InCircle and NM Plus have become as much a part of the shopping scene for the affluent shopper at Neiman-Marcus as Club Z is part of the shopping experience at Canada's leading discount retailer. And, if the numbers were revealed, we suspect that the Neiman-Marcus loyalty reward programs are as much a part of the Dallas store's continuing success as Club Z has been for Zellers.

Three cheers for Extra-Value Marketing!

PART 5

A Global View

18 MaxiMarketing Winners around the World

Provincialism is rampant everywhere in the world. It is part of the human condition. The population of every country sincerely believes that it is wiser and better and more advanced in some way than its neighbors. For instance, there are at least four countries—the United States, France, Britain, and Switzerland—whose people believe that it was they who invented democracy. And possibly the people of Greece would insist that the origins of the democratic ideal go back even further, to the time of Socrates and Plato.

If you closely questioned advertising and marketing people in the United States, no doubt a great many of them would finally confess that, yes, they believe their country to be more sophisticated in that area than the rest of the world. Of course, you would surely encounter similar self-satisfaction in many other countries as well.

But the truth is that no country stands alone any longer. Whatever happens in one part of the world is soon part of what is happening everywhere else. This is now as true for marketing as it is for the rest of what happens in the world economy. We are all part of one global village.

Whether sitting in a Rio de Janeiro hotel room watching CNN on television, visiting a middle-class residential neighborhood in Kuala Lumpur, or cruising down the autobahn in Germany, we can hardly tell any more what country it is, except for the foreign language being spoken in the street and the words we may have trouble deciphering on the billboards.

Ever since our first book was published, we have received invitations to speak at marketing and business conferences around the world. Everywhere we went, we were impressed by the enthusiasm, insights, and ingenuity of many of the local marketing leaders and consultants. Whatever the country, be it Finland, Indonesia, Chile, or the British crown colony of Hong Kong, we invariably learn about a distinctive success in making MaxiMarketing work, an innovative breakthrough we had not seen anywhere else before.

Unlike the cultural factors that often make an award-winning advertising campaign unique to its country of origin, the insights gained from a new Individualized Marketing strategy are usually transportable from country to country. Local regulations and restrictions faced by marketers in each country only seem to inspire greater leaps of creative imagination in devising new adaptations of the basic approach.

The pace of change varies from country to country. But, with each passing year, the worldwide trend away from mass-marketing practices to the new database-driven Individualized Marketing becomes more pronounced. Whether the population is large or small, whether the economy is booming or in deep trouble, whether inflation is raging or under control—none of this seems to slow the universal trend toward one-to-one marketing in the world's developed and developing economies.

As a result, it has now become an article of faith of this book's authors that we can, and should, learn from each other in the global village inhabited by the world's MaxiMarketers. In previous chapters we looked at U.S. success stories and traveled beyond America's borders to spend time with MaxiMarketing winners in Canada, France, England, Holland, and Brazil.

Now, in a whirlwind final swing around the world, we will highlight enterprising companies in Japan, Malaysia, Germany, Norway, Finland, Ireland, Brazil, and Argentina. We want you to see how the principles of MaxiMarketing and the seven keys to business success in the nineties are being used in surprising ways in surprising places.

Now "Guinness Is Good for You" in Germany

How would you like the job of attempting to build market share for an imported Irish beer in Germany, where great beer is a national heritage and there are over a thousand regional and national brews competing for the drinker's attention and loyalty? Bringing coals to Newcastle would be a breeze by comparison. Then to make it even tougher, how would you like to accomplish this with a small sales force and a small marketing budget—too small for the kind of advertising campaign that might be able to move the needle?

The solution that Guinness found to this riddle was to stir up a high degree of consumer involvement with their product—bringing people together to enjoy a real Irish experience. The low-cost lever they used to accomplish this was to make it easy for the tavern owners to get more involved with their own customers, and to sell more Guinness beer to the tavern's customers in the process.

Guinness GmbH came to Germany in 1976, but by the mid-1980s, sales growth had stalled. In 1987 Guinness assembled a database of 4500 owners of taverns who carried their beer but whose establishments were too small to justify visits by the company's limited sales force. Then they sent out a mailing informing these tavern owners of their automatic enrollment in the new tavern owners' GIGFY ("Guinness Is Good For You") Club.

Guinness GmbH pours 80 percent of its promotional budget into the relationship-marketing program for the tavern owners, reserving only 20 percent for traditional media advertising. What we heard from Gavin Forth, the marketing manager, was: "We wanted to increase 2-way communication between Guinness and the sellers because once the product leaves Ireland, Guinness never touches it again. It is imported by local breweries and then goes to the taverns through wholesalers. We needed some way to look after the product."

GIGFY members receive a mailing every few months with tips, ideas, and aids for selling more Guinness. They get discounts of up to 20 percent on unusual, thematic, point-of-sale materials with detailed suggestions on how to put up the displays and organize special events around them. Tavern owners also get suggestions on how to write and send out press releases. One program offered a prize to the pub that got the best press coverage on St. Patrick's Day. A tavern in Aachen blitzed the local papers, got great publicity, and greatly increased sales.

In one of the mailings, the owners received ideas for setting up a dart-board competition. Another time, the mailing included a newspaper ad the owner could use to invite the public to an "Irish" Oktoberfest, a night of card playing, a night of Irish specialties, and so on. A recent mailing offered a cassette of Irish music and a chance to obtain additional cassettes for the tavern owner to sell to his customers. There were also suggestions for involving the customers in voting for their favorite Irish melody.

The mailings to tavern owners call for a response and get a participation rate of around 20 percent. Many tavern owners tell Guinness that they are proud of their membership in the GIGFY Club!

Although exact sales results are confidential, sales are believed to have increased by about 100 percent since it all began, and Guinness attributes this to the GIGFY Club program. We were told by Gavin Forth that in 1992, concurrent with a direct-mail campaign to tavern owners prepared by their agency, Fritsch Heine Rapp & Collins, sales were up 25 percent over the previous year.

Just as Nestlé is not simply selling Buitoni pasta but is selling sunny Italy as well, so Guinness is not just selling Irish beer to Germans but also a touch of the auld sod of Ireland. By getting closer to the tavern owners who sell their product, the company is encouraging Guinness drinkers in Germany to get closer to each other—and enjoy a night of Irish revelry over a foaming mug of Guinness. They are masters of the art of practicing the "bringing people together" key to success—with the novel twist of getting the tavern owner to pay most of the cost.

A New High in TRC Marketing for Lexus

While we are in Germany, let's take a moment to look at an automotive company that is brilliantly building brand loyalty with a total relationship commitment to its customers.

As we have seen, customer involvement and caring enough to really put the customer's interest first are favorably affecting brand preference for many of our MaxiMarketing winners in a way that traditional mass advertising is increasingly unable to do.

We showed you how the commitment of Harley-Davidson to caring for their owners in club chapters and rallies has created a brand mystique that has enabled them to stave off Japanese competition and retain a commanding lead in the heavyweight motorcycle sector.

Now we see Toyota in Germany doing something similar for owners of their top-of-the-line car, the Lexus LS 400. Marketing of the Lexus has set a standard of excellence everywhere in the world the car is sold. And results have far exceeded Toyota's earlier expectations. But only in Germany has involvement with customers after the sale been raised to the level of an art form. Lexus owners revel in the privileges of ownership. It's enough to make their envious friends want to join the charmed circle.

When Toyota decided to launch the Lexus in Germany, they knew that they were going up against three very heavy hitters in the luxury car market: Mercedes, BMW, and Porsche. They decided from the beginning that, in order to compete successfully over the long haul, they needed dramatically different, extra value in their customer-care program. Working with BMC Direct and AZ Bertelsmann, Toyota Marketing Director Achim Schauerte decided to send Lexus owners a series of remarkable gifts and invitations to extraordinary, exclusive events to serve as the icing on the cake of their customer-care program.

All of the mail contact pieces were handsomely produced and were sent to the customer by the dealer, with a personal letter enclosed, signed by the dealer to emphasize his concern for "perfection even in small details."

March 1991: An invitation to a ballooning excursion for owners only, including a picnic, champagne, and an overnight stay in a castle turned luxury hotel, *Schlosse Bühlerhöhe* in Baden-Baden (with appropriate comparisons to the "quiet traveling of the Lexus LS 400"). Some 54 percent of Lexus owners asked for more information, an exceptional response.

November 1991: A gift bottle of the new Beaujolais. Every year on the third Thursday in November, the new Beaujolais Primeur is allowed to be sold in Europe. On this date, the wine is permitted to be transported across the French border. There is a competition among wine connoisseurs to be among those who get the first bottles.

Toyota arranged with a transportation company to deliver one bottle of the new Beaujolais Primeur directly to Lexus owners "with the compliments of Lexus" before anyone else in Germany had yet been able to obtain it. It was a fantastically expensive gift compared to a calendar or a key chain, but a mere trifle compared to the cost of a new Lexus. You can imagine how impressed Lexus owners must have been, and how they might pick up the phone to brag to their friends about the unexpected joys of Lexus ownership.

March 1992: A gift to remind owners of the seasonal time change. At the end of March, there is a one-hour change to central European summertime, similar to the changeover from standard time to daylight saving time in the United States. One day before the time change, all Lexus owners received a reminder to move the time ahead. It was a stunningly attractive Lexus clock *already set at the correct new time.*

September 1992: An invitation to a gourmet weekend in Engadin, Switzerland, in which every course of the elegant dinner was served at a different restaurant. Some 1.8 percent of the Lexus customers actually booked this weekend. They paid their own way, of course, as they did with the ballooning excursion. But the event positioned Lexus as a caring automobile company looking for ways to create really pleasing experiences for people appreciative of the finer things in life. Those owners who actually attended the event and rubbed elbows with other owners felt like members of an exclusive, prestigious club, congratulating themselves on their wisdom and good fortune.

February 1993: A gift of devices to aid mastery of the new postal regulations. On April 1, there was due to be a substantial increase in mailing rates in Germany. Then on July 1 in 1993, there was going to be a fundamental change in the German postal mailing system, a change in which all postal codes would increase from four digits to five. When these changes did take place, they caused a great deal of confusion among the public—but not among Lexus owners. For in February, Lexus dealers had thoughtfully mailed their customers an informative booklet about the changes, a "smart" letterscale, and address stickers already imprinted with the owner's new postal code.

The surprise mailings continue. Being a Lexus owner in Germany is an unending adventure, an experience unequaled by any other car manufacturer we know about. It's money well spent by Lexus in a category with a lifetime customer value of half a million dollars or more.

What is surprising is that none of the other luxury car manufacturers seem to realize what they can afford to pay to keep a customer happy. Lexus cares enough to really put the customer first—and their commitment to the relationship shows up in the loyalty rate at the Lexus dealer showrooms around the world.

Ford Rings Up Car Buyers in Norway

What may seem like an expensive way to entice prospects can prove to be phenomenally economical if the response is high enough. Giving a free telephone to prospective car buyers might seem like a reckless extravagance, even though in this age of mass production of electronics a phone can be produced for just a few dollars. But the Ford Motor Company of Norway showed how such a daring extravagance can pay off.

Ford had a problem in the Norwegian market. They were experiencing a sharp drop in sales and market share for their

Scorpio model. Even their own dealers were losing faith in the car because of its poor image.

An unusual Involvement Marketing campaign was devised, and the first step, as in the Guinness case history, was to involve the dealers. Each of them received a mailing piece explaining the plan, and enclosed with it was a real push-button telephone with a preprogrammed hotline button. If the dealer had any questions about the promotion, all he had to do was to press "1" to get the Ford marketing manager on the line then.

The next step was to do the same thing—mailing a preprogrammed phone to the best carefully selected prospects and then watch sales for the Scorpio double.

By daring to do something real to get involved with targeted, ready-to-buy prospects, Ford found a much better way to be a winner than the usual automotive me-too advertising splattered across the TV screen, with 90 percent of the budget wasted on nonprospects.

Shiseido of Japan: The Relationship Is the Thing

Without a doubt, the marketing of Shiseido cosmetics in Japan is one of the world's most dramatic demonstrations of total commitment to the customer relationship. With annual sales of around $2.7 billion, Shiseido is the fourth-largest personal-care products company in the world.

The launching pad of their worldwide success has been their domestic sales in Japan, where they have carried the art of being a "Caring and Daring" company to new heights. Mr. Kazuaki Kawaguchi of Hakuhodo, one of Shiseido's advertising agencies, told us that in Japan, Shiseido is bigger than the No. 2 and No. 3 cosmetics companies combined. Throughout Japan's economic slowdown and stock market crash in the early years of this decade, Shiseido continued to grow 10 percent a year.

In the 1980s, Shiseido began forging a one-to-one relationship with customers by enrolling 10 million Japanese women in the Shiseido Club. Members were invited to apply for a Shiseido Visa card entitling them to special membership discounts from participating retailers, hotels, and theaters.

Shiseido was one of the first companies in the world to realize the value of having their name on a plastic credit card in a woman's wallet. Shortly after introduction of its cobranded card, one-third of all the Visa cards in Japan flashed the Shiseido logo every time the cardholder or anyone else looked at it.

Each month, one million Shiseido cardholders receive a mini-magazine right in the envelope with the Visa credit card statement. It's chock-full of celebrity interviews, club talk, travel ideas, fun things to do, products to buy, and educational information about Shiseido products. There is lots of "telling" and very little "selling."

Shiseido also publishes a full-sized magazine with a circulation of 400,000 that rivals America's *Vogue* and *Harper's Bazaar* in quality and impact. Shoppers pick up their free copies at leading department stores and at the Shiseido beauty shops located throughout Japan. It's just another example of how this MaxiMarketing winner offers "gain without pain" to the women of Japan.

Shiseido has 10,000 beauty counselors and 25,000 franchise shops in Japan, forming an informational bridge between their products and the users. Then, as a further example of the synergistic activity that permeates this company, there are Shiseido specialty catalogs selling European knits, fine jewelry, and other merchandise directly by mail, and even Shiseido restaurants and a Shiseido Boutique in the Ginza.

To Japanese women, Shiseido is a constant, real presence in their everyday existence. They know and respect Shiseido for its wholehearted commitment to helping a woman in Japan realize her full potential and live a more beautiful life. It is a strategy that has underscored the company's market leadership for more than a decade.

The MaxiMarketing Miracle Maker of Malaysia

Our next port of call is Kuala Lumpur in Malaysia, where an innovative bank is displaying the kind of ingenuity in marketing and service that leaves most other banks in the world behind. It's the AMFB (Arab Malaysian Finance Berhad).

In case you haven't been to Kuala Lumpur, we can assure you of the fact that there are stupendous traffic jams there, too, as in so many other major cities. But AMFB does something about it.

AMFB knows how much trouble it is to buck traffic in order to get to the bank and make a deposit. As a result, they created their special Dial-and-Deposit Service. The customer dials the bank, and AMFB sends a car to pick up the deposit. Maybe there's another bank somewhere in the world that cares enough to do that for you, but we've never heard of them.

AMFB also introduced Southeast Asia's first two-generation home loan: the father-and-son mortgage that's spread out not over just the usual 15 or 30 years as they do it in America but twice that long. It's a win-win situation. The monthly repayments are lower, the home buyer keeps the house in the family from generation to generation, and the bank doubles the lifetime of the relationship with the customer. The lower monthly payments may make it possible for the father and the son to buy a bigger house, to be occupied by both of their families.

Then there's AMFB's Savers' G.A.N.G. for Kids. Children under 12 who start a savings account with just $5 get a free camel coin-bank. Then as soon as their savings reach a total of $50, they become a member of the Savers' G.A.N.G.

> This means all of the exciting Savers' G.A.N.G. goodies are yours for only $3—a special G.A.N.G. T-shirt, G.A.N.G. stickers, button badge, visor, pencil, eraser, ruler, bookmark, timetable, and your very own G.A.N.G. ID card with your picture on it.
>
> You'll also get your Savers' G.A.N.G. magazine, *GANGWAY*—FREE! You can then enjoy all the exciting puzzles, quizzes, stories and contents prepared specially for you. There's even a pen pal column so you can get to know other G.A.N.G. members all over Malaysia.

The pen-pals feature in the kids' magazine is another example of "bringing people together"—the key to success that works so well for Harley-Davidson at their rallies and for Lexus Germany in bonding with their owners at ballooning and gourmet weekend events.

At last count, the Savers' G.A.N.G. was responsible for the opening of 30,000 bank accounts by children. Senior General Manager Koh Pee Seng admitted to *Malaysian Business* that they actually lose money on this service. But the bank is happy to do so because it means getting a customer early and hopefully keeping him or her for life. This is a MaxiMarketer that thinks very long-term.

As explained to us by Lam Song Hen, general manager of operations, the bank's corporate mission is "to entrench its position as a premier finance company providing innovative products and services to its customers" and "to strive to be a caring and responsible corporate citizen."

Thanks in large part to their "Caring and Daring" approach to banking, AMFB has enjoyed a compounded annual growth rate of over 30 percent for the last five years.

A Different Kind of Database for Finland

The United States has enjoyed a history of direct mail going back almost to the beginning of the century. Literally thousands of mailing lists were developed by means of recording names and addresses of mail-order inquirers and purchasers on addressing machine plates or compiling them from public records of various kinds. The U.S. government also has a tradition of compiling and analyzing demographic data from the national census conducted every 10 years and making this data available to the business world.

When the transition began to take place to maintaining name and address files by computer instead of by the older method, the foundation was laid for development of huge commercial databases of U.S. household information from which businesses could make selections for precisely targeted mailings. Something like this is already happening or is about to happen in almost all of the developed economies of the world. But in many of these countries, the development of a large public database has been hampered by the limited scope of direct mail in the past and by strict privacy laws and other government regulations.

In Finland, the largest consumer list company, VTKK, has found a way to treat the building of a database more like the establishment of a club than like compiling a list. Anyone who is intent on developing a national marketing database can learn from their example.

VTKK faced some interesting problems. Finland is a small country, with a total population of only 5 million people. Consumer legislation strictly limits the use of sweepstakes, two-for-one offers, and so on. Lifestyle information cannot be obtained and used unless it is volunteered by the consumer.

Another interesting "problem" that Finland was fortunate to have was that, in the years following World War II, life was *too good* to require heavyweight use of marketing and advertising! Sales success came easy, and there was no great pressure to do better.

But then came the end of the cold war and the worst recession in 120 years. Suddenly, Finns were motivated by the pressure of declining markets to develop more advanced selling methods.

In order to build and offer a lifestyle database, the consumer database division of VTKK launched a novel idea—the Poste Interestante Club. It is "a club of people interested in many activities and hobbies." Through mass media advertising, VTKK invites Finns to join. The main attraction of membership is a free magazine called *Toivelehti.* As with any appealing magazine, it is filled with interesting and useful articles. But it also carries mail-order and promotional offers by companies that want to reach specific individuals in the database.

Naturally, the Poste Interestante membership application calls for information about the member's hobbies, interests, and lifestyle. As a result, an advertiser in the magazine can pick out exactly the right person for the product and the offer. VTKK makes it possible for companies in Finland to more easily pursue the "stop wasting money on nonprospects" key to success.

The effectiveness of the resulting database can be seen in some information shared with us about the results by VTKK Marketing Manager Timo Korpela.

> A book club mailing to names selected from the database got a 4.5 times better pull than the average in their campaign.

Another book company selling art books mailed to selected names and got back 25 times as many orders as usual.

A cruise line sent a mailing to 6000 young single women inviting them to come to a meeting at the office to find out about their "Lady Line" cruise. They received 2000 acceptances, and instead of using their offices for the gathering, had to use the ship.

And all this was happening while the economy was worsening and expenditures in most of the other media were declining.

Any time those of you living outside the United States read something in our books about U.S. marketing institutions and say to yourself, "But we don't have that in our country" or "We can't do that in our country"—think of little Finland. Each country must develop its own unique solutions to the problem of locating, identifying, contacting, and cultivating its best prospects and customers—just as VTKK is doing in Finland through its Poste Interestante Club.

HSM—Daring to Bring the Best to Brazil

Another example of outstanding database marketing and customer-care commitment, this one in the business-to-business selling category, is to be found in Brazil.

In 1987, three smart, well-prepared young business people put their heads together and decided to start a business seminars company with a difference, HSM Cultura Desenvolvimento.

Two of them, José Salibi Neto and Harry Ufer, had the dual distinction of being not only MBAs with experience in working for large corporations but also well-known tennis stars. (They believe their sports background has played an important part in their success, having given them the will to win and the ability to deal with and overcome adverse situations.) The third partner, Marina Domingues, held a BA and MBA. She had begun her career as an attorney and then had focused on the area of business administration.

Their aim was to bring the best-known management and marketing gurus to Brazil—notables of the caliber of Tom Peters, Philip Kotler, Peter Drucker, Theodore Levitt, Regis McKenna, John Kenneth Galbraith, Alvin Toffler, and Philip Crosby. (None of these much-in-demand speakers had ever before shared their knowledge in Brazil. By now, they have all been there, thanks to HSM.)

To accomplish this, the young entrepreneurs faced the familiar problem of the hen and the egg. Namely, they couldn't get the speakers if they couldn't ensure the audiences, and they couldn't enroll the audiences if they didn't have the speakers. In addition, they had to struggle with an economy which at one point was suffering from quadruple-digit inflation and had a currency that shrank 1 percent in value *every day.*

Furthermore, they faced a fiercely competitive market, and in their first year were barely able to do one-tenth as much business as the No. 1 company in the field.

Just six years later, this MaxiMarketing-focused company had become the leading high-level business management seminar organization in Brazil and Latin America, and their volume of business was 10 times that of the No. 2 company in the field. They had promoted approximately 70 international events, attended by over 20,000 executives.

How did they accomplish such a meteoric rise? Basically, through their extraordinary kid-glove treatment of both their noted speakers and their seminar enrollees.

Through exhaustive telemarketing they have constructed a database of over 80,000 business executives, the best and most up-to-date compilation of business companies and executives in Brazil. But it is not just a mailing list. By means of advanced computer technology, they have been able to build up detailed knowledge of all the entries, including what previous events they have attended and what their reactions were.

This information enables HSM to provide a rare degree of personal attention. It is only too common in business seminars and executive development programs to ask the audience to fill out evaluation sheets afterwards, and then do little or nothing with the results. Not so at HSM, where this information by individual response is always fed into the database. Then, whenever a move or improvement is made that might be based on a client's suggestion, a search of the database will reveal if any clients ever suggested it, and if so, who they are. These clients are then contacted, notified, and thanked.

A favorite example they provide is the story of their experience with Salim Mattar, president of Localiza-National, Brazil's leading car rental company. After one HSM seminar he had attended, he suggested that he would like to see Tom Peters in Brazil. A year later, when HSM managed to schedule a seminar with Mr. Peters, Mattar not only received the seminar brochure—he also received a copy of his evaluation sheet which contained his suggestion and a personal letter from HSM pointing out that his request had been answered. Mattar cancelled a trip to the United States in order to go to the seminar.

The company has developed a way to detect when anyone in the database changes job responsibility or moves on to a new company. These people then receive a personalized letter, signed by one of the HSM directors, congratulating that person on this new stage in his or her professional life.

What if HSM brings a speaker to Brazil for a second time and some of their clients who had attended the first time sign up to come again? You might expect the company just to deposit the money and count their blessings. But HSM contacts each of these people individually and explains exactly what the new seminar is going to cover and what parts, if any, will be repeated from the first seminar. Then, if these people still wish to attend the second time, they will know exactly what awaits them and HSM will avoid having a disappointed client.

HSM knows that people who attend a day-long seminar suffer a let-down after lunch. It is much more difficult for the speaker to hold the attention of the audience in the afternoon than it is when everyone is fresh in the morning. As a result, HSM now starts the afternoon session at all their seminars with a 20-minute performance by the best comedian in Brazil.

The comedy show gets everybody laughing and relaxed before plunging back into the material being presented by the day's speaker. Some of the attendees say it's worth coming just for the comedy show. Everyone is much more receptive in the afternoon than they had been before this innovative step was taken.

World's First Left-Handed Handout

Another example of the company's total commitment to giving each participant the best possible experience occurred when they noted a problem with handouts distributed during a seminar. These handout sheets always allowed room on the right side of the page for jotting down notes and observations. But left-handed people found this difficult. To resolve this problem, special handout sheets were designed for "lefties," with extra space on the left instead of the right. A small touch, but it absolutely delighted the beneficiaries.

The recognition and implementation of client suggestions forms a feedback loop which has fueled the growth of this MaxiMarketing winner. As they explained it to us, "All such endeavors to delight our clients and find new ways of doing it are an HSM consistent concern and we allow these clients of ours to know it...As a result, their involvement through suggestions and direct participation in the improvement of this work is getting bigger and bigger, which turns it all into a circle. Our own clients end up helping us to render increasingly better services to them."

For a relatively unknown company to persuade noted business speakers greatly in demand worldwide to travel to Brazil to conduct a seminar was no small trick. They did it by lavishing the same personal care and attention to detail on each speaker as they do on each client. For example, here is the rave they received from Theodore Levitt, the legendary professor emeritus of business administration at the Harvard Business School:

> You organized a remarkably efficient and congenial three days for me in Brazil—made especially effective by your enormously helpful advice and support to make my presentations clear and useful to the audiences.
>
> You attend with great precision to all the logistical details that ease one's way, so as to help one concentrate fully on the subject of one's presentation.
>
> No others have ever done so much and so well for me.
>
> And on top of this, your promotion of my appearance was superb in its effectiveness, professionalism, and good taste.

José Salibi Neto, Harry Ufer, and Marina Domingues dared to start from scratch in a fiercely competitive field and reinvent the seminar business in Brazil. They see themselves as a "Caring and Daring" company that has been able to rise to the top of their field in record time by meeting and exceeding the expectations of both attendees and speakers.

Now they have moved into the market in Argentina, a country with a population of 30 million, about one-fifth that of Brazil. Their first seminar there, featuring Al Ries, drew over 500 enthusiastic attendees.

Following the event, they asked Mr. Ries to write a letter endorsing the appearance of the next speaker. Who might better presell a seminar than the speaker who has just gotten rave notices for his own presentation?

The rise of HSM is an example to inspire any young entrepreneur anywhere in the world—whether selling to business or to the consumer. They are on their way to becoming the premier seminar organization in all of Latin America by concentrating their energies at being best at everything they do and by giving each individual attendee the total attention of the company.

The Mouse That Conquered Ireland

You have just read about HSM Cultura & Desenvolvimento in Brazil; now read the inspiring story of another MaxiMarketing entrepreneur.

Some of the success stories in this book are about large international companies such as Nestlé or LEGO Systems, and if you are part of a very small business, you may feel, "That's all very well if you have their kind of investment capital to play with—but what about *me*? What can *I* do?"

The answer is that each operation, no matter how large or how small, must develop its own unique MaxiMarketing solution based on creatively caring for the customer. We hope that—whatever the size of your venture—you find inspiration and some beginning ideas in what both the large and small MaxiMarketing companies in this book accomplish.

In Ireland, Robert Hayes McCoy provides a delightful example of what a one-person company with virtually no financial resources can do. He has learned how to make a tiny promotional investment bring back a 3000 percent return, and has increased the size of his direct marketing consulting business by 400 percent—growing from a staff of one (himself) to a staff of four.

This may still not seem a very remarkable growth. But McCoy points out that he is operating in a depressed economy without any large advertising agencies and in which many prospective clients don't even know what direct marketing means. A number of direct marketing agencies in Ireland have tried to expand and most of them have gone bankrupt. For these reasons, McCoy is especially pleased that his strategy brings him all the work that he and his partner and small staff can handle, at a good profit.

Furthermore, in an age in which many people in the United States complain about getting too much junk mail and a great deal of business-to-business mail ends up in the wastebasket of the addressee's secretary, company presidents actually call up McCoy and beg to be added to his mailing list.

On a small scale, but still clearly visible, we can recognize here many of our keys to business success today: "tell, don't sell," "gain without pain," "getting real," and "not wasting money on nonprospects."

It all began in 1986, when McCoy wanted to start his own direct marketing consulting business. But he could afford only a very tight start-up budget—so tight that he couldn't even afford colorful brochures advertising his services.

"In fact," he says, "the only colorful promotional item that we *could* afford was the postage stamps that we purchased from the post office." That's when, he says, inspiration, as if it were direct from heaven, hit him!

But let him tell the whole story himself…

> We discovered that the Irish post office generally issues a new postage stamp approximately every 4–6 weeks.
>
> And if you go into the General Post Office in Dublin, the capital city of Ireland, on the very day that a new stamp is issued and buy one of those new stamps and mail it out on

> the same day...it gets a special: FIRST DAY OF ISSUE POSTMARK.
>
> As you can imagine, because of the difficulties involved, not too many of these First Day of Issue stamps are mailed out in Ireland. In fact, all over the world Irish First Day of Issue stamps are considered to be genuine collector's items.
>
> The remarkable thing about these stamps is that they cost the very same as an ordinary stamp. We figured that if we took a bit of trouble and contacted our friends and potential customers every time a new stamp was issued we could create a very cost-effective impact with new stamps...give people a valued collector's item...and, most importantly, create an excuse for keeping in touch with people on a regular basis.
>
> In short, create a wonderful Customer Loyalty Campaign.

McCoy started with a very small mailing list. But the names on it were the *crême de la crême* of Irish business executives.

Then every time he or his partner meets someone who is a potential client, they make a point of exchanging business cards. The very next day, he sends a letter saying in effect, "when I was talking to you yesterday I never got an opportunity to tell you about my hobby. Truth is, I'm a stamp collector. Mind you, I don't just collect ordinary stamps—I collect special First Day of Issue Stamps" and so on.

He then goes on to tell them First Day of Issue stamps are collector's items that tend to increase in value in a very short period of time. Finally, he delivers the punchline: "So, I've decided that every time I'm in the GPO adding to my personal collection, I'll make a point of sending one to you, too."

In some of his letters, McCoy says clever things about the stamps. For example..."Hey, that's a Europa stamp! Take great care of it because First Day of Issue Europa Stamps are worth more money than most."

Other months, he encloses things like his "Fairy Godmother's sequins" in his letters after writing such things as: "I know you are going to find it hard to believe this. That's why I'm sending you some of her sequins as proof." The letter continues, "I was sitting alone in my office the other evening thinking about you...actually, I was wondering how I could impress you so much that you'd definitely want to do more business with

Robert Hayes-McCoy Direct Marketing Consultants immediately, but enough about that for the moment.

"Do you know what happened. . . . .?

"You're absolutely right!

"My Fairy Godmother appeared beside me and told me that I was to invite you out to lunch," and so on.

It's great fun. People write back to him saying all kinds of nice things *and* offering him assignments. People even give him suggestions about what he should say in his next letter.

Mindful that a friend who asks you for something every time he or she writes soon becomes a bore, McCoy artfully varies the letters from a hard-nosed business letter one time to a whimsical, amusing message that doesn't even mention business the next.

Some of the most popular letters of the latter kind are those from "j. mouse." The first letter signed by j. mouse explained that the reason why he was writing was that he had *made a terrible mistake*! j. mouse then explained. (He can write only in lower case letters because, in his own words, "you try typing sometime with one foot on the upper case key and the other on the letter you're looking for!") Here's what his letter said:

> robert wrote you a wonderful witty letter to go with your latest first day of issue stamp but boy is he going to kill me.
>
> he liked his letter so much that he left the computer turned on when he went home last night and he didn't even think of saving it. he wanted to admire it all over again first thing in the morning.
>
> but i didn't know that...and last night i was sitting on his keyboard loving every word of his letter and didn't notice cat creeping up behind me. that's how good robert's letter was!
>
> i got an awful fright!
>
> i jumped and landed on the 'delete' key and robert's very words disappeared in front of my eyes.
>
> i'm in real trouble now. that's why i'm writing this letter to you.
>
> when you get this stamp please write back immediately and tell robert that his letter was the best thing he ever wrote and that you are going to give him a whole lot of business.

and please don't tell him that it was j. mouse that told you to do this.

This first "j. mouse" letter was a big hit. McCoy began to get letters addressed to "j. mouse" and phone calls from people asking to speak to j. mouse. This led to a a whole series of j. mouse letters that became collector's items in themselves.

And j. mouse alone has captured as clients two major financial institutions and a number of other companies.

So let Robert Hayes McCoy and j. mouse serve as a constant reminder to you—it's not how big or how small your company is, but rather how dedicated you are to the identification and cultivation of your best prospects and customers, that really counts.

We have completed our examination of all of the MaxiMarketing winners in this book. They are among the best we could find anywhere in the world, but we know they are by no means the only companies that are using the principles of MaxiMarketing and going beyond MaxiMarketing to achieve outstanding success. (If your company is one of these unrecognized winners, we would be pleased to hear about it from you.)

19
The New Power of "Caring and Daring"

You have read in this book about companies that have successfully dared to be different. Now we'd like to leave you with some final thoughts about the new power of "Caring and Daring" and how you can increase the likelihood of your own success in putting to use what you have discovered.

Let's start off with a fascinating little exercise: Fold your hands together, interlacing the fingers, and look at them. Note which thumb, the right or the left, is on top. Now do it again. But this time make the other thumb come out on top.

If your hands feel uncomfortable, you are doing it correctly. *You are experiencing the discomfort of breaking a familiar pattern.* We discovered this demonstration in a wonderful little book, *The Art of Creative Thinking,* by Gerald Nierenberg. The author says it illustrates the paradox that once you create a pattern of behavior, each time you duplicate that exact pattern, you increase the discomfort level should you decide to change it later. Familiarity breeds hardening of the creative arteries.

Nierenberg gives us the Henry Ford example. "Ford introduced the Model T in 1908 and stubbornly continued to turn out the same car in one color, black, until 1927." Then, maverick General Motors offered car buyers a *choice* of colors. And suddenly Ford was no longer the No. 1 car maker. The product of Henry Ford's original wisdom, repeated sufficiently and often in the same exact way, turned to folly. Later, it would become General Motors' turn in the 1980s to experience how the folly of entrenched thinking can lead to disastrous consequences.

It is always hard to change from doing things in familiar ways that once worked wonders for you. Human nature clings to what worked in the past. But the necessity of change has now been greatly intensified by the extraordinary pace of change in the postindustrial world. Evolutionary change is out. Revolutionary change is in.

Writing about this phenomenon in his book, *The Age of Unreason,* Charles Handy sees the closing decades of the twentieth century as a time of discontinuous change—a total transformation of society and the economy. Handy tells us that, at such a time, change is not what it used to be. It is no longer gradual. To deal with a totally transformed situation, we must be open to startling new ideas even if that idea appears absurd at first sight. In today's world, he tells us, what is required is upside-down thinking.

What is also evident, as we observe the downsizing and job-elimination running rampant in business today, is that staying with the status quo no longer holds the promise of security it once did. At a time of discontinuous change, the business that dares to take big risks in the interest of pleasing its customers is the one actually following the safest course for itself and its employees. The business that "plays it safe" is likely to see market share and job security melt away.

Why Business Panaceas Often Fail

In its efforts to break the ongoing grip of the past, the business community often becomes enamored of a dramatic, new idea or methodology that is going to change everything. The latest quick fix becomes the thing to do because it is fashionable—everybody is doing it. As a result, companies adopt Management by Objective or Total Quality Management or Reengineering the Corporation or Worker Empowerment or whatever the business press trumpets as the latest salvation. But the puzzling outcome is that some companies experimenting with the new approach succeed in making it work for them, *and a greater number often do not.*

Experience with Total Quality Management (TQM) shows what can happen. It was seen as the new thing to do in the 1980s. Now it is getting mixed reviews. A recent article in *The Economist* states: "The quality programs of many western companies are failing dismally."

The Economist cites a survey of American manufacturing and service companies. Only a third reported that TQM resulted in "significant impact" on their competitiveness. In a United Kingdom study of 100 British firms, a mere fifth of those surveyed believed their quality program had achieved "tangible results."

Why does the panacea of the moment so often fail to fulfill its promise the next day?

We believe it happens frequently because there was only a superficial management commitment to the idea in the first place. Then the concept founder's intent becomes corrupted or watered down. There is a failure to realize that the corporate culture itself must change for a turnaround to take place. In a halfhearted attempt at producing change, management misinterprets or misrepresents the real thing.

This is what has happened with some companies that embraced, or thought they were embracing, the new, information-driven direct marketing discipline in recent years.

They conscientiously collected millions of names and addresses of customers or inquirers and data about them in the corporation's computer memory bank. Then they set out to send targeted promotions to identified prime prospects and to find other ways to use the database *in support* of their conventional advertising and promotion strategies. Some of these companies may achieve some tactical goals, but they have entirely missed the point about what drives successful marketing in the Information Age.

To be a MaxiMarketing winner, you must place the database first in your planning. Before you decide what to do with your advertising and promotion, you must know who you want in the database and what you expect to do with the information to increase that person's value as a customer.

If the database is not central to the marketing strategy, a great deal can go wrong. Richard Cross has written about some of the consequences in *The Five Degrees of Customer Bonding*. "It may seem too expensive to senior management. It may fall into disuse. It may be assigned to an unqualified outside manager. You may be allowed access to only a portion of the data."

The road to an extraordinary return on the database investment is frequently complicated by a shortsighted focus on the data rather than the "datamotion"—how you turn the information into knowledge to solve problems and move the marketplace.

Without first having a clear understanding and wholehearted belief in how the database can become the basis of a total commitment to meeting the needs of customers, an in-house database can indeed become a costly exercise in futility.

And the success of what you do in carrying out this new "Caring and Daring" interactive strategy will depend on your degree of willingness to abandon the familiar and embrace a new vision.

Getting It Absolutely Positively Right

With today's escalating tempo of competition, just getting customers is hardly enough. The trick is to "get 'em and keep 'em." The success stories described in the preceding chapters showed how this can be done when management puts its full weight behind a major corporate investment in going beyond mere customer satisfaction and exceeding customer expectations.

The companies we chose to present certainly are not the only practitioners of Database Marketing, Involvement Marketing, Existential Marketing (the "Get Real" concept), Extra-Value Marketing, and the other keys to business success we touched upon. Recently, we learned of a case that shows once again what a genuine commitment to a visionary strategy encompassing this approach can do.

Federal Express has compiled a database of more than 20,000 companies who are its steady customers. They have built a program called Powership to keep from losing these customers to such rivals as United Parcel Service. Each of these good customers has been given a free computer, linked to Federal Express's headquarters in Memphis. Now, when the customer has a concern or a question, these shippers can do their own checking with their Fedex-supplied computer on the whereabouts of any of the dozens of packages they send on a given day.

Powership is not viewed by Fred Smith, the founder and CEO of Federal Express, as a nice little promotion or just another add-on to his multifaceted marketing activities. Says Vice-President Laurie Tucker, the executive who oversees Powership, "Over the last two-and-a-half years, Fred Smith has made this program the No. 1 strategic priority for our company."

And every month Federal Express polls another 1000 of its Powership customers on ways the company's relationship with them might be improved.

Has Powership paid off? You bet it has.

"There has been an outpouring of customer loyalty," reports Tucker, "and we have seen increased volume because of the system. We are constantly building on our success with Powership. We are always looking for new ways to delight or make our customers value us even more."

With Powership, Federal Express is caring for the customer's best interest in a daring new way—yet another example of the new power of "Caring and Daring."

Many Ad Agencies Are Slipping—While a Few Soar

Disenchantment with the dominant role advertising once held in building a brand is spreading throughout the business world. Many top executives now believe that advertising has become much less effective due to the splintering of the marketplace into ever smaller niches.

Not to be outdone by the fascination of their clients with each new methodology for fixing what ails the business, agency management has come up with its own panacea—integrated marketing communications. Early in the decade integrated marketing was on the lips of just about every mainstream agency executive.

Ad agencies would no longer position themselves simply as fonts of creativity. They would go where the client was increasingly spending money in the 1990s. Overnight, agency managers swallowed their disdain for sales promotion and direct marketing and repositioned the famous-name creative agencies as the place to go for integrated marketing services, supplied by various subsidiaries under the agency corporate umbrella.

But, in their heart of hearts, agency management never gave up the belief in "good old advertising" as the real thing. After paying lip service for a while to integrated communication, Madison Avenue is back to pushing creativity as its reason for being once again—while clients continue to prefer buying their integrated marketing services piecemeal from the best specialist they can find for each discipline.

With such a powerful vested interest in big-budget, image-building TV commercials, there aren't many agencies ready to take a leap into the Information Age, go back to square one and start over. Madison Avenue has been slow to refocus on the need of most clients today for a fusion of advertising and marketing disciplines, built around information-driven customer relationship strategies.

One-way bombardment of the marketplace to gain share of mind remains the order of the day, just as it has been for the past 40 years. The use of double-duty direct-response advertising that builds brand image *and begins developing a customer feedback loop* is still the exception rather than the rule. Helping clients get involved with, and stay close to, prospects and customers is not a top priority in agencies obsessed with proving their creative prowess. Staying with yesterday's agenda contributes to stalled growth and growing client disaffection.

By contrast, some of the new, young agencies are doing very well because they are not prisoners of the past. One striking example is the meteoric rise of a direct-response advertising agency, Bronner Slosberg Humphrey (BSH) of Boston.

When *Advertising Age* published their list of the world's Top 50 advertising organizations early in 1993, BSH was the only agency on the list that had grown by more than 30 percent in the previous dismal year for ad agencies. The BSH growth rate of 34.7 percent stood well above No. 2, Chiat Day of Venice, California, at 25.4 percent and No. 3, Cheil Communications of Seoul, South Korea, at 22.1 percent.

The newcomer to the Top 50 list was founded just 10 years earlier by a 22-year-old Boston University undergraduate whiz kid, Michael Bronner. American Express became his first client when he dreamed up and sold them a service establishment cooperative mailing idea. In 1987, a headhunter located for Bronner an exceptionally talented partner and creative director, Mike Slosberg.

Slosberg had unique dual qualifications. Having first risen through the ranks at a general agency, Young & Rubicam, Slosberg—in a surprise move—was installed into their direct marketing subsidiary, Wunderman Worldwide, as president. When Bronner and Slosberg were joined by a third partner, Steve Humphrey, who also got his start at a general agency, the fledgling agency became Bronner Slosberg Humphrey and was poised on the runway for takeoff.

By 1990, the firm was billing $127 million. Then, in recession year 1991, billings almost doubled to $223 million. BSH won a dozen awards that year, and Slosberg was picked as Creative Executive of the Year by *Adweek.* In 1992, BSH was named New England Agency of the Year by *Adweek.* Billings climbed to over $300 million. This, at a time when most agencies were marking time or slipping backward, as the power of brand advertising waned and ad budgets shrank.

BSH is not selling the old-time agency razzle-dazzle of bombarding a faceless market in order to manipulate consumer perception of a branded product. The firm has gone back to square one and dared to build an agency based on a new kind of razzle-dazzle: influencing the behavior of known consumers in ways that solve client problems with measurable results.

BSH limits its work to a small group of only eight blue-chip clients including: AT&T, American Express, Seagram, Disney, Federal Express, L.L. Bean, and Quaker Oats. IBM was added to this elite roster in early 1993. Most of the agency's growth has come from expanded budgets by its short list of clients rather than from taking on new ones.

Commitment to Change Makes Great Clients

One of the secrets of Michael Bronner's success is his refusal to take a client who is not committed strategically to direct relationship marketing at the top management level. This means the agency is willing to withdraw from competition for a new account rather than enter a relationship in which one-to-one marketing is not given real strategic importance. Reportedly this is exactly what happened in a pitch for a famous brand packaged-goods account. Bronner also said, "No, thanks," when invited to go after a pricey foreign-car account.

Says one of their clients, Richard Shaw of Seagram, "The reason for their growth is the agency's incredible dedication to their clients' business and their vision of what direct marketing can accomplish."

We visited Michael Bronner at the BSH office in Boston, and from our conversation with him gained some insight into what he believes a business must do to succeed today.

"What we see as the most effective strategy for megasize companies," he told us, "is to think smaller by reorganizing around customers with similar needs. Each market segment needs its own marketing team with an accountable P&L for that segment. Then the team can access the larger infrastructure of the corporation for the leverage needed to carry out the program. The corporate players who best understand the customer in each segment break through the wall of consumer resistance to meet needs better than the competition."

What he said struck a responsive chord. We had argued in *MaxiMarketing,* seven years earlier, "The advertiser's management insists on being able to love the advertising but neglects to put anybody in charge of loving the prospect." The kind of corporate reengineering Bronner was advocating clears the management decks for customer care on a segment-by-segment basis.

"Small companies do, in fact, operate this way," he continued. "Every large company started small. What they face later is how to stay small and flexible despite their size. *What they must do is use the company's size to the advantage of the customer—and not (and this is where so many big corporations go astray) to the sole advantage of the company."*

Bronner said that they try to run their own business that way. "By keeping a small client base, we can think like a dedicated small agency for each client." He knows that the steadfast consumer loyalty of the past to a company or brand, "for better or for worse," is just not there any more. The answer, he believes, is "to find an approach to caring for the customer that can't be duplicated and to put it at the heart of the company's culture. It's something that's really hard to do. But when you do come up with the right answer, it can be a true source of competitive advantage."

Bronner Slosberg Humphrey and other rapidly growing response-oriented agencies such as Devon Direct, one of MCI's Friends and Family agencies, and Berenson, Isham & Partners with HBO and the Saucony Walking Club on their client list, are refreshing additions to the agency scene. They provide independent strategic marketing thinking and great creative input for interactive advertising on TV, in print media, and through direct mail.

In Brazil, the agency that handles advertising for the Amil Group, Promarket, has demonstrated just how far such a new model agency can go in answering all the needs of a modern-day client. Promarket swept 21 of the 39 awards for TV advertising creativity handed out by the Brazilian Association of Marketing and Advertising Columnists while, in the same year, pioneering the delivery of outstanding database services, telemarketing, and direct-mail promotion for their client's many businesses.

Once you strip away the prejudice that keeps the advertising establishment from seeing response-oriented agencies as real agencies and direct response as real advertising, the Promarket all-purpose agency just might be the forerunner of the "Advertising *and Marketing* Agency" of the future.

We will see different agency models emerging to meet changing client needs. But any shop that can deliver responsive top-flight creativity and the marketing know-how needed to build a strong customer bond is going to have a distinct competitive advantage.

Our Three Commandments for Maxi-Performance

We said in our previous books, and we will repeat it here, that we can't tell you what to do for your specific business, because each situation and each problem is unique. But we can suggest some ways to think about what to do.

In that spirit, we want to pass along to you the following guiding commandments for putting to effective use the insights gained in reading this book.

I. Thou shalt do more than enough.
II. Thou shalt make a passionate commitment.
III. Thou shalt find a unique solution for *thy* company or client.

Let's take a closer look at each of these guideposts separately.

I. Do More Than Enough

In our discussion of Nestlé packaged-goods marketing in France, we pointed out that the best brand-building today has a fourth dimension. In addition to how *high* the number of advertising impressions made, how *deep* the hold that the image advertising achieves on public consciousness, and how *wide* the distribution, there is also the degree of *involvement* the prospects or customers experience with the brand or with each other. This means not only how intense the involvement is, but also how many *different forms* of involvement there are.

It is no longer enough to do one or two things right and think you've done enough. Today you must do more than enough. The rising tide of advertising clutter and the rising pressure of competition both demand it. Your chief competitor is probably moving toward the new individualized marketing, too—you've got to move even further.

Are you thinking of starting a frequent-buyer program for your product or store, as Zellers has done so well? That *might* be very good.

Are you considering putting your company name on a cobranded MasterCard or Visa card and letting your customers earn points with their purchases, as General Motors has done? That *might* be very good.

Are you about to meet with a publication's advertising salesperson to buy just the 30 percent of the circulation that is right for your product, as Seagram has done? That *might* be good, too.

But if you put just one daring new program in place and call it a day, you may still lose out to a competitor who does not just *one* thing to build the brand and the relationship, but does much more.

Look at The LEGO Company, with its 12 different contact points for interaction with the market, running the gamut from their LEGO Builders Club and Shop-At-Home Catalog to the LEGOland theme parks and LEGO Imagination Center.

Look at Shiseido, with its cobranded Visa card *and* its monthly mailing to the home *and* its full-sized beauty magazine *and* its specialty catalogs *and* its beauty counselors—and everything else they do.

Look at Nestlé Baby Foods in France: not content to just establish highway rest stops, not content to just provide phone counseling for anxious parents by licensed dieticians, but doing both. And a lot more.

To move the needle with MaxiMarketing today, you've got to implement your "Caring and Daring" strategy with a wide range of activities focused on meeting the needs of your market as they have never been met before.

Yes, there are corporate investment considerations and limitations to take into account. But on the plus side, there is a powerful synergy—we call it Super-Synergy—which comes from the interaction between the components of a multi-involvement program. Just think of the millions of dollars your company may be wasting on advertising to nonprospects. These millions could finance multiple in-depth programs for prospect cultivation, brand building, and customer bonding.

II. Make a Passionate Commitment

You may say that it is easier said than done. You're right. But we don't see any way around the need for it.

When we asked Michael Dell what differentiated Dell Computer from the competition during the years of its spectacular rise, he replied, "We have a tremendous, passionate, commitment to taking care of the customer. That passion absolutely is the difference."

The absolute difference! A passion for taking care of the customer! One of the striking things about his reply was the absolute conviction with which it was delivered, without a moment's hesitation.

Here is a 28-year-old multi-multimillionaire, fighting the battle of his life against a rejuvenated Compaq and a reborn IBM, who still finds time to pick up a phone on his desk and listen to calls from customers. Michael Dell is still driven by gaining his own personal insights into pleasing the customer.

And we told you about the passion Fabienne Petit of Nestlé France has for taking such good care of the parents and their babies. About Mike Keefe of Harley-Davidson, who looks at the commitment to the customer as "fun and a passion and kind of our reason for living." About the passion of José Salebi Neto and his partners for providing every HSM Cultura seminar attendee with the personal attention they would lavish on a good friend visiting their homes.

It is well past the time of thinking about customer satisfaction as a corporate goal and time to start thinking of customer astonishment as what you want to achieve. That's what Dr. Ferreira de Rocha of Amil did when he laid out $5 million for helicopters and ambulances *before* he knew whether his Rescue Health Plan would have any takers in Brazil. His passion for creating a truly astonishing service propelled the Amil Group into a new cycle of growth.

If you are not the CEO in a position to lead your troops in that kind of passionate commitment, you can still, in the words of the old hymn, "brighten the corner where you are." You can still care passionately about pleasing your prospects and customers and be the start of a widening circle of influence in your company. Remember that the Puget Sound Fund of the Puget Sound

Bank did not originate at the top, but was endorsed and solidly backed by top management after its worth became apparent.

III. Find a Unique Solution for Your Company or Client

When you read about the 10 million phone customers enrolled in MCI's Friends and Family calling circles, or Nestlé's restoration of the Casa Buitoni in Tuscany, your heart may sink rather than rise. Why? Because you have collided head-on with The Law of the Unique Situation: namely, the specifics of a spectacular success in one category is quite often seen as not readily transferable to another.

"That's all very well," you may grumble, "to talk about getting phone customers to recruit other phone customers for you, or enhancing a pasta brand's appeal by rebuilding its ancestral home. But I'm selling mouthwash or running a dry cleaning store or selling office machines. How can *my* company do what those companies did?" And the answer is that it can't, of course. You've got to make good by adapting the thinking behind the success of our MaxiMarketing winners in finding your own unique solution to your own special problem. It can be a demanding process—but also a rewarding one.

That's why we have said and written many times that "the kind of creative ingenuity which has heretofore been lavished on mass advertising is now needed for the creation of trail-blazing marketing strategies."

Advertising Age, in a front-page story run in the summer of 1993, put a spotlight on this new reality. The message from IBM to ad agencies competing for their $90 million personal computer account was that "the promise of creative advertising may have gotten the finalists in the door, but it is going to play a smaller role in actually winning the business. Strategic thinking has emerged as the key."

A new day is dawning along Madison Avenue.

The focus on a unique solution to your own special problem is both a challenge and an opportunity. You can be certain there is a unique solution of your own waiting to be uncovered. And when you find it (with the help of the seven keys to business success today), you will have an advantage that is difficult to overcome.

MCI started with the unique problem of being an overwhelming underdog and found a way to use "corporate jujitsu" to come up with an offer that AT&T is still trying to match two years later. Buitoni started with the problem of selling premium pasta at a premium price and found a unique solution in its Tuscany-based heritage.

To capture the mind and heart of the consumer or business client in your category, you must find the right solution to a problem that is specific to your company.

The success of each company described in the preceding pages began with the same blank sheet of paper you face when thinking about a new direction for your company. To get your own creative juices flowing, ask yourself: "In what way might I adapt what Guinness, Lexus, AMFB, Ryder, Fidelity, HSM, Seagram, Harley-Davidson, Shiseido, and the others have done in responding to a challenge faced by my company?" Remember to be willing to go back to "square one," if necessary, and to take another look at what business you are really in.

Never forget the power of caring enough to really put the customer first.

Think of all the ways you can use Existential Marketing to "get real" and Database Marketing to stop wasting money on nonprospects and Extra-Value Marketing to offer customers gain without pain. And if that still doesn't do it, think about the MaxiMarketing winners who broke through today's media clutter by bringing people together with Involvement Marketing and how some of them used Information-Age Marketing to put telling ahead of selling.

The keys to success you have seen highlighted in these case histories can become the keys to your own unique success.

If there is one supreme lesson to learn from the experience of the innovative companies profiled in these pages, it is never to settle for less than devising your own daring solution to answering customer needs. Just doing things a little better than before or stealing a page from the competitors' most recent achievement is not going to get the job done and is certainly not going to turn you into or keep you the leader in your category.

If you want to drive the competition crazy and set in motion a really impressive jump in sales and profits, our MaxiMarketing winners from around the world have shown how to make it happen. Now it is your turn to redefine the playing field in your own competitive arena and walk away a winner. Above all, you must develop and encourage a passion for caring for your customers and your prospective customers and exhibit the daring required to leap into the future a step ahead of the competition.

We wish you well in what can become the most important undertaking of your business career.

Index

Note: The *n.* after a page number refers to a note.

About the Authors

Stan Rapp and Thomas L. Collins are coauthors of the best-selling *MaxiMarketing* and *The Great Marketing Turnaround,* which together have sold more than 250,000 copies worldwide, have been translated into 14 languages, and have influenced the practice of marketing on 5 continents. During their years in the advertising agency business, they cofounded and led Rapp & Collins, today known as Rapp Collins Worldwide—a $600 million network of agencies that is part of Omnicom. Their strategic consultancy serves a distinguished list of clients in North and South America. They speak, write, and consult internationally from their base in New York City.

AN INVITATION FROM THE AUTHORS

We are interested in having this book begin our own one-to-one relationship with those readers who wish to practice the MaxiMarketing approach and expect to apply the keys to business success presented in the preceding pages. In addition, our search for MaxiMarketing winners continues. If, at some future time, you believe that your company's performance is deserving of such recognition, do let us know by faxing or writing to the address below.

MaxiMarketing Information Center
333 East 30 Street
New York, NY 10016
Attention: Stan Rapp
Fax No. 212-779-1856

I am interested in (check one or more):

☐ Receiving information about training for expert application of database marketing and MaxiMarketing practices.

☐ Receiving information about the one-day MaxiMarketing Idea Generating Workshop customized to my company's specific needs.

☐ Receiving information about future availability of a *Beyond MaxiMarketing Newsletter* with ongoing reports and analysis.

☐ Receiving information about how to order the classic *99 Idea Killers Poster* to display in my company to encourage innovative thinking.

Name________________________________ Title ________________

Company ____

Address ____

City ____________________________ State__________ Zip ________

Fax No. _________________________ Phone No. ________________